SUNDAY MISCELLANY

To Leah –

Enjoy! – This

and Life –

Best Wishes,

[signature]

SUNDAY MISCELLANY

a selection from 2006 – 2008

edited by CLÍODHNA NÍ ANLUAIN

RTÉ

Sunday Miscellany
First published 2008
by New Island
2 Brookside
Dundrum Road
Dublin 14
www.newisland.ie

ISBN 978-1-84840-015-3

The quotations from W. H. Auden are reprinted from *Collected Auden*, edited by Edward Mendelson, by permission of Faber and Faber Ltd.

The quotations from Louis MacNiece are reprinted from *Collected Poems*, published by Faber and Faber Ltd, by permission of David Higham Associates.

Poem 'Original Sin on the Sussex Coast' from *Collected Poems* by John Betjeman © 1955, 1958, 1962, 1964, 1968, 1970, 1979, 1981, 2001. Reproduced by permission of John Murray (Publishers).

'My First Basque Village' by Paddy Woodworth was adapted from a passage in *The Basque Country: A Cultural History* (Signal 2007, Oxford University Press 2008).

'Brooklyn Heights' reprinted by permission of United Agents on behalf of Andrew Motion.

'Fiabhras' by Seán Ó Ríordáin reprinted by permission of Sáirséal Ó Marcaigh.

British Library Cataloguing in Publication Data. A CIP catalogue record for this book is available from the British Library.

Printed and bound in the UK by CPI Mackays, Chatham ME5 8TD

New Island received financial assistance from The Arts Council
(An Chomhairle Ealaíon), Dublin, Ireland

10 9 8 7 6 5 4 3

CONTENTS

June

July

August

INTRODUCTION

Sunday Miscellany on RTÉ Radio I is one of Ireland's best-known and most listened to radio programmes. For decades, its simple formula has attracted thousands to tune in — and it draws new listeners all the time. *Sunday Miscellany* is a radio hour of new writing contributed by a feast of emerging and established voices. The writing and music speak for themselves, hold their own. They follow the programme's opening through to its closing, heralded by Samuel Scheidt's *Galliard Battaglia*, the programme's instantly recognisable signature tune. At the heart of the success of *Sunday Miscellany* is its regularity on the air, at the same time every Sunday morning.

It is two years since the last *Sunday Miscellany* anthology appeared in 2006. During that time, over 700 more audio essays and new poems have been recorded. Hundreds more contributors have made their way to studios in Dublin, across Ireland, in other parts of Europe and in America, to sit before the microphone and share their minds and imaginations with us. Over a hundred more *Sunday Miscellany* programmes have been produced and broadcast.

This latest anthology once more illustrates what got contributors going, what mattered to them – personally and publicly. It is an imagined mirror of that time as it was reflected through the programme. Licence has been taken in laying out the book in twelve monthly sections since it is a selection from nearly two years of the programme. The book opens with a feeling of beginning and renewal. It ends in similar spirit to reflect that *Sunday Miscellany* continues on again as another year begins.

Some contributions take on topical ideas or happenings as their starting point – the 2007 Irish general election, MRSA in our hospitals, the retirement of Fidel Castro, the Rugby World Cup 2007, the SSIA savings initiative or the social and political tensions in Zimbabwe. Other contributions don't consider the immediacy of time but rather bring us out of the time in which we hear the programme. Listeners – and increasingly this includes those tuning in through the Internet – say the programme speaks directly to them, catches them and remains with them after it is over. They hear it in all sorts of places – relaxing overlooking the Mediterranean, in Bermuda, in a convent in the West of Ireland, in their cars while driving to work or to Sunday Mass or Service, or in their garden in the Cork suburb of Glasheen. Wherever or however they heard it, it mattered enough for them to contact the programme to say that a piece meant something and that they would like to savour it again. The selection in this book takes account of many such requests. It is intended to make the best of companionable reading over and again for those who open the book and enjoy their own random selection of essays and poems wherever they read it.

Making *Sunday Miscellany* has its own patterns of work in bringing this weekly programme together. Reading and considering the scripts that come in as open submissions, and merging these with commissioned writing direct future programmes. Planning is vital to strike a balance through the year between those containing the expected mix of subjects and those dedicated to anniversaries such as the centenary of the birth of the sculptor Séamus Murphy, the bicentenary of the publication of *Moore's Melodies*, the fortieth anniversary of 1968 – the year of the gentle revolution – or the 400th anniversary of the birth of John Milton and of the Flight of the Earls. In addition to these specific anniversaries *Sunday Miscellany* also contributes to particular projects marked across the RTÉ schedule like Seachtain na Gaeilge, European

Broadcasting Day, Inter-Cultural Week, as well as such calendar perennials as St Patrick's Day, Easter and Christmas.

The nature of listening to radio means that many experience *Sunday Miscellany* in intimate company or alone, just as recordings for the programme are typically made in the quietness of a studio with only the contributor, the producer and sound engineer present. In 2007, *Sunday Miscellany* took to the road for the first time. The programme was recorded live in front of an audience, also for the first time. Participants in Listowel Writers' Week were commissioned by *Sunday Miscellany* to present new material accompanied by musicians at an event held in St John's Theatre in the town as part of the festival. So popular were the occasion and its radio broadcast that they were repeated with another selection of writers and musicians in 2008. A number of these spoken contributions now appear in the book. While many are set in Listowel, they brilliantly relate as much to the stuff of simply being alive as to the particulars of that place.

An aspect of *Sunday Miscellany* and of this book is the eclectic mix of figures — contemporary and historical — referred to by contributors. In no particular order, they include Ernest Hemingway, Maeve Brennan, Máirtín Ó Cadhain, Gary McMahon, John Donne, Barbra Streisand, Teresa Deevy, Sylvia Plath, Jem Roche, John McGahern, W. H. Auden, Georgia O'Keeffe, Ronan O'Gara, William Hogarth, John B. Keane, Maureen Kenny, Oliver Goldsmith, Edmund Hillary, Elvis Presley, St Charles of Mount Argus, Patrick Ireland and Jesse James. The nature and make up of contributors to this anthology are no less varied, including as it does actors, journalists, secretaries, barristers, poets, a mask maker, a senator, a physicist, a life coach and a children's minder.

Benedict Kiely died in 2007. It was widely remembered in the talk and the words written about him how his voice for years was synonymous with *Sunday Miscellany*. I included a recording of an RTÉ archive piece of him in the programme the Sunday following his passing. I had previously included the same piece the Sunday his own County Tyrone were playing in the 2005 All-Ireland Senior Football Final. On the first anniversary of his death Gerald Dawe contributed a newly written essay on Benedict Kiely to *Sunday Miscellany*. I have included both of these in this anthology to remember those no longer with us who contributed to *Sunday Miscellany*, and to savour again the legend that Benedict Kiely was to so many RTÉ Radio listeners for years.

All-Ireland hurling and football final Sundays are special on *Sunday Miscellany*. Phone messages left by emotional listeners, e-mails and letters saying what those programmes mean and the requests for copies of these scripts are enormous. Although the same handful of counties have dominated these matches in recent years, the variety of contributions, the breadth of passion, the anticipation of the joy and the unmentionable devastation of what winning or loosing means continues to be shared by contributors with listeners across the globe on those memorable September Sundays. This anthology includes some of these essays from 2006 and 2007. Indeed, sport is such a regular fixture on *Sunday Miscellany* that it is a subject that appears throughout this book. The celebration of human relations, of physical achievement, of the importance of memory and of its participative nature is captured in contributions on baseball, boxing, soccer, rugby, skiing and sailing.

No project is completed without the help and support of many people. I would like to thank in particular the broadcasting co-ordinators associated with *Sunday Miscellany*: Amanda Coyne, Laura Leigh Davies, Fionnuala Hayes and Jarlath Holland. Thanks are due to the many sound engineers so central to recording the programme. Liz Sweeney produced the programme for some of the period covered in this book. She is to be thanked for the many timely contributions in this anthology, including a commemorative piece following the death of the scholar and writer Seán Ó Tuama and another marking the centenary of the birth of playwright Henrik Ibsen. I would like to thank Malachy Moran, RTÉ Archives and Services Manager; Lorelei Harris, Editor, Arts Features and Drama; Ana Leddy, Head of RTÉ Radio I; and Adrian Moynes, Managing Director, RTÉ Radio, whose encouragement of this publication makes such a difference.

Once more, it is a pleasure to thank New Island, and especially Deirdre Nolan and Edwin Higel, for their work on the book and ensuring the handsome production of its content. I would like to thank Finola Jones of mother's tankstation for her assistance in providing the image of the painting for the book's cover by contemporary Irish artist Mairead O'hEocha.

My very special thanks go to Brian Fay and our children, Eoghan and Nora, whose patience and support knows no bounds.

I would like to thank all those who continue to send in material for consideration to the programme, as well as those whose writing appears here and on whom this book and the radio programme depend.

Finally, I would like to thank the thousands of listeners who tune in to *Sunday Miscellany* every Sunday morning. This book is, most especially, for you.

Clíodhna Ní Anluain
Producer and Editor
Sunday Miscellany
RTÉ Radio I
August 2008

JANUARY

EARLY ANECDOTE

Gerard Smyth

In Januaries of snow, Junes of harvest weather
School years passed like a carnival parade.

It was still the age of pen and paper
and the movie poster for *Lawrence of Arabia*.

Through backstreets behind the brewery
my snow-prints followed me, turning corners

slogging along or stopping when I stopped
in the granite shade of hopstore walls

those mornings when I headed off, hurrying
to reach the yard before the hand-bell made its call.

Carrying in my bag the tattered atlas
and the narrative of Caesar's war in Gaul.

THE WAKING CITY

Vona Groarke

For whatever reason, you just can't sleep. It's four a.m., you have a flight at nine, tomorrow will wear you out and you should sleep. You try, you really try, and once or twice, you feel it creep up on you, but it's like a shadow and something carried over from the evening before insists it isn't time yet for darkness and lost hours. Outside your window, lamplight stains the footpath and your windowsill and your hand when you hold back the hotel blind to watch the street for even some small evidence of another life. This city, you see, goes on without you, filling in its night-time hours behind closed doors and curtained windows: nothing is on show, not up the street that only a few small hours ago, you tottered up on too-high heels, all set for the evening ahead. Not down the street, towards the arch and the river, where something, at least, is moving along, allowing itself to change.

You pull on clothes. Faint light is just coming into its own. You think again of a newborn calf unpacking itself from folded legs, trying to find its feet. Like origami in reverse. It isn't even cold. You head first for the docks: if anywhere won't have quite given up on the night before, it will be here. The engines of the navy ship are grumbling away about the years and years it's been since they had anything like fun. No one's on deck. A retinue of yachts and fishing boats trades gossip by the wall. Their names flutter like charms on a bracelet: *Shanghri-La*, the *Derring-Do*, the *Milicent*, *Lán Grá*.

You pass a pub with no shutters and no lights. You're looking in the window at the chrome of upturned chairs glinting in a mirror that occupies the full breadth of one wall, and then, when you look harder, at four sets of eyes fixed on you from the corner of the bar: the staff making a night of it, the work done, the place cleared and nobody ready yet to call it a day. You move on.

There's a huge pile of scrap metal at the end of the pier. Rusty fragments of cars and gates and cylinders and pipes and sheet metal and something that looks like a turnip mangle with the words 'Pierce & Son' just legible, poke out of a mass of burnished copper, that in this light, could almost be a midden haul of newly unearthed antiquities: golden torcs and filigree silver and an ambered reliquary with flecks of soil still clinging.

Down by the arch, the river holds sway. You walk the path alongside, flanked on the right by new apartments with all their curtains pulled tight and no light within. You notice a derelict warehouse you never saw before. You're counting its windows when the brakes of the bin lorry at the end of the path pull you up short and you have to start over. 'D'ya see those churches, that one and the big cathedral, well they got the whole thing wrong, you know, the whole bloody thing just back to front,' he says behind you. The binman has a theory that is something to do with Sundays being Saturdays and the Sabbath being observed on the wrong day. He quotes chapter and verse and doesn't look like he'll draw breath anytime soon. 'Good man,' you say, 'you've obviously looked into it anyway', and before he can register the interruption, you take off. You don't own the morning any more.

A couple swings out of Cross Street singing a song together in a language you don't recognise. They stop ahead of you in front of the record shop and call up a name to the open window above the sign. A blond head pokes out and then a key is thrown that clatters on the road and has the two of them scrambling to beat each other to be the one to pick it up. The woman wins and dangles it in front of the man's face while he tries to get it off her. They don't notice you. You walk on.

Back towards the hotel, a man is wedging open the door of his corner shop. He nods at you and you nod back. A man in a security uniform comes out behind him with a two-litre bottle of Coke and a bouquet of chocolate bars. He nods at you too and, just like that, the morning is suddenly more about the day ahead than it is about last night. You walk into the foyer: the night porter is washing floor tiles. He looks up to tell you the forecast is beautiful.

THE EMPTY ROOM OF FASHION

Emer O'Kelly

Something I read recently has reassured me that I'm coming back into fashion: at least my living room is. Minimalism, said the excited, breathy tone of the article, is on the way out: clutter is back. Recommendations followed on how to achieve 'the look', with a list of the designer shops where clutter, suitably and falsely aged for immediate chic, could be purchased. Curled up in the corner of my big (and old) couch which seats three comfortably, four at a pinch, I glanced around the not-very-large room. Ten tables, three assorted armchairs, an occasional chair, three stools and twenty-eight paintings (I've started on the third row) caught my eye. The chimney alcoves are filled with books to the fortunately high ceiling. As an interior designer friend of mine said, in the mysterious language of his trade, 'There's a lot of stuff in that room, Emer.'

Somehow, fashion is unlikely to get quite that cluttered. But, then, I've always equated empty rooms with the empty minds of those who live in them, which allows me to feel superior to the fashion for minimalism and hard surfaces. A nest of cushions, a book (maybe two), newspapers, needlepoint, a glass of wine, the TV and CD remote control immediately to hand; they're *de rigueur* for an evening spent at home.

I've always gone for clutter: I like having my life's concerns visible around me, as I like displaying the objects that friends have given me as gifts, even if they're not what I would have chosen myself. I remember talking some years ago to someone who was enthusing about her new drawing room: it was to have a single couch, or as she called it, a sofa, and three paintings. That was it. Where, I asked hesitantly, would she kick off her shoes and curl up with a book? I watched with some amusement as her pretty face puckered bewilderedly at the sound of the alien word.

Fashion is tyrannical, in décor as well as clothing, and those who follow it seem to live in terror. The thought of being described as 'so last season' is a death threat, and home can have no familiarity: it must be updated at the whim of design fads. New kitchens every five years are the prerogative only of those who don't cook: cooks like familiarity. I even knew somebody once who said with threatening pride that if anyone tried to boil an egg in her new kitchen, their lives would be forfeit. She meant it, too, as she lovingly itemised every top-of-the-range gimmick and appliance, its designer name and its heart-stopping price tag. The new owners will need to update, say the property supplements about the kitchens in charming old houses where the current owner has produced superb meals for six people every day for forty years. The new owner will be unlikely to sully her hands with more than opening a designer cookbook to look at the pictures before consigning it to a shelf, never to be taken down. But she'll be bang up to date.

'Isn't it strange,' the late Sybil Connolly once mused to me, 'that people who are obsessed with style so seldom have any?' Miss Connolly, as she was always known to her staff, knew what she was talking about. The doyenne of the Irish fashion industry, who was the first woman to give us an international profile way back in the 1950s, was never fashionable herself, but always supremely stylish. As a result, the clients for whom she catered on the international market kept her magnificent ballgowns for twenty years, their beauty and glamour never dating. She was ladylike in the most old-fashioned of ways, but had a tongue like an adder when she chose: the remark about style and the lack of it was aimed at two particular Irish journalists who were indeed fashion-obsessed. On another occasion, in what turned out to be her last television interview, several years before her final illness, she wore what she confided was a twenty-year-old dress, consulting me as the interviewer about what jewellery I thought would be suitable with it. I knew more about television than she did, she said sweetly, but I wasn't about to advise Miss Connolly about anything, and kept my mouth firmly shut. I knew style when I saw it, and it had nothing to do with fashion.

Maybe that's why I rejoice in my instinct for clutter: it's my clutter, and at least it's individual. White walls, wood floors and flat-pack furniture may be fashionable, but they're unsettling in their sameness: how do people know they're in the right house? And if there *is* a rush to the designer shops for distressed clutter, will that become uniform too? Miss Connolly, who also designed a range of homewares for Tiffany's in New York, must be turning in her grave.

A MONK

Michael Harding

I have a young Tibetan friend, Losang Rabsal, who is a monk. He seems so happy in his monastic life, and in his celibate vocation, that I once asked him to tell me the circumstances of how he became a monk.

First he laughed.

Then he went silent.

And finally he became very serious and began speaking.

'There was always snow,' he said, 'in Tibet.'

When he was growing up.

He was his mother's only child, though there were cousins his own age in the nearby tents of his relations. It was a huge family of many people in many tents, surrounded by an abundance of sheep.

His father was old. He was small and thin and full of wind. Like a snake standing erect, with huge ears, and in his throat a constant whistle of wind. In those days, all the young children would eat dried fruit, which they called 'old people's ears'. Rabsal called them 'Father's ears'. They lived in the hills, with tents and animals. His father sat on the grass in summer, motionless, like a log of wood in the forest.

There was always something suffering in him that his son could not understand.

In the depth of winter, the extended family would all settle in one sheltered place. Sheltering the animals. The children playing with bells. The women stirring soup. The men smoking pipes and taking snuff.

The coldest part of the night was just after dark. Until bedtime. Rabsal's young cheeks burned with the cold air. And he sat in the corner of the tent dreaming of monasteries.

He did not desire cattle. He did not desire horses. He did not desire yaks. He did not desire a wife or child or to be famous or to be praised by the village. The only thing he desired was a monastery.

How wonderful to be inside the walls of a monastery. Learning to read. With a warm stove and an old Mongolian teacher to shorten the evenings. With stories like 'The Empty Pot', and 'The Upside Down Pot', and 'The Pot with the Hole in the Bottom'.

At night, he would sometimes stand out with the horses and the horses kicked the wind because they were angry at the cold air. 'I am also disappointed,' he told the horses. 'You wish for shelter. But I wish for a monastery. We are not so different.'

He rubbed the horse's nose, and stared into its eyes until the horse settled and then he would fall into the snow laughing.

His father was withering away. Turning into air. A shadow in the corner. Always in the dark of the tent now. On the bed. Yellow in the face. And a putrid smell from his urine. He was in pain when he moved. His legs swelled with sores. And his tooth ached in the middle of the night. One day, he turned to his son and said, 'You were born dreaming. You will never get a wife.'

'I don't want a wife,' his son blurted out. 'I want to go to the monastery.'

It was not something Rabsal intended to say. The words just walked out of his mouth.

The old man laughed till it hurt his ribs and he coughed black phlegm up as his laughter turned to choking. That was the first time Rabsal had ever revealed his desire to his father, and he was glad, because it made his father laugh, and because the following day his father was dead. And because such words had walked out of his mouth, at such a moment, Rabsal knew they must be true, and he knew it was time to walk to Lhasa and enter the monastery.

MARMALADE

Hedy Gibbons Lynott

There is something about the making of marmalade. Those who
indulge in it constitute a kind of secret society, their communication
system underground, their involvement hidden. Vendors of Seville
oranges never seem to advertise, but a kind of bush-telegraph signals the
fruits' arrival and some basic human desire, perhaps for light, a whiff of
spring, even a promise of summer, drives marmalade's acolytes out into
the cold, dead days of January. Lurking at the back of the greengrocer,
we smile conspiratorially at each other, a little sheepish that in this
twenty-first century, when we could so easily pick a jar off a supermarket shelf, we still have an urge to 'create' from those gnarled, ugly, citrus
our own tangy hoard. Perhaps it runs in families — that urge, lurking
beneath the surface through the generations, as compelling as any
genetic code.

It may have been my grandfather, James Houlihan, eventually
invalided from the Royal Navy after the First World War, who started it
in ours. When, on 8 February 1908 his ship, HMS *Kent*, weighed
anchor at Plymouth en route for China Station, he would have been
below decks, peering into the roaring maw of a furnace, shovelling in
more coal. Long practice and attention to minute changes must have
taught him just the right moment to add more fuel, to coax their best
from the thirty-one Belleville boilers that propelled his ship.

Loading coal at Malta, Trincomalee and Singapore, along the route
by which oranges originally made there way to Europe, I wonder did

James Houlihan see much of that bitter-sweet fruit. I like to think that, on shore leave in Hong Kong, his choice of the colourful Chinese bowl as a gift for his new wife was not just a random one. I don't know if Ellen ever made marmalade, ladling the aromatic concoction into that small hand-painted bowl, thinking of her husband sweltering at some furnace halfway across the world, but I do know that every year between January and February, for as long as I can remember, the smell of oranges cooking pervaded our home.

There is something about the making of marmalade that is mindful. Weighing and measuring, slicing and simmering, testing to ensure the pithy skin is truly soft before adding sugar; standing guard beside the saucepan while heat permeates the mixture, until ever-so-slowly the bubbles rise to the surface and the tsunami of creamy yellow foam surges across the pan. The temptation to stir the mixture any more than is necessary to prevent burning must be resisted while waiting for the precise moment to adjust the heat that will produce a slow, rolling boil.

A slow, rolling boil. To some, it might seem like watching paint dry. But there is an unmissable moment in this process when it is just right to take the pan off the heat, a moment when the viscosity of the pectin brings about jellification in the mixture. In other words – that fleeting, magical, setting point. Pre-empt its arrival and you will be drinking, rather than eating, marmalade. Exceed it, and you will be hacking the stuff out of a jar. Get it right, and that piquant mixture of rough and smooth, bitter and sweet, dark shot through with brightness, reflects life itself.

My mother always conducted a 'tasting' of her newly-made mar-malade. Into my grandmother's Chinese bowl, with its exotic blue and gold figures on their bright orange background, Mam ladled the hot liquid, with strict instructions to hovering 'tasters' to let it cool. After a suitable interval, she dipped the porcelain ladle into it, and holding that first spoonful up to the light, turned it this way and that, checking colour, transparency, set. Then, sliding the marmalade onto her tongue, she rolled it round, biting and swishing and chewing with the concen-tration of a sommelier. Impatient observers until then, we simply lashed the not-quite-set-yet preserve onto thick, buttery toast.

Stacking the last jar of the last batch of this year's marmalade in the cupboard, I place the Chinese bowl on my kitchen table. Looking into its amber contents, I can hardly wait for that first vivid spoonful.

THE STRAP

Pat Boran

Like a Christian Brother of old, my father kept a leather strap, and was known to use it. It was not enough simply to use a leather strap: in the confines and privacy of one's home, it was necessary to be known to use it, the power being as much in the threat as in the application. More of a belt than the apparently custom-made straps the Irish Christian Brothers liked to carry, wide and undulating as the tongue of a cow, my father's strap was, I recall, about nine inches long and made of a flat leather band, folded over onto itself lengthwise, then sewn along the length so that there was a slight but distinct seam down the middle.

Seam side up or seam side down, however, my father's strap, when it bore down on your fingers, left your hand on fire, your eyes on fire and terrible confusion in your heart. For it was clear, from early on, that my father loved us, even us three boys for whom the leather strap was all too often taken down from the shelf where it rested between the scissors and combs, to be removed from its double-strength elastic band and allowed to unfurl itself like, I always thought in a fearful, distracted way, the serpent in the Garden of Eden.

To be fair to him, my father had grown up in a different time, a time in which such forms of discipline were not uncommon and where if you were not receiving corporal punishment at home, you were almost certainly receiving it at school. My father's generation had a war in common, and childhoods of scarcity and hardship in which men disciplined their sons the way a farmer might a beast who had strayed off the path. There were crude and sometimes cruel solutions to problems that ought to have been solved in other ways.

And yet, incredibly as it now seems to me, for a long number of years, my father's strap was wielded in our house, and many evenings I sat there in the front room, or the breakfast room as it had once been called, squeezing a still-burning hand and gazing out through the lace curtains at Main Street, Portlaoise, like a prisoner gazing out between steel bars.

And there must have been shame in the beatings too, for my father and for us, because I remember how dark a thing it felt to tell it to a friend one day in school (would we have been eight or nine?) who confessed to me that his father did it too, but preferring a stick or his open hand and, once in a while, his fist ... Still sucking on gobstoppers in the bicycle shed, it suddenly became clear to us that we were very likely a whole school, a whole generation of young lads, being routinely beaten, and beaten down, for no real reason and with no real purpose, and little chance of it coming to an end. The strange thing was that it was nearly always the beatings, the straps and the sticks themselves, which were the enemy. Only when a school friend swore revenge on his father, and looked as if he meant it, did it dawn on us that the solution to such a widespread problem lay in individual, particularised action.

So it happened that, one day, long enough after such a beating to be calm and clear about how to proceed, my younger brother and I decided to destroy my father's strap. We simply made up our minds that this particular chapter of our lives had come to an end. The details are sketchy, but I do recall that *Sesame Street* was playing on the television upstairs as we made our way down to the kitchen, hearing the fifth-last and the third-last stair board creak as they had since we were born. By chance, my father was away somewhere, gone to a nearby town on business, and, despite the ominous warning that 'He'll miss it', from our mother, who had always been horrified by its sight, I stood on a chair and took it from its resting place.

My brother, as I recall it, opened the front door of the range, and, holding the strap in the tongs from the open fireplace upstairs, I lifted it inside, this black coil of darkness, this leather, hand-held weapon of domestic terror. And we stood and watched it for a minute or two, twitch and straighten, spark and twitch, rise and snap and spark again, until the flames at last took hold of it and, bathed in the sheer heat of the moment, we shut the door of hell on it and moved well back.

All lives, simple or complicated, are full of mysteries. One from my own is how did my father react when he found his leather strap had vanished? For apart from looking for it, and threatening now and then to get another — which he never did — he never asked us directly if we'd taken it or what had become of it.

As if he knew. As if maybe he'd needed to have the decision made for him. As if it had long been clear, even to him, that the strap's time, if ever it had one, was long since gone. Soon his sons would be young men, his daughters, young women. He and his wife would be a late middle-aged couple, growing old in patterns they had built for themselves.

And, in the midst of all this change, at its mercy one might say, sometimes letting go turns out to be a kind of blessing: for without his leather strap, my father's own beautiful hands, even while ours visibly toughened, slowly softened again.

THE SIR EDMUND HILLARY BIRTHDAY CLUB

Joe O'Toole

So Sir Edmund Hillary has left us. It was a year ago this month that, arriving in New Zealand, he gazed out at me from the Auckland newspapers' front pages. Sir Edmund Hillary at eighty-seven years of age, returning from what was expected to be his last trip to the Antarctic ice.

That evocative photo image transported me back half a century.

I was almost seven years old when my father read from the *Sunday Press* the story of Edmund Hillary becoming the first man to conquer mighty Mount Everest, to stand proudly on what they called 'the top of the world'. He told me that Mount Everest was five miles high. Five miles. My child's mind struggled. That's from Dingle to Lispole straight up in the air. As he read the story, a new world of crampons, pitons, ice axes and more emerged. Well, we climbed every foot of that ice mountain with Edmund Hillary hammering home every spike, tying every safety rope and sucking the rarefied air until, frostbitten and weary, we reached the barren icy summit with himself and Sherpa Tenseng.

He was an instant hero, but we like our heroes local so there was an immediate natural affinity between the ice man Edmund Hillary and Abha-na-Scail man, Tom Crean. In that way, Edmund Hillary took his place among the pantheon of West Kerry greats. Somewhere along the way, I had made the interesting discovery that Tom Crean and Edmund Hillary shared the same 20 July birthday. More importantly though, it was also my very own birthday. We three were linked inseparably and forever in my fantasy youthful birthday club.

Now, in New Zealand 2007 with these memories flashing and flooding through my mind, I pondered the chances of meeting with the great man. The Irish consul enthusiastically agreed to help and, within a few days, confirmed the stunning and unexpected news. Sir Edmund would be delighted to meet and, better again, Lady Hillary had generously invited us to afternoon tea at their home.

Their Auckland home nestled in sumptuous bougainvilleas. The front door was welcomingly ajar when we arrived and a cheery 'Come on down' was the response to our speculative knock. Lady Hillary, a friendly, attractive and sophisticated woman without airs or graces, greeted us.

'I was just baking us some scones,' she said. 'Ed is in the lounge', and she handed me the tray.

He was erect, large-framed and taller than I had expected as, with a twinkle in his eye and a welcoming smile, he put us at our ease, explaining that his hearing was not as good as it used to be. Gentle, charismatic, understated and softly spoken, his presence filled that room. As we enjoyed Lady Hillary's home-made scones, Sir Ed explained that it was the two Irishmen, Crean and Shackleton, who were his great heroes and role models. It turned out that his grandfather and Lady Hillary's grandparents were Irish and he had been to Abha-na-Scail in the Dingle Peninsula and paid homage to Crean, the one he most admired. He laughed heartily at some local West Kerry stories about Tom Crean. He had never realised and was delighted when I pointed out that he shared the same birthday with Tom Crean and he smiled indulgently when I told him that it was also my own. 'You and Ed must exchange birthday cards this year,' Lady Hillary suggested. We did.

Later, he recalled vividly his extraordinarily surreal experience when, years previously, he had first walked into the century-old huts constructed by Scott, Shackleton, Crean and others, and which are still there to this day undisturbed on the ice.

'I was on my own,' he told us. 'When I walked into those huts for the first time, I might have emerged from a time machine. Things lay exactly as the exploration teams had left them nearly a century earlier. It was as if they had walked out the door just a few minutes previously. Cutlery and delph on the table, basic tools on the floor, the men's trousers and other clothes on the shelves and canned food, especially tins of beans, ready to be opened. It was eerie. I could feel their presence around me and with me and then I saw a figure come towards me with his arms out, I knew it was Shackleton and he smiled before he faded away. In all my life,' he continued, 'I never had a similar experience. I'm neither mystic nor overly spiritual and you may make what you will of it but, for me, it was real.'

There was a quiet moment after he had finished speaking. His last words to us were a question. 'Would you ask the Irish government to support the preservation of the Antarctic huts in memory of those great Irishmen?'

We did, and Ireland responded generously. And that was how I came to meet my hero, this previously remote global icon, Sir Edmund Hillary. New Zealand by birth, Irish by blood, one of our own.

I'll be sorry not to be sending him a birthday card this year.

Wii are family

Sue Norton

The only thing — and I mean the *only* thing — my nine-year-old son wanted for Christmas was a Nintendo Wii. 'You have to stand up and jump around to play it,' he kept insisting. 'I'll just ask Santa for it,' he said.

His father and I have resisted buying him electronic toys for years now, for all of the predictable — and predictably middle-class — reasons: he'll get sucked into an electronic vortex, we'll have to plead with him to come eat dinner, do his homework, walk the dog. He'll go off his books, his football, his neighbourhood spy-club. He'll go off us. And for the mother of all middle-class reasons, we finally gave in — all his friends have Wiis. What's a parent to do?

When he unwrapped the package on Christmas morning, his head nearly fell off. None of the gifts in the Santa pile had contained a Wii, so he concealed his disappointment and went on to open the presents from Mom and Dad. He thanked us for the binoculars, the scrapbook, the goalie gloves, the Eoin Colfer book. And then his little sister crawled off to retrieve a hard-to-reach package cornered under a back branch of the tree. Thoroughly devoid of expectation now, he peeled back the paper and saw that upper case '*W*' and then the two little '*iis*'. He rubbed his own eyes in disbelief, and, like I said, his head nearly fell off. He jumped all around the room screaming, 'A Wii, a Wii, I can't believe you got me a Wii!' And he really couldn't believe it. I think he thought Santa had brought him new parents.

We are a month past Christmas now and I'm wondering if I have any regrets. Well, we're out €240. That's regrettable. We're also out one or two high-minded principles about the ill-advisability of video games for children and about the repugnance of global consumerism. Nintendo for my child? I hardly recognise myself.

And to be sure, we have to call Declan five times for dinner. But, in truth, that's only one or two more times than before he had the Wii. What's probably more unsettling is that he hasn't even opened the Eoin Colfer book. Any chance he gets, he plays the Wii. His little avatar, his 'Mii', looks nothing like him. Declan's Mii has brown skin and an afro. So that's kinda cool. The Miis that he made representing me and his dad look for all the world like hip, attractive people. So he and his Wii have warmed my heart and flattered me, all in one go. (Believe me, no set of binoculars was going to achieve the same effect. Even if Declan had peered at us through them backwards, we would still have looked straight-laced and middle-aged, only far away.)

And what I've really liked about the Wii is that it has brought us up close. Up close to Declan. I still think that it – and its PlayStation, Gameboy and PSP cousins – is daft. But now I have a son whose parents are less remote. He thinks we're cool now. He doesn't expect us to be cool all the time – like about vegetables, homework and bedtime – but he knows we're *capable* of being cool. He knows we'll forsake our better judgement just to tickle him pink from time to time.

I'm never, ever going to buy him a toy gun. That, I'll stick to. And if he ever wants some gratuitously violent Wii video game, he won't get it. But, every so often, I hope we will remember to show him that we're not rigid, we're not doctrinaire. We are not, like our avatars, one dimensional and pre-programmed. Wii … are family.

BUILDING BRIDGES

Gemma Tipton

There's something very romantic about bridges. There's the connecting thing – the idea of getting you across something that seems impossible – or impassable – to the Other Side. There's the human ingenuity, the skill and the will to build this thing. Bridges are good. You might even say they're morally good – for how can bringing people and places together be bad?

I think it's easy to get excited about bridges. There's the one between Copenhagen and Malmö, you can see it from the air as you fly in. It's called the Oresund and it opened in 2000, connecting Denmark and Sweden together for the first time since the Ice Age, dancing across the sea as it goes. It's also the second longest suspension bridge in the world. People who are into bridges seem to like statistics. Third tallest, most arches, number of rivets, most tonnes of reinforced concrete ... Perhaps it's one way to get our heads around the sheer wonder bridges can evoke. This wonder, I think, comes close to philosopher Edmund Burke's idea of the Sublime – something that produces awe and a little bit of terror. He calls it astonishment – 'that state of the soul in which all its motions are suspended ... The mind,' he says, 'is so entirely filled with its object, that it cannot entertain any other.'

Well, on that note, if you want the Sublime, it has to be the Millau Bridge in France (and yes, it's the tallest in the world, one of the pillars is higher – indeed – than the Eiffel Tower). Above the clouds, it *is* truly breathtaking. Norman Foster, who designed it, said he wanted it to have 'the delicacy of a butterfly'. It's hard to imagine, until you see it, how beautiful concrete and steel can be. The closest we get to anything like that in Ireland are the Foyle Bridge in Derry and the Boyne Bridge in Drogheda. Lit blue at night, the Boyne Bridge glows like a magical thing. No, it doesn't float above the clouds, and, no, driving over it doesn't feel like flying a car, but it still gives a little hint of that astonishment that fills the mind with nothing but itself – for a brief moment at least.

There's this other idea in philosophy that says something is beautiful if it's perfectly designed for its purpose. Burke doesn't agree with this. When he discusses the sublime and beautiful, he says there isn't a connection, only coincidence. But the coincidence with bridges is strong. Their beauty comes from a grace – the kind of grace you get when all the parts are working perfectly together. The beauty of an arch comes from the fact that if it were even the tiniest bit different, it wouldn't stand, or bear the weight it's meant to.

And it's the bridges with the extra bits that lose that sense of grace and don't quite come off – like Santiago Calatrava's James Joyce Bridge over the Liffey in Dublin, all extra wings and white bits. I prefer the Millennium Bridge – the first time I saw it was on a misty night, and it ran flat, like a magic carpet over the river, little blue lights glowing against the foggy haze. We're getting another Calatrava bridge in Dublin soon, farther out towards the sea. I hope it doesn't feel like the first – something he had left over from a design for somewhere else. I hope it's as amazing as some of his other designs.

The great Victorian bridge builders, such as Isambard Kingdom Brunel (and you get the idea his mother had him marked for greatness when she named him), spread suspension bridges out like draped ribbons across rivers and gorges. There is Telford's Menai and Brunel's Clifton, which still cause drivers to stop their cars and wonder. Part of it is their grace and part of it is their size, but even though size matters, smaller bridges can do it for you too. There are those little ones in Venice, and also in Venice Beach, California, where tobacco millionaire Abbot Kinney recreated the Italian city's bridges and canals down the road from Los Angeles. Americans seem to have a habit of falling in love with foreign bridges. There is also London Bridge, now in Arizona, after another millionaire, Robert McCullough bought it and transported it brick by brick in 1968. Today, it's second only to the Grand Canyon as a tourist attraction there. From the ridiculous to the sublime, you might say.

Yes, there is definitely something very romantic about bridges. Romantic *and* sublime. When the Channel Tunnel was first opened, the novelist J. G. Ballard said, 'Yes it is amazing. But imagine if it had been a bridge ...'

FEBRUARY

BROOKLYN HEIGHTS

Andrew Motion

That Sunday morning in Brooklyn
My love side-stepped into Oscar's bar
For coffee before our day of pleasure
While I sat on the blue bench outside
still slow with love and breakfast.
It was only then I noticed the stranger
dressed for church in a charcoal suit
And starched shirt unlocking his bike
from railings close to my right hand.
Good morning, I said, and meant it,
But he had his mind on other things,
His chain tingling through the spokes
And turning link by link to solid silver
As he pulled it free. Or was that only me?

I used to be too slow, always, or too quick,
so my shots at everything fell wide
of where they meant to strike and stick.
The truth of love is letting love decide.

In the same moment my love re-appeared
And settled her warm head on my shoulder,
The smart stranger hoofed off from the kerb

Letting his own weight carry him smoothly
Along the bare black river of new tarmac.
It was a part of our happiness to watch him
coasting away from us in his own good time,
until a gust of wind blew loose the seeds
from sycamores across the road. I thought
of angels, and of angel-brightness blessing
where it fell. Although from where we sat
It looked more like an inexplicable cascade
of single pale propeller blades which sliced
The solid air to ribbons, and ourselves as well.

BENEDICT KIELY (1919–2007)

Gerald Dawe

In May 1945, the twenty-six-year-old Benedict Kiely published a fascinating book, *Counties of Contention*, subtitled *A Study of the Origins and Implications of the Partition of Ireland.* The study was reissued in 2004 by the original publishers, Mercier. Kiely published two other studies, the groundbreaking *Poor Scholar: A Study of the Works and Days of William Carleton (1794–1869)* in 1947 and *Modern Irish Fiction: A Critique* in 1950. In 1999, *A Raid into Dark Corners and Other Essays* appeared under the imprint of Cork University Press. Notwithstanding his importance as a maker of fiction and a memoir writer, Kiely's critical writing is important for a number of reasons, other than the insight that these works reflect upon his imaginative writing.

From a generational point of view, Kiely represents that great wave of post-independence writers who were caught up in the artistic, political and cultural assessments of Irish nationalism, its achievements and failures, and who analysed these directly or indirectly as writers.

It is curious to compare the writing of Ben Kiely in his late twenties and his contemporaries – both immediate, including Anthony Cronin and Robert Greacen, and somewhat older, such as Seán Ó Faoláin, Frank O'Connor, Patrick Kavanagh, John Hewitt – with the younger writers of today, few of whom would be drawn to politically sensitive issues – sectarianism, or more recently, inter-culturalism, for instance – in the same way that, for example, the partition of Ireland was such a burning issue to Kiely's generation. Even fewer today would, I imagine risk the wrath of their peers with a critical study of contemporary Irish fiction, such as Kiely wrote almost sixty years ago.

I recall reading his study of William Carleton (*The Poor Scholar*) in the early 1970s. I was a graduate student at University College Galway, researching a thesis on Carleton under the supervision of the Professor of English at the college, the late Lorna Reynolds.

Kiely's book was an absolute godsend because, in those days, only a handful of academics and writers (including Patrick Kavanagh, Anthony Cronin, John Montague and Thomas Flanagan) had written about the Tyrone novelist. Others who had heard of Kiely dismissed him as an historical curiosity, a thoroughly minor figure in the landscape of nineteenth-century Ireland, not much worth bothering about.

The Poor Scholar had an extraordinary dramatic impact and opened the door upon a world that was, in literary and cultural circles of the time, very much under the shadows of a neglected, fugitive, indeed strangely repressed, past.

And then a few years later, in 1977, Kiely's magnificent short novel *Proxopera* appeared, one of the masterpieces to have emerged out of the dark days of the Troubles. Indeed, the novel can be read as a kind of critique of *Counties of Contention*. It is much more than this, but it does interrogate some of Kiely's earlier assumptions.

Read together, *The Poor Scholar*, *Counties of Contention* and *Proxopera* provide a unique insight into the history of Northern Ireland: hope and reality, the legacy of sectarianism, political failure and political violence as seen and interpreted by one writer standing alone, and make a lasting testament to the impact of all these forces upon the imaginative traditions.

But back in the late 1970s, this awareness was all a long way off.

We used to assemble in the Great Southern Hotel in Galway on Sundays for a swim — kids, parents and friends. It was a ritual. The pool sat on top of the hotel, by the rather plush restaurant and neat cocktail bar, and often, when the kids were finishing off, we'd have a drink before heading our various ways home throughout Galway town and county.

One early afternoon, shuffling through the Sunday papers, coffee and sandwiches at the ready, the lift to the top floor opened, and I recall hearing, as if it were only yesterday, the distinctive voice, referring to 'my sister', and then spotting the shock of hair passing by, followed by a group of Americans en route to the bar. There was a kind of pop-star quality about Ben. No matter whom he had in tow, electricity seemed to follow him and the atmosphere intensified, as if something quite brilliant was about to happen. Which of course it did, for Ben, whom I only got to know briefly towards the end of his powerful life, was a shape-changer in conversation.

I never knew anyone like that before or since. His memory of all kinds of oral and written literature was second to none. He knew all the great European and American classics. And he had also read all the stuff that no one else had. He was an expert without being pompous about it.

When I had started my thesis on William Carleton in the 1970s, he was one of only two people who responded to my queries. He was a mentor before the term was invented. I recall at a dinner in his honour, organised by Ben's stalwart friend and supporter, John Wilson Foster, his regaling (a Ben word I suspect) me with advice about nineteenth-century Irish poetry in English – for decades a No-Go area. And when we left him home, the walking cane waved in the air with a wonderful flourish.

Ben was a chieftain. He belongs among the blessed of this earth. I hope some day all his work – the fiction, the criticism and the memoirs – will be available to the younger generation of readers of literature in English.

For Ben Kiely deserves that – a new audience to listen to him and learn, and, most importantly of all else, to enjoy, to relish the voice of a good man talking about what he knows and loves. I cherish the few hours I spent in his company.

SWEET OMAGH TOWN

Benedict Kiely

You may recall the traveller in Oliver Goldsmith's poem who wandered,

> remote, unfriended, melancholy, slow,
> Or by the lazy Scheld or wandering Po,
> Or onward where the rude Carinthian boor
> Against the houseless stranger shuts the door.

He found that his heart remained untravelled and, over long distances, turned in affection to his brother and at each further remove from home, he dragged 'a lengthening chain'.

That was a thought that seemed to be much in the mind of a writer so French in his style and so Irish in his heart, and who may in his boyhood have heard the songs and harp music of Carolan. For in the wisest and most delightful series of essays ever put together in English he makes his imaginary citizen of the world, Lien Chi Altangi, a man from Honan, write from England and to his friend and mentor in the Orient and at the far end of two continents: 'The farther I travel I feel the pain of separation with stronger force: those ties that bind me to my native country and you are still unbroken. By every remove I only drag a greater length of chain.'

This attachment to place, to the home places, even the mythologising of place names, is not confined obviously to ourselves, the Irish, nor even to island people. But it is possible that it may be more emphasised in the case of island people, and made more poignant when their destiny takes them far from the island of their earliest associations and affections, Ithaca or Ireland.

Aodh de Blácam in his most valuable book *Gaelic Literature Surveyed* linked Seathrún Céitinn's famous syllabic exile poem with poems of the early and middle Irish and talked of the magic of its vision.

> Hail to her nobles, her counsels;
> hail, all hail to her clerics:
> hail to her gentle women:
> hail to her poets and scholars.
>
> Hail to her level places
> and a thousand times to her hillsides:
> oh, lucky he that dwells there,
> hail to her loughs and waters.
>
> Hail to her heavy forests,
> hail likewise to her fish-weirs:
> hail to her moors and meadows:
> hail to her rafts and marshes.
>
> Hail from my heart to her harbours,
> hail too, to her fruitful drylands;
> to her hilltop hosting:
> hail to her bending branches.
> O writing, my blessing
>
> Though often strive the peoples
> in that wealthy holy island —
> westward over the surging flood
> bear, O writing, my blessing.

Through that poem, de Blácam found it possible to look back to an early nature poetry whose 'peculiar and magic virtue' was to concentrate within a lyric 'a vision of a spacious region. We are given an image of Alba or of Éire as the Creator (we think) might see it; or as some hunter who had ranged all its hills might imagine it in peaceful memory at life's end.'

In an Ossianic poem, for instance, describing the reveries on the life of the warrior running through the mind of Fionn, places are mentioned as far apart as Assaroe on the Erne, and Slieve Gua in the Decies, Slemish in Antrim and Erris in Mayo.

It was a desire of the son of Cumhall to listen to the sound of the wind in the trees of Drumderg, to sleep to the sound of the current at Assaroe, and to hunt in Feeguile of the wolf litters.

The warbling of the blackbird of Letterlee, the wave of Rury beating on the strand, the belling of the stag from the plain of Maev, the sound of the deer on Slieve Gua, the whistle of the seagulls beyond in Erris, the rushing of the three streams by Slemish ...

Places so loved, names so often repeated as if they were charms and words of power and invocations of the very spirit of place, gathered about them their own sanctities and mythological significance.

One of the most curious samples of that itinerary literature that was our predilection comes from my own county of Tyrone, the 'Seachrán Cairn tSiadhail' – the Carnteel rambler. Carnteel is a spot on the road between Aughnacloy and Benburb and the poet saw there his vision on a bright morning and set off for twenty-eight verses, in an almost intoxicated celebration of the place names of Ireland.

It was a mode that passed on to popular balladry in English, to roam through Roosia and likewise Proosia and sweet Kilkenny and distant Spain, and to return in the end to that first, best country and to see the smoke rising above your own rooftree.

About my own home town, there is, as far as I know, no song in Irish, but some unknown balladeer did the needful in Sax-Béarla, in a song I've heard sung by Davey Hammond and Gerry Hicks and Seán Ó Baoill and the words as I have them now, I owe to Paddy Tunney.

> From sweet Dungannon to Ballyshannon
> From Cullyhanna to Old Ardboe
> I've roamed and rambled
> Caroused and gambled
> Where songs did thunder and whiskey flow
> It's light and airy
> I've tramped through Derry
> And to Portaferry in the County Down
> But with all my raking and undertaking
> My heart was aching for sweet Omagh town.

POETRY MAKES NOTHING HAPPEN

Stephen Matterson

'Poetry makes nothing happen.' That phrase is one of W. H. Auden's
most widely quoted, and yet it is, on its own, a rather misleading senti-
ment for understanding Auden.

'Poetry makes nothing happen' appears in his elegy for W. B. Yeats, a
poem that Auden wrote in February 1939, a month or so after Yeats'
death, and only a few weeks after Auden's arrival in the United States.
For many of Auden's readers, 'poetry makes nothing happen' must have
seemed like a statement reflecting a shift in his own poetry, a move away
from the public commitments that his renowned work of the 1930s had
so clearly and so brilliantly embraced. Auden's moving to the United
States seemed like a flight from that earlier self and its commitments,
an act of turning his back upon both England and on the 1930s, the
period that he was soon to label a 'low, dishonest decade'.

While there is some truth in this perception, it is very far from being
the whole story. The phrase 'poetry makes nothing happen' is quoted far
more often than the whole, long sentence in which it appears, where
those four words are nuanced and developed towards a searching exam-
ination of what poetry is and does:

> For poetry makes nothing happen: it survives
> In the valley of its making where executives

Would never want to tamper, flows on south
From ranches of isolation and the busy griefs,
Raw towns that we believe and die in; it survives,
A way of happening, a mouth.

Poetry is a 'way of happening'. It's a mouth, we turn to it for the expression of things we find difficult to say, for things that touch us, move us, delight us. Rather than locating the importance of poetry in its immediate historical and public effect, Auden sees it in a larger, historical perspective, which is the difference between making something happen, and a 'happening'. He refers to the astonishing range of poetry and the themes and ideas that it can accommodate; like a river it will flow through valleys, ranches and towns, bringing life and meaning, reaching and touching lives. Lives that include my own, as I realised when I first read Auden's long poem 'New Year Letter', in which he wrote, as he often did, of the landscape in which I was growing up: 'those limestone moors that stretch from Brough/To Hexham and the Roman wall' where the river Eden 'leisures through its sandstone valley'; 'Always my boy of wish returns/To those peat-stained deserted burns/That feed the Wear and Tyne and Tees.' Poems don't just speak to us, they speak for us.

Auden's poem in memory of Yeats ends with a kind of rhapsody. As so often happens, one poet's elegy for someone else turns out really to be about the poet, and about what poetry means. In this darkening world of 1939, Europe is clearly heading towards another catastrophic war:

In the nightmare of the dark
All the dogs of Europe bark,
And the living nations wait,
Each sequestered in its hate;

Rather than being silenced by this terror, this dread, there is more need than ever before for the voice of the poet, a voice that can connect us to each other, to the world, and to history; this is what 'survives', raises us above ourselves, above the immediate, and above our failures. Auden, born 100 years ago in 1907, ends his elegy for Yeats with a vision of the work of the poet in the public world, and Auden concludes his poem with the two lines that appear as his own epitaph on his memorial plaque in Westminster Abbey:

Follow, poet, follow right
To the bottom of the night,
With your unconstraining voice
Still persuade us to rejoice.

With the farming of a verse
Make a vineyard of the curse,
Sing of human unsuccess
In a rapture of distress.

In the deserts of the heart
Let the healing fountains start,
In the prison of his days
Teach the free man how to praise.

THE FOTTRELL PAPERS

Melosina Lenox-Conyngham

It is ironic that some of the most important source material of the Dominican Order in Ireland should have been preserved for over two hundred years in the house of an Ulster Protestant. George Butler Conyngham, my great-great-grandfather, lived at Springhill, County Derry, where he was a landowner and a magistrate. His portrait shows him to be no beauty, with a long nose, a double chin and a stiff white wig.

In 1739, at Toomebridge on the northwest shore of Lough Neagh, he arrested two Catholic religious whom he thought were the Catholic Archbishop of Armagh and the Catholic Bishop of Derry but who, to his disappointment, were Fr Fottrell, Major Superior of the Irish Dominican friars and Michael MacDonagh, Bishop of Kilmore, on their way to make a visitation to the Dominicans in Coleraine. He had them imprisoned, but soon they were able to escape and hurried back to Dublin. A reward of £200 was offered for the recapture of Dr MacDonagh who left hastily for Rome where he spent a year before returning to Ireland.

I would like to think that their escape was because of remorse suffered by my ancestor for having persecuted Roman Catholics, but I fear it was pique at not having detained bigger fish, for he flung all the papers that had been taken from the two priests into a cupboard in the library. For the next two hundred years, they remained there, in the battered leather portfolio that Fr Fottrell had been writing on when he was arrested.

These documents included the provincial archives of the Dominicans for the previous four years with various letters, addresses, notes and sermons. In one address to a community of nuns, Fr Fottrell condemned the use of ruffles and, particularly, headdresses which had scandalised the laity and he was shocked to see young nuns walking for a considerable time with secular men in the garden.

Fr Fottrell's companion, Michael MacDonagh the Bishop of Kilmore, had joined the Dominican Order in Coleraine, studied in Italy and then taught at the college in Rome. When there, he was made confessor to the youthful Bonnie Prince Charlie.

In 1730, he returned to Ireland as Bishop of Kilmore; an appointment that caused 'amazement' in Ulster because of his youth and that he had been elevated over those with superior credentials. However, he was a discreet and prudent man, though, according to one complaint received, his zeal overcame his judgement when he intervened on behalf of his double first cousin, 'a fighting, drinking and disreputable parish priest', who had a papal bull entitling him to the Deanery of Derry. According to a report sent to Rome, the cousins rode into Derry and entered the cathedral, which was full of Protestants celebrating the birthday of King George I. To the great surprise of the congregation, Michael MacDonagh gave the priest public possession of the deanery. They then rode off like mad men towards Dublin boasting and drinking so heavily, that his double first cousin fell off his horse and broke his leg.

Dr MacDonagh said those descriptions were 'abominable and execrably calumnies' of what had happened and gave his own version of the event in which he said that when travelling in Derry, he had met the cousin who had a fresh papal bull for the Deanery of Derry. With another priest, they had gone to a locked room in the city where the cousin took the oath and they then went quietly to the postern gate of the cathedral where the bishop put his cousin into possession of his deanery without anyone, Catholic or Protestant, being the wiser. He added indignantly that it was before breakfast four days later that the cousin's horse stumbled so that he fell off but that he did not break his leg.

After the incident at Toomegridge, Fr Fottrell and Bishop MacDonagh eventually returned to their pastoral work and though they suffered persecution, it was not again at the hands of my great-great-grandfather.

ROOM 511

John O'Donnell

They met just once at a fishing competition. There is a photograph of the two of them together. They are surrounded by hangers-on but both men seem oblivious to the fuss. The younger man is lean and trim and wears his trademark peaked army hat and appears to be listening intently and respectfully to whatever advice the older man, paunchy in a battered sailing cap, is murmuring into his ear. It is 1960 in Havana. The competition is the grandly titled International Swordfish Fishing Tournament, a competition invented by and since named after the older man in the photograph, Ernest Hemingway. And the younger man is the 1960 tournament winner, a man named Fidel Castro.

Years later, we are in the Hotel Ambos Mundos in Havana. A copy of the photograph hangs in Room 511, a room which has since become a kind of shrine. The small corner room has three windows giving out onto the streets below and the room itself is as spare as anything its most famous occupant ever wrote when he lived here for part of the 1930s. A bed. A couple of shelves of books. On the day we visit, a couple of typed pages from *Death in the Afternoon*, complete with proof corrections marked in pencil (the pencil too is there) in Hemingway's own handwriting, lie on a little table. Beside these pages is the Royal typewriter at which Hemingway stood to type *For Whom the Bell Tolls*. A leg wound sustained during his days as an ambulance driver in the First World War made it uncomfortable for him to sit for any length of time.

'Show me a great American writer,' the saying goes 'and I'll show you a great American drinker.' But our Cuban guide solemnly insists: Hemingway never drank while he was writing. True, the stories of boozing and brawling seem a long way from the quiet of this little room. We look again at the picture. It is tempting to think of both men as being at the height of their powers at the time the photograph was taken. Here is Hemingway, aged sixty, the Pulitzer and Nobel Prize winner. Here, too, is Castro the revolutionary and recently elected Prime Minister, the thirty-three-year-old law graduate who had led the Revolution against the oppressive military regime and who would go on to lead his country through the next half century.

Our tour completed and tips distributed, we climb the stairs to the rooftop terrace of the hotel, order the obligatory mojitos, and gaze out over the skyline of the city, so many of the once-beautiful buildings now crumbling, on the brink of collapse. What could Hemingway have been saying to Castro all those years ago, as he murmured into the newly elected leader's ear? It would be wonderful to think Castro was receiving advice on how to hook and hold a marlin from the writer of *The Old Man and the Sea*. But the truth may be shabbier and far less romantic. In 1940, Hemingway bought Finca Vigía, an idyllic farmhouse just outside Havana where he lived and wrote with his third (and later fourth) wife for twenty years. But after the revolution in 1959, the Cuban government decided to expropriate property owned by US citizens, including – it appears – Finca Vigía, The Cuban government has always insisted that Hemingway *donated* the house as a generous gesture to the people of Cuba. But maybe Hemingway had no option but to leave. It is said this meeting in 1960 was no more than a last opportunity for Hemingway to meet with Castro and plead to be allowed to keep his property. Some say Hemingway even allowed Castro to win the fishing tournament so desperate was he to hold on to his Havana home. If so, the plan backfired completely. Perhaps Castro used the occasion as a publicity stunt; an opportunity to see and be seen with one of the greatest writers of the century.

Either way, nothing happened. Hemingway left Cuba shortly after the photograph was taken. Just over a year later, he was dead. Perhaps it was unsurprising that the writer who proclaimed that 'a man does not exist until he is drunk', should himself be a long-time sufferer from high blood pressure and liver problems. Hemingway also suffered from paranoia and manic depression, which his medical advisors in their wisdom treated with ECT. Hemingway blamed this electro-convulsive therapy for 'putting him out of business' as a writer by destroying his memory.

Having left his beloved Havana, on 2 July 1961, he took one of his favourite shotguns from the basement gun cabinet of his new home in Ketchum, Idaho. He pressed the barrels against his forehead and pulled both triggers. His legacy is, of course, the writing; the terse vivid prose that says so much in so few words. The legends also survive; so, also (in a somewhat dilapidated state), does Finca Vigía. And so does Room 511 in the Hotel Ambos Mundos, the hotel of 'both worlds'; where there is a bed and a typewriter and a picture of one man asking to be let stay in the world he loved and another man who would change the world in which they both lived forever.

ROCK 'N' ROLL

James Cotter

In February 1992, Guns N' Roses announced they'd play Slane Castle later that year. As soon as I heard it, I knew with the absolute certainty of a fifteen-year-old that it would be the best day of my life.

The tickets went on sale one Saturday morning. Me and Ed, my best mate, decided we should queue before the shops opened. Sure, Slane could only hold about 80,000 and there'd be at least 2 million who wanted to see the best rock 'n' roll band ever. I mean, even the Pope got a million.

So when that Saturday arrived, we got up at 4.30 a.m. and Eamonn, my long suffering dad, drove us into Grafton Street. Although not quite a million, there were several hundred people in the queue. It was an intriguing slice of society; long-haired students and leather clad ne'er-do-wells mixed with Axl-Rose-loving schoolgirls and the occasional down-and-out, who, although not particularly interested in paying £50 to go to a field in Meath, seemed to enjoy the whole queuing process. Especially the yelling-at-passers-by bit ...

Now, queuing today isn't what it used to be — these days if you are fifteen and stuck in a queue, you'd probably have your Sony mini-games-console with you to play wireless *Hyperkill-Murder-Deathball 3000* with the other queuers and when your batteries wore out you could always hook yourself up to your MP3 player. If the worst came to the worst, you could amuse yourself by texting all your mates with wake-up messages.

But this was 1992 and all those gadgets were but distant gleams in the eyes of Japanese designers. We had nothing. We stared glumly at the queue ahead of us, then, after an hour or so, just to shake things up, we turned round and stared glumly at the queue behind us. There were a few nice-looking rocker girls there but, despite our long hair and moody stares, they didn't seem to want to talk to us. To be fair to them, if you saw what I looked like back then, you wouldn't want to talk to me either.

Ed, combining the worst of both his geek and rocker tendencies, had fitted two small speakers inside his jacket which he hooked up to his Walkman. Preparing to impress the crowd with this futuristic clothing, he pressed play. Unfortunately, he'd forgotten to change the batteries. The tortured noise that squeaked from his jacket may once have been Metallica, but forced out of a Walkman at quarter speed through two tinny South Korean speakers, it sounded nothing so much as a funeral dirge being sung by Alvin and the Chipmunks after six pints and a valium.

Eventually, the shop opened and, to our great relief, when we reached the front of the queue, they still had tickets. It later turned out that if we'd wandered along on the morning of the concert, they still would have been able to spare oh, 9,000 or 10,000 for us – a point my dad didn't tire of making for months afterwards.

When the day of the concert came, me and Ed were on the first bus down to Slane and, when the gates opened, we raced down that long green field and got to the very front of the stage. As I looked up at the hundred-foot-tall stack of speakers that towered above me, I knew this really was going to be the best day of my life.

The sun beat down and the first supporting band came onto the stage with a yell of 'Bishop Eamon Casey, fair fecks to ya!' The crowd cheered, Ed and I looked at each other and nodded, yup, we were rebels against society, fearlessly rocking out and laughing at the establishment.

The day went by in a haze of screaming and sweat, scary toilets and noise. Noise so loud, every time a cymbal hit I felt a physical pain in my chest. I loved it.

As we made our way home afterwards, two red faces in a sea of sweaty black denim, we agreed it was probably the best gig ever performed by anyone, anywhere. We knew we were at the defining event of our generation, the Woodstock for rockers. In the back of the bus, we heard people talking about an upcoming Nirvana gig. We scoffed quietly, Nirvana were all very well, but they didn't speak for our generation, sure this whole grunge thing was just some Johnny-come-lately fad. But Poodle-haired rock, we knew, was eternal.

When I got home, hard-as-nails-rocker that I was, I told my mum all about the perfect day I'd had. The only problem, I frowned, was a bit of ringing in the ears – but it was a small price to pay and, sure, it was bound to go in a day or two.

Fifteen years later and I'm still waiting for the ringing to go. But if that's the worst thing I did to myself during my teenage years, I got off lightly. After all, one of my mates has a Def Leppard tattoo.

I got a call from Ed the other day; he lives in Spain now and is in the middle of starting his own company. I waited to hear him complaining about the cost of this, or the time it takes to do that. But all he said was – Guns N' Roses are playing in June; man, get tickets quick, they're bound to sell out!

THE IRISH CASANOVA

Catherine Brophy

There was a time when the only foreigners living in Ireland were the Italian fish and chip families, the Chinese takeaway clans and the occasional European or American woman married to an Irishman. I knew several of these women, women brought up in exotic, faraway places like Vienna, Marseilles, Amsterdam and New Jersey, and I could never figure out what it was that possessed them to marry Irish men.

'Oh but Irish men are so romantic,' they said, 'so poetic.'

In my experience, they were never romantic and the 'poetic' ones were literary poseurs who wore smelly clothes and who'd trample to death any *cailín* who stood between them and their drink. One of them tried to impress me in Grafton Street once by lifting his chin, running his hands through his dandruff-speckled locks and declaiming in sub-Mac Liammóir tones, 'I must arise now and go for I must return to the womb.'

He was heading for Amiens Street Station to catch the train home to his mammy.

And to make matters worse, whenever I travelled in Europe, dark-eyed Italians would press their hands to their hearts and declare that my eyes had ensnared them. Torero-hipped Spaniards insisted their lives would be ruined if I didn't give them my love. Mustachioed Greeks vowed that I was their goddess Athene. Heady stuff for a convent-bred girl. And I lapped it up!

But I wasn't a complete eejit. I knew they didn't really mean it and that they said the same things to any young woman they met, but, still and all … I wished and I wished that Irish men could learn to be just a bit more romantic. To start opening doors, offering a single wild flower, noticing that actually, I do have nice eyes. But whenever I said this to fellows I knew, they guffawed, dug me in the ribs and asked if I was going for a jar.

Oh well I thought, we're a slave nation. We've no tradition of courtly love, no Romeos, no Don Juans, no Casanovas to offer our men folk direction.

And then, one bright Sunday, I went into the National Gallery of Ireland and there he was. No, not the love of my life, but a full-length portrait by Joshua Reynolds of Charles Coote, the first Earl of Bellamont otherwise known as 'The Irish Casanova'.

And not only that, he was a Cavan man. No disrespect to the men of Cavan, grand lads and great talkers, but Romeos – I don't know.

Charles Coote, however, cut a swathe through the women of Ireland. He deserted his wife – well you can't be a decent Casanova with a wife in tow. Then, he cut an equally wide swathe through the sophisticated social scene in London, fathering daughters wherever he went. His men friends thought he was pompous, big-headed and not much of a public speaker, but even they recognised that he had a way with the ladies. At one point, he courted a tradesman's daughter who wanted a ring on her finger before she'd submit to his charms. So, he dressed up his servant to look like a parson and they held a fake wedding. Sure, you wouldn't get better in a play.

Go and look at his picture in the National Gallery of Ireland and you'll see it all there. A plain enough lad, God bless him, but with oodles of oomph, who obviously saw himself as God's gift. He's standing there with his hand on his sword, legs crossed to show a fine muscled calf, dressed in a suit of white satin. His long hair flows free and his hat sprouts a bouquet of huge, high, white feathers.

'Look at me,' he seems to be saying, 'amn't I pure gorgeous out.'

He has pink rosettes on his shoes, a huge, mayoral-type chain on his chest and over his shoulders is draped a luscious, pink satin cloak with the large sunburst crest of the Order of the Bath. Actually, the cloak was originally red but that's faded with time and somehow the pink seems perfectly right, for the one thing that Romeos, Don Juans and Casanovas can do is flaunt colours that most men would shun. And get this; the gorgeous pink cloak is tied with a cord which has great golden tassels dangling down over his thighs. It's as though he were saying, 'Now don't worry ladies, I've got what it takes.'

I laughed when I saw him. Such a peacock.

But no wonder he'd had no effect on the men that I knew in my youth. He was the Earl of Bellamont, a member of the Ascendancy and a horse Protestant who'd put down a minor rebellion. And what Irishman worth his porridge and spuds would look to the likes of him for lessons in charm?

JOHN DONNE:
LOVE'S LOST CHRONICLER

Emer O'Kelly

When John Donne died in 1631, his reputation was already established as a great poet. A hundred years later, it had plummeted, largely thanks to the robust criticisms of Samuel Johnson, who bluffly disapproved of his predecessor's 'metaphysical conceits'. This actually had nothing to do with metaphysics per se: it expressed Johnson's disdain for poets who flaunted their learning, the 'conceits' being the use of learned or even far-fetched images. The conceit for which Johnson himself is best remembered, of course, is his less-than-objective definition of 'patriotism' in his dictionary as 'the last refuge of a scoundrel'. Poor Donne, on the other hand, was a genuinely tortured scholar who spent the latter years of his life as Dean of St Paul's in London absorbed in notions of faith and possible damnation, exploring both in his religious poetry. If his wraith is out there somewhere, he probably sees the reputation he now holds as yet another flail for his always lively conscience: today it's not the tormented intelligence of the man who lived as the scientific age began that we remember. Our familiar is the solemn-faced, austere soul who still wrote some of the most tremulously passionate and joyously sexual poetry ever known.

We sometimes forget that it was not until the dawn of the era of family values under the pretty and pudding-faced Victoria and her lumpish German husband Alfred that sex became disreputable in literature.

In the seventeenth century, notions of 'courtly love' frequently palpated more than the lily-white breasts of the privileged and modest objects of its pure desire.

> This bargaine's good; if when I am old, I bee
> Inflam'd by thee,
> If thine owne honour, or my shame, or paine,
> Thou covet most, at that age thou shalt gaine.
> Doe thy will then, then subject and degree,
> And fruit of love, Love I submit to thee,
> Spare mee til then, I'll beare it, though she bee
> One that loves mee.

The longing is like a drawn-out breath, just as the tempest of frustration rages in 'Twicknam Garden':

> Make me a mandrake, so I may grow here,
> Or a stone fountaine weeping out my year ...

> O perverse sex, where none is true but shee,
> Who's therefore true, because her truth kills mee.

Then there is the perfection of new love, untarnished by mundane experience, the sun rising daily to be addressed in expectation of more glory as in the poem of the same name:

> Thy beames, so reverend, and strong
> Why shoulds't thou thinke?
> I could eclipse and cloud them with a winke,
> But that I would not lose her sight so long ...

> Aske for those Kings whom thou saw'st yesterday,
> And thou shalt heare, All here in one bed lay.

> She's all States, and all Princes, I,
> Nothing else is ...

> Shine here to us, and thou art every where;
> This bed thy center is, these walls, thy spheare.

When Donne married the niece of his patron's wife, he destroyed his burgeoning career as a rising courtier and diplomat. He had abandoned the faith of his father, Catholicism, around 1593, shortly after his brother died in prison, committed there for having harboured a priest. The Donnes had always been a Catholic family; Thomas More, the accuser and scourge of Henry VIII, was a relative of John's mother. But it would seem that it was genuine doubt of conscience which prompted Donne's apostasy rather than a fear of ruining his career. He was an intimate of Sir Walter Raleigh and the Earl of Essex, the Queen's favourite. But none of that mattered when, on becoming secretary to Sir Thomas Egerton, the young careerist married Ann More, Lady Egerton's niece. He was imprisoned only briefly, but years in the wilderness followed. Ironically, when he returned to court favour, James I insisted that he embrace the ministry, and he was ordained in 1615. His beloved Ann was to bear him twelve children before the final birth killed her in 1617, only two years after favour began again to shine on her husband.

But Donne seems never to have forgotten her or the joys they had shared, although the celebration of both in poetry had long been abandoned for more lofty themes when he died. But even though he wrote of the ecstatic pleasures of her bed, John Donne had an encyclopaedic storm of knowledge of the pain as well as the joy of love. Did he stroke thighs other than Ann's, before or during marriage? Did he suffer the pangs of unrequited love or the chill of a swan neck turned from him in cold rejection? Certainly, he knew with exquisite precision about the dolorous side of love:

> I brought a heart into the roome;
> But from the roome, I carried none with mee:
> If it had gone to thee, I know
> Mine would have taught thine heart to show
> More pitty unto mee: but Love, alas,
> At one, first blow did shiver it as glasse.

Nor was he a stranger to the double entendre, as in 'A Valediction: forbidding mourning' he writes of two souls:

> If they be two, they are two so
> As stiffe twin compasses are two,

Thy soule the fixt foot, makes no show
To move, but doth, if the other doe.
And though it in the center sit,
Yet when the other far doth rome,
It leanes, and hearkens after it,
And growes erect, as it comes home.

And as he preached his way to death from the pulpit of St Paul's, passionately and eloquently according to contemporary accounts, it's hard not to wonder in the twenty-first century how many members of the solemn-faced Dean's seventeenth-century congregation knew that he had once sighed onto the page:

Licence my roving hands, and let them goe
Behind, before, above, between, below.
O my America, my new found lande ...

HOLDING HER

Sharon Hogan

I feel her
nearly
                    immediately.

She rests, quietly.

Warm,
          high in my
belly,
                         a gentle orange dawning
                              like light through honey
                              like   spooling toffee
                                             sweet light
warm.

I know at once it is a girl.

She rests there
          nestled in her tiny, glowing
cradle
                    humming in the centre of my being

humming in my heart, too,

                    and hands
                                        hips
                    lips tongue
toe-tips.

I talk to her
constantly,
secretly.

Do you see that? —
                              a white moth landing on my sister's straw hat

Can you hear that? —
                              wind-chimes at the
Garden Centre
                              resonant, reverberant

I didn't mean that —
                              a flash of anger
at myself —
                                                  it might confuse

the small self
sleeping inside me

We won't worry about that —
                                        suddenly sensing

the solidarity of
Two.

It feels that for
the first time,
maybe,

I am not alone.
I am
accompanied -

by myself,

and by this invisible,
                         infinitesimal,
                                    burgeoning
Being
Who
silently,
                              subtly,
utterly,

teaches me of Love.

I learn that

that
which dims her warming flame
also dims
my own

that

that
which nourishes me
helps her to flourish

- like so,
we grow together:

she, hidden-ly,
small-ly,
                              heartbeat by heartbeat
I, palpably,
in depth and breadth,
                                    in heart and force and feeling

For eight weeks.

Then I wake
very
early.

I feel her let go.

I feel her
Rolling like a warm brown tear
          Down through my body,
Out of my body,
          Drawing wisps and tendrils of herself
          From my hands and teeth and eyelids

Where she had lodged

Until I am empty.

I see her
          Lying in the base of the bowl
          Small, red-brown cluster
          Against white ceramic.

          Nameless.

She is gone.

A year later
To the day nearly

I feel a coldness
In the place where she had lain.
It is a silvery, steel-ly whiteness
That cuts, ice-water-coloured,
Straight through my solar plexus.

I wish I could have held her.

THE GRAVE OF SYLVIA PLATH

Michael O'Loughlin

When we think of England, or at least when I think of England, I think of cities and motorways, the London Underground with its multicultural crowds. So, as I sat in the little train that runs between Manchester and Leeds, that idyllic green heartland of hills and valleys, woods, and quaint villages came as a revelation to me. Moston, Rochdale, Smithy Bridge, Todmorden, the solid Anglo-Saxon names of Yorkshire delighted me. But when I reached my destination, the small village of Hepden Bridge, it all began to seem familiar. The canals and sturdy stone bridges, with the brown moors in the distance, the mist on the small chimneys tucked into river valleys, these I knew from the poetry of Ted Hughes, in particular his book with photographer Faye Godwin, *Remains of Elmet*.

This was no coincidence, as the reason I was in this literary area was directly related to Ted Hughes. I was to give a reading at his former home of Lumb Bank, not far from his birthplace in Heptonstall. The old mill owner's house is now a branch of the Arvon Foundation, providing creative writing courses for people from all over the world. As I sat sipping a glass of wine in the library, surrounded by thousands of poetry collections, the director introduced me to a large black tomcat. 'This is Ted Hughes,' he said. 'We're now on our seventh.'

After the reading, I remarked to the director that the group included quite a few Irish people. He told me that they were being inundated with applications from Ireland. 'It's those SSIA government savings things,' he told me. 'People now have money to develop themselves.' It's an ill wind that blows no good, I thought.

After a restless night, in which I dreamt that the stream flooding the valley below was a hurricane, I woke in the dark just before dawn. I had a special task to do before returning to Dublin.

It was a grim, damp morning. The sheep huddled on the moors and the clouds enveloped the trees. As I sweated up the hill, I passed the occasional square stone farmhouse, with an old Land Rover invariably parked outside. Everything seemed old, neat and untouched for centuries, in contrast to the jumble of visual styles you would see in the Irish countryside.

In the small village of Heptonstall, people were just waking up. As I walked along the wet, narrow street paved with large slabs of stone, I could see into the old weaver's cottages, where people were preparing breakfast. There was no one on the street. Then a door opened and a young man emerged. He was wearing jeans and a leather jacket, but the front of his head was shaved and a long blond plait hung down his back. His face was half-covered by tattoos and half a dozen piercings. He looked like he had stepped straight out of an ancient Saxon chronicle.

The churchyard wasn't hard to find. A beautiful old church, with a ruined mediaeval monastery beside it. When I stepped into the ruin, a crow, perched on one of the exposed roof beams, cawed loudly and flew off. It was very quiet in the rain, there wasn't a living soul about. The church itself was surrounded and hemmed in by a jumble of large stone gravestones. But what I was looking for wasn't there.

Poets are inveterate sniffers around graveyards, I suppose because a lot of the work has already been done for us. I crossed a country lane into a windswept, flooded field on the outskirts of the village. This was the new graveyard, which took the overspill from the village. After a few minutes patrolling the densely-packed rows of almost anonymous graves, I found what I was looking for: the grave of Sylvia Plath. It looked the same as all the others, if anything, more neglected and anonymous. The small stone was decorated with a string of carved pearls, as seemed to be the custom of the graves around here. The simple stone gave the name Sylvia Plath Hughes and her dates but, below it, these lines: 'Even amidst the fiercest flames the golden lotus can be planted.' As I shivered in my unsuitable clothes in the mud, I could not help thinking that the fierce flames would soon have been doused by the low-lying clouds and the golden lotus was nowhere to be seen.

I retraced my steps through the village, with mothers arriving to deposit their children at the local school. And after breakfast at Lumb Bank, I left Yorkshire again.

A few hours later, when I sat in the gleaming modern glass and steel of Manchester airport, it all seemed like a dream. Had I really been to England at all? And then I looked down at my shoes and saw they were still caked with the mud and grass of Heptonstall churchyard, a souvenir to bring back to Ireland.

MARBLES

Gerard Smyth

Playing marbles in the avenue,
I loved their colours rolling on the path,
the spherical motion, the smack
when glass hit glass. We had fistfuls of them,
collections stashed in cloth bags
that we clutched like a treasure chest.
We exchanged and traded them.
Bluebottle blues for bloodshot reds.
It was part of the camaraderie of boys back then.
Kaleidoscopic, polished to the lustre of a gem,
sometimes they'd spill and fall,
pirouetting in all directions, slipping
through the grill and down the rain-shore.
A loss for which there was no consolation.

MARCH

EMERALD

Karen Ardiff

Two thousand six hundred million years ago, in what is now Zimbabwe, emeralds were growing. These were among the oldest gemstones to form in the world and they had a turbulent birth.

Beryllium, vanadium and chromium, which combine to create this fiery green jewel, are concentrated in different parts of the earth's crust. The emerald should not exist at all, but the earth is not a stable place. Monumental tectonic processes, the kind that move continents and thrust mountains out of the deep, played matchmaker to these frisky elements. They found each other and crystallised.

Have you ever seen a really big one? I haven't, but my mind goes into overdrive as I contemplate the powerful punch that The Mogul Emerald must pack. Discovered in 1695, and owned by Indian maharajas and maharanis, it weighs 217.8 carats. Count 'em. Two hundred and seventeen carats. Never mind the point eight, which is what so many people have in their engagement rings. This thing is ten centimetres high and has flowers engraved on one side of it and prayers (yes, prayers – plural) on the other.

It's worth imagining this gem, as in all likelihood you and I will never get to see it. It was sold on 28 September 2001 at Christie's of London to an unidentified US buyer for $2.2 million. A snip if you ask me.

It saddens me to think of it lying in a bank vault somewhere, because an emerald is a garden.

The extreme forces of nature which create an emerald fill it with inclusions and faults. It is so rare to find a nearly flawless emerald that the finest are worth more than diamonds. But they are prized for certain of their flaws too, specialists referring to an emerald's inscape of delicate fronds and fissures as a 'jardin'. There is a six-spoked star in the fiery heart of one of the rarest varieties. Imagine that.

For me, though, what is most telling about this gem is that the best indicator of its value is colour. A perfect pale green jewel is not worth nearly as much as a more flawed gem of a deep and vibrant green. The kind of green that you and I know as, well ... 'Emerald Green'.

As we edge into spring, it's easy to see why the human heart responds to that luscious, intense colour. It is the chromatic antidote to SAD, the winter blues. The glorious spring yellow of the daffodil and lesser celandine is subtly preceded by a swell of glowing foliage. From now until the summer starts, smothering you with the scent of Meadowsweet and Lady's Bedstraw, you (or at any rate, I) will be cheered on by green things crowding our way.

Already little streams in the Phoenix Park near my home are choked with watercress and, underneath the trees, cushions of leaves are preparing to bear the delicate spring wild flowers: those inauspicious, shy ones that you noticed as a child. The ones that you picked for your mother that didn't survive the afternoon in a glass of water on the kitchen table.

Green has been many things through many ages. It was the colour of Venus, the Greek goddess of beauty and love – a strange assignation it seems now, when red is the Hallmark standard for passion. But it makes sense. Green is the colour of newness and freshness and if these are now traits too exclusively connected with the idea of female beauty, it is not the fault of the spring.

There is another darker side to the colour green. It has always been associated as much with sickness and decay as it has with quickness and fresh youth. It is the colour of infection and putrification – a dichotomy beautifully explored by Dylan Thomas in his poem 'Under Milk Wood'.

But there is a vital distinction that is embodied in the emerald. Green is terrifying when it is opaque. That is why gemologists celebrate a tender, modest jardin at the heart of a darkly glowing jewel. But when the inclusions overwhelm the irridesence and threaten to make the gem cloudy, something hard-wired in us over millions of years makes us balk.

Beauty is a translucent thing. Which is why joy, which makes a person glow from within, is so uniquely attractive.

What sets us apart as a species (although there are many tender creatures on the earth) is our capacity to carry our love over through the dark, opaque moments of our time with each other. If we couldn't do this, only the young could ever love.

AN GHAOTH ANEAS

Colm Ó Snodaigh

An ghaoth aneas
Bíonn sí deas
Is cuireann sí rath
Ar shíolta.

An ghaoth aduaidh
Bíonn sí fuar
Is cuireann sí fuacht
Ar dhaoine.

An ghaoth aniar
Bíonn sí fial
Is cuireann sí
Iasc i líonta.

An ghaoth anoir
Bíonn sí tirim
Is cuireann sí
Brat ar chaora.

Tháinig Pádraig suas na trí chéim déag go ciúin. Isteach leis tríd an chistin chuig an seomra ina raibh an pianó suite. Seanphianó caite dubh, réasúnta i dtiúin. É suite go compórdach sa chúinne idir an fhuinneog, a d'fhéach amach ar an ngáirdín cúl, agus na seilfeanna a bhí lán le bíoblaí glasa, crua-chlúdaigh an Irish Texts Society.

Shuigh sé síos ag an bpianó mar ba ghnách leis go rialta agus thosaigh ag seinnt go ciúin cúramach, *An Ghaoth Aneas*. Gach nóta glan agus cinnte. Gach mothúchán á rá go soiléir tríd an gceol – a mhéaracha ag luascadh go leochaileach ó nóta go nóta gan stró.

Bhí mo dhearthár Rossa, trí bliana d'aois ag an am. Bhí sé suite go sona sásta faoin mbord ag spraoi lena bhréagán, ach tar éis nóta nó dhó de sheinnt Phádraig stop sé den spraoi agus thosaigh ag gol. Bhí mo Mhamaí sa chistin agus nuair a chuala sí an caoineadh tháinig sí isteach chuige.

'Cad tá cearr a pheata?' ar sí agus í á bhreith isteach ina baclainn.

'Tá Pádraig brónach,' arsa Rossa.

Nílim cinnte cén fáth go raibh Pádraig brónach an lá úd. Ach tá a fhios agam gur tháinig sé abhaile oíche amháin timpeall an ama seo agus iomarca dí ólta aige agus gur bhris sé gach fuinneog ina sheomra. Crá, briseadh croí – bean a loic go dona air ba chúis lena fhearg is a dhuairceas an oíche úd – deoir do ghach scealbhóg gloine. Gach seans go raibh an díomá a bhraith sé, toisc tréigint na mná, fós ina chroí agus nótaí ceansa an cheoil á seinnt aige.

Bé *An Ghaoth Aneas* ceann des na céad píosaí ceoil a d'fhoghlaimíos ar scoil. Droch-fheadóg stáin le gob dearg i measc tríocha fheadóg eile ag screadaíl go tréan. An chéad nóta 'C' ag iomaíocht leis an 'C ghéar' a sheinneadh leath den rang mar bhotún. Is dócha freisin go raibh sé ar cheann des na céad píosaí a chóirigh an chéad ghrúpa ceoil ina raibh mé, do fho-bhabhtaí Shlógadh – píosa ceoil simplí ach álainn a bhí éasca go leor a sheinnt gan ach na bunscileanna seinnte smachtaithe againn. Bhí an píosa céanna de ghlanmheabhair agam, ní amháin toisc gur mhinic a sheinneadh Pádraig é ach freisin toisc gur seinneadh an leagan álainn ar 'Ó Riada sa Gaeity' san tigh go mion minic.

I dteach trí stór cois farraige, trí mhíle ó dheas ó lár na cathrach, a d'fhásas aníos. Teach álainn trína chéile. Seisear buachaill fiáin le fuinneamh. Thíos staighre ag bun an tí a bhí seomra Phádraig. Ba cara lem thuistí é a thóg seomra ar chíos. Ritheadh muid thar a sheomra gach maidin agus bhuaileadh cúpla dorn ar a dhoras – 'Dúisigh Pádraig.

Dúisigh. Tá sé in am dul ar scoil.' Ba mhúinteoir é agus b'iondúil dó a bheith níos deireanaí ná muidne.

Bhí ceol go smior ina chnámha. Ceol clasaiceach — Mozart, Bach, ba chuma ach é a bheith oilte. Jazz — stopadh sé comhrá le héisteacht le giota ar an raidió. Sean-nós. Rac — ba í a chóip de 'Let it Be' a thug an chéad spléachadh dom ar na Beatles. Fuaim dhraíochtúil a chuir glion-dar orm. Fiú bhí téipthaifeadán aige agus dhein sé mé a thaifeadadh ag canadh nuair a bhíos a sé. Bhí éascacht ag a mhéaracha ar an bpianó — stíl mhall shollúnta, beagán ar nós stíl an Riadaigh.

Bhí sé an-mhórtasach asainne i Kíla as ár gcumadóireacht agus ár seinnt agus is minic a chuirfeadh muid suíochán i leataobh dó i gceann de bhoscaí an Olympia. Níor shroich sé gig na Nollag seo imithe tharainn i Sráid Vicar áfach, óir teip ar a shláinte cúpla lá roimhe agus shleamh-naigh sé uainn chun na síoraíochta.

Gaoth fhuar anoir a bhí ann lá na sochraide. Lá binbeach láimhíneach i reilig Mount Jerome i ndeisceart na cathrach, in aice na canálach. Shiúlamar go mall ón séipéal chuig an reilig agus ansin an cúpla céad slat chuig an uaigh. Thosaigh an sagart ar a chuid.

Ach tar éis dó stopadh d'fhanamar uilig timpeall ar an uaigh — mí-shásta leis an chaint ró-ghonta a thug sé, mí-shocair mar nár tugadh bealach dúinn ár mbrón a rá nó a thaispeáint, mí-shocair nár dúradh níos mó faoin duine álainn seo. An duine álainn seo a gheal croíthe lena shúile spleodracha. An duine álainn seo leis an gcuimhne rí-ghrinn. Fear féasógach, fear maith, fear stuama, fear scléipe, fear spéaclaí, fear comh-luadair, fear codladh. Duine ceanúil mothálach a gortaíodh ró-éasca. Cara clainne.

Tháinig mo mháthair anonn chugam.

'Can rud éigin, in ainm croim,' ar sí. 'Tá ceol éigin ag teastáil.'

Chuir mé mo mhála síos ar an gcré tais in aice liom agus thóg amach mo fheadóg stáin Francach. Thosaigh mé ag seinnt go mall, ag déanamh iarracht gach mothúchán a rá tríd an gceol — *An Ghaoth Aneas*. Líon mo shúile le deora — an tráth seo bhí mise brónach.

DAD'S FEET

Enid Reid Whyte

They say that real memories – ones that tie together into a story – don't happen until we are of school age. Before then, it's snapshots. But over time those snapshots often tie into longer and more cogent memories, like my dad's feet.

Mom always searched for the right socks for him for as long as I can remember. And some of those earliest memories are of her darning the holes he wore in them. Darning is a thing of the past and, in the 1950s, she darned over what we Americans called a darning egg – I believe they were more mushroom-shaped in Ireland. They were dark socks, heavy cotton and had a subtle argyle pattern just on the sides.

Subtle and conservative like his sack suits because he was in sales and never cared to make any sartorial statements. Heavy socks, because his feet were always cold. 'Why does Daddy wear heavy socks?' 'Because his feet froze in the war, honey,' she answered. Another question, 'Why did his feet freeze in the war?'

Somehow through the years, and never directly heard from my father, we learned that he had been captured at the Battle of the Bulge. Taken from a field hospital where he was recovering from shrapnel wounds in the hip; his glasses had been taken from him; he'd been put into a box car; taken somewhere; and then force-marched to a POW camp near Nuremberg. He was wearing only a pair of rubber galoshes – no socks. His feet were never warm again.

In the 1960s, he was diagnosed with Hodgkin's Lymphoma. In medical tests, dye was injected into his insteps and we children were fascinated by the blue colour the dye turned his slender and rather elegant feet. His familiar warm cotton socks comforted him. In the hospital off and on for the remaining sixteen years of his battle with Hodgkin's, his silly sense of humour often was displayed by the socks he wore. We all searched for the novelty ones he put on to celebrate any occasion when bedridden. Red white and blue socks for national days, red for Christmas and lavender for Easter.

Then, later, pressure garments including socks that went up to his knees meant he had to discard his beloved comfy argyles. My mother and I took it in turns to hand-wash them in hospital so that the elasticity remained in these expensive unattractive items. He wore pressure sleeves too; he always remarked on how fashionably co-ordinated he was and referred to them as 'his dainties'. We all learned how to help him in and out of them.

When my mother made her daily visits to him in hospital, she always patted his feet first, as they were the first bits of him you saw when you approached his bed. They'd exchange a kiss, talk quietly, she'd see to his needs and then, when it was time to go, she'd stand at the foot of the bed stroking his feet as they exchanged a few words of farewell.

When he died in 1979, aged fifty-five, he was buried in the grounds of our tiny eighteenth-century country church. The church is so small the coffin was in the aisle right next to us during the funeral and the pews are so small, we couldn't all sit in the same one. I was directly behind my mother. My father had chosen the hymns, 'Oh God, Our Help in Ages Past' to start and the middle hymn was 'Abide with Me'. During it, I saw my mother's hand steal out of the pew and reach over to pat my father's coffin, right over where his feet must have been. Tears streamed down my face and I only just managed to collect myself by the final hymn, 'The Strife is o'er the Battle Won (Alleluia)'.

A life lived and somehow to his first daughter marked by her father's feet. At the interment, the rest of the mourners seemed to back away from the graveside. Trying to figure out why, with shifty looks down and behind, my family noticed that an Eastern Black Snake, large but harmless unless you're a rodent, had stirred itself out of hibernation on that unusually warm March day. My father's feet would never have backed away from it, nor would they have trod on it. He would have used his equally elegant hands to gently pick it up and show his much-loved children what wondrous, useful and beautiful things God had made for us. Then, he would have let it go.

FOCAL COSANTA

Aifric Mac Aodha

Leagtaí blaoscanna each
Faoi chúinní halla an damhsa tráth,
Go mbainfí macalla as sála bróg,
Go mbeadh na fallaí ramhar le ceol.

Ba choscrach an radharc iad, a chuid:
Lucht ána an ghuairneáin mhóir.
Ní liginn a ndoircheacht lem'ais,
Ach ghuínn go bhfanfá im' chomhair.

IN MY DEFENCE
Aifric Mac Aodha

Horses' skulls used to be placed
Under dance floors long ago:
They coaxed an echo from a heel
And helped the sound ring whole.

Whatever spurs your grand whirl –
I know it for its starkness, dear:
Don't think that I'm not wary,
For all that we're up here.

I BELONG TO GLASGOW

Leo Cullen

My father was a singer, my mother was a singer and the sewing machine was a Singer. So went a funny line when I was young. It was a line I had reason to consider because I didn't think it was funny.

Delia Murphy, ballad singer, distinctive radio voice of the 1940s and 1950s, had a sister who also sang and also recorded with HMV records. And just like Delia, whose career was curtailed through being the wife of a diplomat, her sister also put a halt to her troubadour days. Living in a country hotel with her hotelier and horseman husband, she gave up the world of concert hall and recording studio to be at his side. 'Career' was not an option for a married woman in those times.

It didn't stop her singing though. We, her children, heard her constantly. She sang in the hotel bar at night, where the old boys aired 'The Wild Colonial Boy' and sometimes she pulled out her records and the old boys' faces burnished whiskey colour in appreciation. And every day that I went gallivanting around the countryside with her in the car, tallyhoing to hunts and to point-to-point meetings or visiting stables to see ponies, every day, she sang her repertoire of songs through the open window: 'Hello Patrick Fagan, you're the apple of my eye.' Was I impressed? She was only my mother ... what son is ever impressed with a cracked mother, singing her head off? Especially when a song went: 'Let him go, let him tarry, let him sink or let him swim/He doesn't care for me and I don't care for him.' Well I didn't care for her either! Whereas Delia, Delia was somebody special, who arrived stage centre into our hotel, a mystery of feathers, fox furs and leather gloves. And hadn't Delia escaped from diplomatic life in Australia, in order, for a few heady years, to resume her career? The wild colonial girl, was Delia!

'Sing along with me, laddie,' my mama used to say, wheeling around bends of the road, driving into the sun. I wouldn't sing. I glowered and pretended the flat countryside round Templemore was hugely entertaining. 'Just look at that interesting bullock scratching its tail end against the post. Just look at that excited dog chasing those disobedient sheep,' with such silent directives I tried to distract myself. She sang anyway. Mad as a hatter. 'You're an old cod!' she said.

I didn't want her singing. It was a silly pursuit. Why was it silly? Dada said she had a sweet voice, sweeter than Delia's; it was just that it hadn't yet grown as mature, as stage polished, as Delia's. Was it how I thought that if maturity grew into it, she would return to the circuit like her sister? And then I wouldn't have her for me. Was that why I thought she was silly? My considerations on the issue were not at all articulate. Meantime, she kept her hotel staff in impeccable livery – she kept a standard for the Tipperary hunting set and the town's little bourgeois band of diners. And she kept me – was I afraid I would be deprived of life fluids, that my little root hairs would go aquiver? She kept me in apple tarts.

But then there came a silence. No Mama. No longer her voice sang through the high ceilings of the hotel; no longer she lullabied my little brothers and sisters in their lofts. No longer was her presence felt. She wasn't well, I was told. But where was she? There was a strange atmosphere about the hotel. The commercial travellers grumbled at breakfast. The staff grew snappy and shushed me out of the steamy hot kitchen. Until, one day, when I was idly looking out through my nursery window onto Bank Street, I saw a funeral move towards the church, a slow procession accompanied by church bells, and some grown-up who was in the room with me sadly made the sign of the cross on my forehead. Was it that which made me go into Mama's bedroom? Anyway, there she was in the bed, welcoming me with open arms. Well, I joined her in song that day. We raised the roof that day. The barroom on the floor below never heard such laughter. 'I belong to Glasgow, dear old Glasgow town,' we sang together, pretending to be drunk. 'Somethin's the matter with Glasgow for it's going roun' and roun'!' We collapsed in the bedclothes with laughter. And then I returned to the nursery and watched the funeral tail away.

For years, I was sustained by that memory; only later did I puzzle over the sequence of events: how on an afternoon I had watched my mother's funeral pass down Bank Street, we could also have sung together in her bedroom. Is it too much to ask that, any more than little laddies' root hairs can quiver, little ladies can have transcendent experiences? That my mama had come back to me for an ould song? Or did I make up the whole thing? I don't know.

What I know is this: She was Angela Murphy, younger sister of Delia Murphy, wife of a horse trainer, hotelier, and businessman, mother of five children. She was a hostess, horsewoman and happy spirit. And she was a singer. Not a sewing machine sort of Singer. A real alive, a fine sort of singer.

DOING SOMETHING IRISH

Vona Groarke

In the spring of 1905, Charlotte Pickford Hennessy Smith took her son and two daughters to the offices of a Broadway agent. Her daughter, Mary, the famous silent movie star, would later recall, 'We scrunched down in our clothes to appear as small as possible, the idea being that, if they wanted us taller, we could always straighten up.' There was a problem: the agent needed two boys and a girl, but Charlotte vouched for her children's ability to cross-dress convincingly and the family was hired.

In November that year, the musical *Edmund Burke* opened at Brooklyn's Majestic Theatre, starring Mary, Lottie and Jack Pickford, along with a singer known as the 'Father of the Irish Ballad', whose voice was then earning him in excess of $100,000 a year. Chancellor 'Chauncey' Olcott played the role of Lord Edmund himself. The show, which was decked in shamrocks, buckles and brogues, was not overly in thrall to the historical events of its real subject's life: instead of the author of *A Philosophical Inquiry into the Origin of Our Ideas of the Sublime and Beautiful*, we have a hero who saves the Prince of Wales from would-be kidnappers, in return for which feat of derring-do, the prince promises to produce a comedy by Oliver Goldsmith and to give Burke a seat in the House of Commons. That show closed after twenty-eight perform-ances, but, for the most part and for the next twenty years, Irish-themed musicals were major, bankable hits and their most famous, most popular and best-paid star was undoubtedly Chauncey Olcott.

Olcott was born in Buffalo, New York, in 1860. His mother, Margaret Buckley, had been born in Ireland and had sailed to America with her family when she was eight years old to live in what Chauncey would later describe as an 'Irish shanty' on the banks of the Erie Canal. Neighbours recalled the young Chauncey being hoisted onto a table at the Washington Hose firehouse to sing Irish ballads. At the age of nineteen, he made his debut with Emerson and Hooley's Minstrel Company in Chicago, but though popular in his minstrel roles, it was the Irish ballads he performed as an encore that brought down the house. He soon graduated to Broadway shows with titles like *Barry of Ballymore*, *Isle of Dreams*, *The Heart of Paddy Whack* and *Macushla*. Under the headline, 'Romance in Green: Flowers and applause greet Chauncey Olcott at the Liberty', the *New York Times* reviewed his 1907 production as:

> Four acts of blarney, with the star as the Irish hero, soloist, and center of innumerable escapades such as would undoubtedly have finished a man of any other nationality, composed the play last night at the Liberty Theater, where Chauncey Olcott appeared in 'O'Neill of Derry'.

As well as performing, Chauncey Olcott was a noted composer. Songs he co-wrote include 'Mother Machree', 'A Little Bit of Heaven', 'Sure They Call It Ireland' and 'When Irish Eyes Are Smiling', but his most famous solo composition is 'My Wild Irish Rose', written for his Broadway show, *A Romance of Athlone*. John McCormack had a hit with the song but, in more recent times, it has been covered by artists as diverse as the Ink Spots, Keith Jarrett and Daniel O'Donnell.

Olcott was enormously successful, owning a house next door to Mrs W. K. Vanderbilt on East 57th Street. His funeral at St Patrick's Cathedral in 1932 was attended by the governor of the state and the mayor of New York City. His life was also the subject of a 1947 Warner Brothers motion picture, *My Wild Irish Rose*, the trailer for which presented 'the rogue with the brogue whose escapades made those naughty 90s blush'.

The film is a largely forgotten period piece: the scenes with Denis Morgan blacked up as a minstrel would probably cause a few raised eyebrows in contemporary audiences, and the depiction of Irishness is probably not one most Irish people would recognise, except, perhaps, from other Hollywood films. Chauncey Olcott may not have been a great artist, but he was one of the first to see an artistic opportunity in his Irish heritage that hadn't much to do with shame or ignorance. It may well be a sentimental and simplistic story, but it was, at least, a way of being warmly recognised.

Perhaps that's why his music still has some currency: if you check YouTube for one of the songs he popularised, you won't find a Chauncey Olcott recording of 'Macushla', but there are many versions by Rufus Wainwright, singing in green lederhosen, camping it up mightily. Tinkering with Irish stereotypes can be great fun, of course, but first, you need to catch yourself a good cliché and, when you do, you might just find that Chauncey Olcott was there before you and has made a song of it, and that you recognise the tune.

CRAOBH AN DOMHAIN

Éamonn Ó hUallacháin

Céad bliain ó shin go díreach i mbliana, ar Lá 'le Pádraig 1908, is ea throid Éireannach don uair dheiridh do Chraobh Throm-mheáchan Dornálaíochta an Domhain. San sean Theatre Royal i mBaile Átha Cliath a tharla sé, nuair a thug Jem Roche as Loch Garman aghaidh ar Tommy Burns, an Ceanadach a bhí mar Churadh an Domhain ag an am. Ní fada a mhair iarracht Jem, faraor; neomat agus 28 soicind, le bheith beacht, sa chéad bhabhta. Ní raibh ariamh, roimhe nó ina dhiaidh, troid ba ghiorra do Chraobh seo an Domhain. Tháinig dorn dheis Burns anuas go crua ar shúil chlé Jem le luas lasrach, agus ní fhaca sé ag teacht é. De réir chuntas an ama, chuaigh an tÉireannach síos faoi mar a lámhachadh é. Nuair a tháinig sé chuige féin, de réir a chéile, ní raibh fhios aige cad bhí tar éis a tharlúint dó.

Dúirt Jem gur mhaith leis troid ar aghaidh agus deirtear go raibh Burns sásta seans eile a thabhairt dó, ach shocraigh an moltóir go raibh go leor feicthe aige agus stop sé an troid. I ndiaidh an troda cuireadh ceist ar Roche caidé a mhíniú ar an méid a tharla.

'*Rinne sé ró-thapaidh é, sin an méid*' an t-aon mhíniú a bhí aige. An míniú a bhí ag Burns ná gur shiúil Jem isteach sa bhuille ab fhearr dár chaith sé ariamh ina shaol dornálaíochta. Ba bheag an sólás é sin don ghabha as Loch Garman. Ba ócáid an-díomách i saol spórt na hÉireann an oíche chéanna sa Theatre Royal. An t-aon dream Éireannach a bhain aon sásamh as an oíche ná iad siúd a chonaic bualadh Roche, a rith amach ar an tsráid agus a dhíol a gcuid ticéidí go glic leo siúd a bhí fós ag ciúáil le fáil isteach.

Ba mhór an difríocht idir an díoma ag deireadh an lae agus an dóchas lenar thosaigh sé. Bhí pictiúirí de Roche sna fuinneoga uilig thart ar Loch Garman agus bileoga faoi ar fud an chontae. Nuair a tháinig a thraein isteach go stáisiún Bhaile Átha Cliath chuir slua ollmhór fáilte roimh an fear téagartha, dathúil seo ó bhruach na Sláine. Bhéic siad le bród nuair a dúirt sé leo go raibh sé chun ceacht a mhúincadh don fhear as Ceanada. Dúirt a bhainisteoir Nick Tennant nach bhfaca sé cén chaoi go bhféadfadh Jem an troid a chailliúint, go raibh sé orlach níos airde agus dhá chloch níos troime. Ach bualadh a bhí i ndán dó, díreach faoi mar a tharla don chéad Éireannach a throid don chraobh chéanna, naoi mbliana roimhe sin, Tom Sharkey as Dún Dealgan.

Ach cé gur chaill sé an troid, chuaigh Jem Roche ar ais go Loch Garman mar laoch. Bhí na sluaite roimhe ag stad na traenach agus hiom-praíodh ar ghuailneacha é, taobh thiar de bhannaí ceoil, go dtí a theach i Slaney St. Bhí náire air féin gur fheall sé ar a lucht leanúna ach ní mar sin a chonaic a mhuintir an scéal agus níor tháinig aon laghdú ar an ghean a bhí ag a phobal féin dó ainneoin gur theip air i mBaile Átha Cliath.

D'fhan Jem Roche mar Churadh Throm-mheáchan na hÉireann ar feadh chúig bliana eile agus d'éirigh sé as an dornálaíocht i 1913 gan an craobh sin a chailliúint. Chuaigh sé ar ais ansin chuig an spórt eile a chleachtaigh sé ina óige, an Pheil Ghaelach. Bhí sé ar fhoirne peile a bhuaigh craobh an chontae sular thosaigh sé ag troid agus i 1913 chuaigh sé mar thraenálaí d'fhoireann peile Chontae Loch Garman. B'iontach an rath a bhí ar a chuid iarrachtaí. Bhuaigh Loch Garman craobh sinsir na hÉireann ceithre bliana as a chéile idir 1915 agus 1918. Níor sáraíodh an gníomh sin ó shin.

Fiú Mick O'Dwyer agus na sárchiarraigh a bhí aigesean sa ghlúin seo, níor éirigh leo níos mó craobh as a chéile a bhuachaint ná mar a bhuaigh an fhoireann a bhí ag Jem Roche, breis is nócha bliain ó shin. B'fhéidir go bhfuil ceacht ansin áit éigin. Más mian leat an lámh in uachtar a fháil ar pháirc na peile, bíodh iar-dhornálaí mar thraenálaí ar d'fhoireann!

Nuair a bhí a laethanta spóirt thart, ní dheachaigh Jem ar ais chuig a chuid oibre mar ghabha ach chuaigh sé mar gheall-ghlacadóir, agus bhí an-aithne air ag rásaí capall ar fud an deiscirt. Chónaigh sé i Loch Garman i rith a shaoil lena bhean agus cúigear clainne. Óg go leor a bhásaigh sé, tamall gearr roimh Nollaig, i 1934 agus gan é ach 54. Gortú beag ina chois nár thug sé aire dhó, agus a chuaigh nimhiúil, a leag ar lár ceann de mhórlaochra spóirt na tíre seo sa chéad bliain seo caite. Nuair a hiompraíodh a chorp faoi dheireadh go reilig Bhaile na Croise bhí banna píobairí ann arís ag siúl roimhe, faoi mar a bhí i laethanta a chuid glóire.

ST PATRICK'S DAY
IN OLD SAVOY

Tony Quinn

Green of various shades pervades the house. The sitting-room walls are decked with Tricolour tapestries evoking Irish slogans from sport and culture. Shamrock images and national symbols proclaim identity and heritage. Posters quote traditional proverbs from song and story, old words, sean fhocail: May the road rise to meet you. *Go n-éirí an bóthar leat.* The road did rise to meet us when we had driven up to the hillside house.

Inside, green, white and orange balloons float from the living-room ceiling. The oven exudes aromas of fresh baking. Festive fare placed on a jade-coloured tablecloth tempts nibblers. A young mother puts a leprechaun hat on a child's teddy bear. A little boy is garbed in a green football jersey asserting 'I'm playing for Ireland'.

Such stereotyping and paddywhackery often annoys me but on this felicitous occasion, the ambience and context erode my prejudices. The young mother in the room is my daughter, Jeannette Patricia, a marketing executive for a multinational company in Geneva. She lives over the border in High Savoy, France, and we are here for a double celebration, her birthday and St Patrick's Day, *lá breithe agus Lá Fhéile Pádraig.* She was born in 1973, the year Ireland joined the Common Market, now the European Union. Her Christian names reflect French and Irish traditions.

The three-year-old boy in the green football jersey is our grandson Ruairí. His name recalls that of Irish high kings and also of Rory

O'Donnell, Earl of Tirconaill who passed nearby during his flight to Rome. Ruairí speaks English and also *cúpla focail as Gaeilge* with a local French accent, peculiar to Savoy. That region, between Lake Geneva and the mountains was under Italian influence before merging with France in the nineteenth-century. Diverse cultures still converge in the alpine foothills. Our son-in-law, Geled, proud of his Celtic ancestors boasts that, like himself, St Patrick was a Welshman.

Jeannette opens the literary and musical presents we brought her. Joyce's book of short stories, *Dubliners*, evokes nostalgia for her native city. When she plays songs from the Dubliners CD, the patriotic ballad, 'Kelly the Boy from Killane', reminds me that my mother's people came from Wexford. There, our ancestral townland was called the Springs and, by coincidence, our daughter's house is on the route des Tattes, the road of the springs. Family roots are deep and wells of heritage are brimful with memories and connections. At the party, we munch brown bread with smoked Atlantic salmon, washed down by black porter, but thankfully not green beer. Our daughter's business colleagues join in the celebrations. *Sláinte, santé,* cheers. This is globalisation and intercultural dialogue in practice. Most of the English-speaking guests, part of the Irish Diaspora, are expats from Britain, America and Australia. Their ancestors emigrated from the Emerald Isle to labour on farms and in factories. We listen to festive tunes and exchange greetings for *Lá Fhéile Pádraig.* The French neighbours also enjoy Irish music. When U2's music booms, the guests are excited to learn that our family home is near Bono's house, below Killiney Hill. From the patio, green balloons float on the evening breeze. We hear cow bells ringing from the spring pastures below verdant forests fringing snow-peaked Alps. But these are not the hills of home. The educated young Irish now travel abroad to avail of lucrative career options. However, emigration can still be a lonely experience, and during St Patrick's Day festivities, Irish exiles celebrate heritage, remember roots and indulge in nostalgia.

As we bid adieu to High Savoy for the return flight from Geneva to Dublin, Jeannette Patricia wishes us bon voyage: *Go n-éirí an bóthar libh ... Go gcoinní Dia i mbos A láimhe sibh, go mbuailimid le chéile arís.* May the road rise to meet you ... May God hold you in the hollow of His hand, until we meet again.

MAGPIE

Enda Wyley

The day builds itself piece by piece;
the newt joins the owl, then the porcupine,
quince on its branch bends over a ruby ring,
colour seeping across the living room floor

until the jigsaw's yacht sails to its zebra end
and we go walking, your hand a small ball
in my palm poised to roll where any adventure lies,
hidden in parks, wild gardens, up doorsteps, behind pots.

Your eyes, beady berries on Raymond Street's trees,
see everything – and then, just there, *muck-pie, muck-pie,*
you call to the ebony-white bird that tussles
with the daffodils, that pecks for sparkling light

like diamonds through the railings. Our day
building and renewing will not stop.
Blueberries devoured, cod stew and sleep
the warm milk of waking, later the afternoon

becoming a city of wooden blocks up to the ceiling –
only the great moon in the sky and the twinkling star

will drag you in song from your industry.
Then night has you nestling close to my neck,

your lips whispering the day's things softly.
Muck-pie, muck-pie, your little fingers pulling
at the jade on my chain, feel relentless to me
like the jay all ready to steal and fly away.

RAIN IN BOSTON

John F. Deane

There have been days of rain here in Boston. It comes as a surprise to me who prepared long and hard for snow and frost and ice. I am brought back out of the unfamiliar to days I had thought long faded out of memory and have been smitten again by the vagaries of the mind. Do you remember those long rainy days we would sit inside and watch through half-fogged windows, boredom holding us, tired of the books? Oh yes, you were bustling about, forever busy, a lot of it unnecessary, passing the time, I think, as if time were a threat and not something that would run out for you, as it will for me, some time, and who knows when? Things here are strange, familiar too. Small hard banks of snow remain and, no, there's no sign yet of spring. I remember how excited you used to be as the buds appeared, as if suddenly, on the fuchsia hedge. Here the winter holds, it has longer arms, winds stretching down over Canada with thin and chilling fingertips. I remember that story of the Snow Queen you used to read to me, well over half a century ago, I was stirred by the tale of ice lodged in the eye and heart, throwing a different view of love about the world, where the Snow Queen ruled in her palace of ice, where the Northern Lights, the aurora borealis, was a kind of chill and lovely firework display.

And then there are the birds, or not. During the snowstorm that came through like a vast, rushing express train some weeks ago, all the birds seemed to have disappeared, as if they had caught that train and moved on south. There was an eerie silence in the garden and, among the trees by Boston College, a dreary absence. I heard a chuckling sound one day and saw a congregation of sparrows in under the shelter of a bush where the snow had never reached; they were setting up a rumpus, a debate, no doubt, on weather but all of them were chattering at once with not a word of sense amongst them. I stopped and watched, feeling, well, here are familiar creatures, behaving as they did when you and I stood out one winter and flung them tiny moistened crumbs of bread. You must remember? How we shooed the eager cat away indoors? And when that bully magpie came, scolding and threatening from the garden wall, how you took pity on it, too, aren't they all God's little creatures, you said.

Isn't it strange how you may be walking down miles-long Commonwealth Avenue and all that you can think about is the backyard of home, the blue-black apron of your mother speckled with the tiniest of daisies, and the squabbling of house-sparrows, familiar as the old rusty gate you swung on.

Then, today, along with the rain, there came a kind of clearance, that work of sunshine to get through and you can sense a glow in the world, a light that sings already deep in the heart, like the promise of lilac back into the world. And there he was, the cardinal bird, perky red crest and aggressive red beak, there in flesh and feather, a brilliant red with a black bib that takes nothing away from his preening glory. I took his coming as a welcome to this stranger from the west of Ireland, a loud halloo as if to say, Now just you wait, all this dull, damp city of Boston will clarify itself and will become a playground filled with sunshine and good cheer. And there, right beyond the cardinal, the catbird, oh yes I had heard of him, grey and secretive, but with that strange and haunting cry like the mewing of a sorry cat, and he called out, that sharp-shriek mewling sound and all I could think of was your phrase, 'Little boys should be seen and not heard.'

And here I am, talking to you, and you have been gone now a quarter of a century. Something about the heart, and its ongoing will to lift into bright skies of hope and love, something about walking here, in a strange city, growing aware of a love that was offered to me so many years before I grew aware of it, and relished it. Thank you. And God speed.

THE BLESSINGS OF A PAIR OF WOOLLEN TIGHTS

John O'Donnell

There are many accessories one might consider essential accompaniments to an international sports event. Team colours; a scarf; a coat with a naggin stashed away inside. Maybe even a little radio. But I am still wondering how it was I came to be standing outside Lansdowne Road at 2.50 p.m. for my first ever home international on Saturday 14 March 1970. I was nine, alone and ticketless but wearing underneath my 'longers' a pair of black woollen tights.

The tights had been my mother's idea. As always, she was full of practicality and compassion. 'He could be standing around down there on his own for hours trying to get a ticket. And the terraces. He'll freeze!' My father was more circumspect but knew better than to differ. 'Just make sure you don't tell any of the lads in school,' he murmured.

Ireland were playing Wales in Ireland's last match of the season, a match that seemed to be little more than a formality for the great Welsh side travelling to Dublin to win the Triple Crown. A glance at the Welsh team-sheet would have any self-respecting Irishman up half the night with worry. J. P. R. Dawes. 'King' Barry John. Gareth Edwards. Merve 'the Swerve' Davies. We had ... well, we'd lost to France, in Paris. We'd also lost in Twickenham to England, despite the best efforts of the surprise recall to the team, a somewhat pudgey Tony O'Reilly. Maybe, as the former Irish scrum-half Johnny Quirke put it, 'Heinz beans *were* haz beanz.' An unconvincing win against Scotland hardly set us up to take on what was almost certainly, at the time, the best team in the world.

But tickets were impossible to find. Perhaps they had been snapped up by Welsh fans eager to celebrate a Triple Crowning glory. Or maybe Irish fans wanted to see whether these Men of Harlech were mere men or truly gods. The only hope, according to my father, was to turn up early and see if anyone was selling. At 12.30 p.m., I stood at the railway gates outside the grounds. No ticket touts. Nobody at all, in fact, except a man with a bunch of keys, opening the turnstiles. 'You're here nice and early,' he nodded. 'Trying to get a good place inside to watch the game?' I explained I had no ticket. 'Did he know of anyone, or did he have a spare one himself?' 'Oh no, not a chance; the tickets were all gone weeks ago. Don't know what you'll do.' From my pocket, I produced my trump card. The crisp new orange ten shilling note my parents had bestowed on me was unblemished; it was also about five times the value of a schoolboy terrace ticket. 'Any chance you could let me in; I'd take up very little room?' In the best traditions of the IRFU, the man was sympathetic but unyielding to this sorry attempted bribe. 'Sorry sonny … nothing I can do.'

The fans began to arrive. They swayed and laughed as they poured down from the trains or ambled up Lansdowne Road. All of Ireland, it seemed, was here as well as half of Wales. Trussed up in my anorak, green scarf and hat, green jumper, shirt and vest and black wool undergarment, I began to sweat. My few plaintive attempts to ask if anyone was selling a ticket met only with pitying smiles and shaken heads. An hour passed. Another hour, and more. The ground was almost full; I could hear the band inside, the announcements over the tannoy. There were no late changes on either team – or on the ticket front. I stood disconsolate, a small, unhappy, perspiring stone in the middle of the streaming crowds. In front of me, disappearing green and red; and then, brown – the brown coat of my father's old Cork friend Dan Daly. Out-half for Dolphin and (my father once declared) the best never to have played for Ireland. 'What ails you, child?' he asked. I told my tale of woe. He eyed the turnstile. 'Come here.' He nudged me up to the little barrier. Suddenly I was airborne, held aloft by two huge hands that it is said never dropped a pass, soaring over the barrier and down on the other side into the ground. 'This little fellow's lost his ticket,' I heard Dan's broad Cork accent explain behind me to the bemused turnstile operator.

I never found out what, if anything, Dan gave the man. But I would pay a hundred times face value to meet Dan Daly again now, to thank him for what he started. On the occasion of my first ever Five Nations match, Ireland, against all the odds, hammered Wales by fourteen points to nil. The scores included a memorable try by the late, great Ken Goodall and a marvellous try in the corner by Alan 'Dixie' Duggan. An iconic photo by Dermot Barry captures Duggan in full flight, diving for the line. One man is already on the pitch, arms open wide to embrace the flying hero. Above him, high on the South Terrace is a smiling red-faced nine-year-old boy dressed up like Scott of the Antarctic, giving thanks for Duggan and for rugby, for the helping hands of Dan Daly and the blessings of a pair of woollen tights.

TERESA DEEVY AND THE INDIAN ACADEMIC

Emer O'Kelly

It's about as bizarre as you can find, and I have no idea how it came into my possession. A book called *Sixty Years of Realistic Irish Drama, 1900 to 1960* sounds perfectly normal. A study from a learned perspective, perhaps; more likely one from an intelligent journalistic perspective, published, quite obviously, here in Ireland or in Britain or the United States. But no, this is a work written by one N. Sahal; modestly, the given name is not revealed. It's published by Macmillan, something you might expect for a work on Irish theatre. But this is Macmillan and Company, Bombay, Calcutta, and Madras. The copyright date is 1971, the introduction signed by N. Sahal himself in Jodhpur, India, and dated December 1970. The foreword is signed by A. G. Stock in August 1970, with an unexpectedly mundane geography: Somerset, England. A. G. Stock refers to N. Sahal as Dr Sahal, and tells us he is his one-time colleague at the University of Rajasthan in Jaipur. That was where his doctoral thesis was registered, a decade before the book finally reached publication, by which time Dr Sahal had moved on to Jodhpur. The institution, he gratefully acknowledges, provided a subsidy of a thousand rupees towards the Macmillan publication, an extension, Dr Sahal tells us, of the thesis. The journey has taken ten years, and you can read the frustration in the carefully phrased list of thanks and dedications, from his supervisor Dr R. Dwiveda, to the late Dr Una Ellis-Fermor of the University of London, who helped him fix the subject.

But why? Dr N. Sahal at the time of publication had never left India; he had never visited the Abbey Theatre, never met any of the play-wrights whose work he deals with in such detail and with such empathy and sympathy. As A. G. Stock points out, mentally and geographically India and Ireland are far apart, and Dr Sahal knows Ireland only through its literature. But Stock also points out that both India and Ireland have '... long imaginative traditions, which entice a certain type of artist and intellectual to brood over the past instead of looking real-istically at the present. And India, like Ireland in the Abbey's early days, can still be touchy about its public image.' No change there then, at least where Ireland is concerned.

But what is extraordinary for the twenty-first century reader is the comprehensiveness of the study of the twentieth-century realists who superseded the Yeatsian vision for our National Theatre, refracted through a sphere of geographic distance, refined by academic distance and quite obviously driven by passionate interest born of an instinct impossible to pinpoint. N. Sahal acknowledges a predecessor: the work by A. E. Malone on Irish drama published in 1929 'but never revised because of the author's death'. He believes Synge to be 'not devoid of realistic elements' and Lady Gregory, 'though mainly a writer of farces, to be more of a realist than a sharer of Yeats's ideals', and has included them for what he calls brief discussion, along with 'more pronounced realists'.

O'Casey towers in this work, and there are separate chapters on St John Ervine, Lennox Robinson, Paul Vincent Carroll, George Shiels, M. J. Molloy, T. C. Murray and many more, their work now neglected and discarded as reminiscent of an Ireland we prefer to forget. Many of them seem to have entered into enthusiastic correspondence with Dr Sahal during the 1950s, and their insights make interesting footnotes.

But it is the study of the almost totally forgotten Teresa Deevy that leaps from the page. 'Realism in the plays of Teresa Deevy has become intensely psychological and at times even fantastic ... with ambition versus contentment the recurring theme,' Dr Sahal writes. It is a number of years since Teresa Deevy was brought to the attention of Irish audi-ences when her play *Katie Roche* was revived at the Abbey in the 1970s with Jeananne Crowley in the lead role and directed by Joe Dowling. More recently it was revived by the Peacock with Derbhle Crotty in the lead role and directed by Patrick Mason. But, for Dr Sahal, Deevy is pivotal in mid-twentieth-century Irish theatre and he justifies his stance admirably, dissecting, detailing and analysing work as long out of print as it is out of memory.

Deevy was born in 1894 in Waterford. She was denied the opportunity to attend university when she went severely deaf, and went to London to learn to lip-read. There, she came under the influence of Shaw's work. 'Not his over intellectual and ruthless analysis of social evils, but his new approach and some sparks of his vivacious wit,' writes Sahal, somewhat witheringly of the great Fabian. Lennox Robinson and Denis Johnston both encouraged her after she came home in 1919. And a whole series of plays that were essentially feminist and anti-religious in structure and theme were staged before disappearing into the maw of nationalist consensus. Katie Roche, for instance, refuses to end her friendship with a young man even when she is married. It is innocent, but society can't conceive of that, and Katie is subjected to a witch-hunt at the hands of her pietistic neighbours. It's a comedy, and all ends happily if ironically, which is possibly why Deevy did not find herself subjected to the fiery breath of the dragon censorship. But genuine free-thinking seems to have pervaded all her plays.

She entered into voluminous correspondence with the young academic in Jodhpur throughout the 1950s, and seems to have sent him the typescripts of unpublished plays, as well as answering all his queries and analysing her own dramatic theses from her silent world. 'Teresa Deevy has taken her cue from Chekov,' says Sahal. 'Psychological penetration is her strength, and artistically good-humoured detachment her manner and style; she never makes her drama a debating forum.'

Perhaps that is the key; western academics in our time detach drama from its performance almost as a matter of course, and plays that are 'not coldly analytical but warmly passionate' are automatically suspect. But for one academic, seeking the truth in Irish drama from across the world, and waiting ten patient years to have his work published, Teresa Deevy exemplified a kind of genius that came close to O'Casey's.

One wonders what would have happened had the deaf old playwright who never heard her fluid and penetrating texts spoken, ever met the precise and studious young Indian lecturer who admired her literary fierceness and independence so much.

REMEMBERING JOHN McGAHERN

Denis Sampson

When I arrived at John McGahern's house for the first time, almost thirty years ago, I found John turning the hay. There was an old tractor in the shed, but he was doing the job by hand. In the warm August afternoon, we worked together round the small field that runs down towards Lake Laura. We walked the field and paused to look out over the lake. Some cows had waded in to cool off.

Constable might have painted the scene, Hardy might have described us or Heaney put us in a poem. I think John would have been pleased with such immortality, if he had not already accomplished it for himself. In his first years as a writer, a painter friend introduced him to Constable, to the letters and the life as much as the work. He liked the Romantic painter and spent a lifetime searching in words for the sources of light in a dark landscape, for intimations of heaven in the hell he had been given.

I have to admit, however, that on that day, I did not really belong. I was young. Leitrim and heaven were not really my landscapes. I had grown up on a farm a hundred miles down the Shannon valley, but I had been brought up to go away, into education and wherever that might lead. My older brother was the farmer, and even when I saved the hay years before, my head was already in books. I had sweated over many fields, and put methylated spirit on my welts, but I knew I would never return from far-off places to root myself, as John had done.

Far from the land, in Canada, I discovered his first books. Some years went by, and, then, I had the good fortune to meet him in Montreal. Now, in the summer of 1979, I had driven up to the farm. I had spent a long time searching for it, as all I had was the postal address. It didn't even mention the nearest village. Of course, he and Madeline had no phone then. They had indeed withdrawn to their own lake district.

But perhaps 'withdrawn' conveys the wrong impression. He had distanced himself from the cultural traffic of cities, and from the kind of daily wonders that newspapers record, so that he could more fully create his own heaven. It was more than escaping from distractions, or freeing himself from gossip and intrigues. As a historian of the human heart, he did find gossip useful, but, for him, the talk of his old neighbours across the lake, or in Earley's pub in Mohill, was more useful than the gossip of Grafton Street. More useful because the art he wished to create had to be grounded in the work and the suffering and the wild humour of local life.

John's formal conversation was often pointed by a favourite expression from memory: a couplet from Yeats, a phrase from Beckett, an epigram from Proust, a definition from Auden. As he quoted the words of those he admired, a reverent stillness entered the room and a silence followed. It was as if there was no more to say on that subject. So sure was his reading, and his rereading, that he created his own company.

I had the feeling that he had come not only into his own place, but that he had also found his own time. It was the time of my childhood, of his childhood, of Constable and Wordsworth, of the timelessness of memory and art. In the company of Yeats and Beckett and Proust, he would refine his own style in this place. His writing room was not cork-lined, but it was in that room that he won his immortality. His kind of philosophical contemplation brought to light a supreme reality in the hayfield and the lake. He wanted to bring the history of his own deepest feelings and the history of his community and time into relation with such a sublime reality.

I could never become a farmer, but in John's work I found images of my humanity and my nature. When I visited the farm, I came to stay, for it was in his novels and stories that I discovered my sublime home.

APRIL

WALLS, ISLANDS AND WELLS

Joseph Woods

for Mo Irwin

Can this be right? How last Sunday
to walk the Great Wall to a point
where it crumbled, merely a week
passes and this Sunday to be brought

round Omey island, face the Atlantic and out
there a conference of swans, at our back
a hexagon fortress built for a writer.
Here a holy well with an alcove of supplications:

a dolphin's vertebra, a bag of miraculous medals,
smooth stones with girls' or women's names
scribbled upon them, a soother and a single sock,
everything one could wish for.

Then a ruined church of pink-granite
half-sunk in sand whose gable must glow
in the evening sun. But before the tidal
road back what stops me in my tracks

are sand-grains shifting with the speed
of an hourglass, revealing what sand
has been secreting,
the half-concealed Imperial yellow shell.

AT MOON'S CORNER

Gerald Dawe

When I visited Galway the second time, I stayed. In those days of the early 1970s, no one quaffed water from designer bottles but the bus driver used to stop, along with his passengers, at a pub in Roscommon for a couple of pints and a whiskey before resuming the cross-border journey from Belfast to Galway. There was a border then too. Gardaí, Irish defence forces, UDR, British soldiers, RUC, Customs and Excise men, and various others, whom we probably didn't see, peered out of makeshift roadside bunkers.

It was a furtive time. Five years of killing, bombings, reprisals, and assassinations, the raising of streets, riots and looting, political crisis. Madness was in the air. No one really thought it would all become a way of life but in the café in Cavan (passengers changed bus services there, from Ulsterbus to CIÉ), it felt as if life had not altered terribly much over the generations of tea and sandwiches, knowing nods and silent recognitions. But buses were now being hijacked, set on fire, stopped and searched, re-routed and bus stations had taken on a haunted, frightened aspect, surreptitiously at first and then, after the appalling destruction of Oxford Street Station in Belfast, it was more than fear caught hold of glances. That bag? That box? That bicycle? That car?

When the bus pulled in alongside the steps to Éamonn Ceannt Station, I felt a dizzy sense of freedom – freedom from the dark streets of home; freedom from the ceaseless rant and rancour; freedom from the closing down of the city in which I had grown up; freedom from the thugs and bullies. There was also a feeling of having escaped, just in the nick of time. The Belfast I had left behind was of a very confused summer that included doing final university exams during the Ulster Workers' Council strike, juking through UDA barricades; several months working in the Central Library and moving across the deserted city at night to the small flat I shared with an American pal in an east Belfast estate.

Eyre Square had an autumnal glow and a fresh breeze in the air. Back then, the shape of the square had a very real sense of welcome to it. The houses, offices, hotels and shops seemed to set the tone for the rest of the townscape. I can't recall one tacky shop or hoarding. The many canals and bridges and high stone houses and warehouses, which, in those pre-tax-incentive development days of the early 1970s, were roof-less and windowless, made the city seem small and compact. I dumped my bag in the American Hotel and punctually headed to University College Galway, my first port of call, to introduce myself to my profes-sor, Lorna Reynolds, and to the Dean, the classics scholar, 'Ma' Heavey.

The walk by Moon's Corner, the post office, down to the Law Court and library and over the Salmon Weir Bridge, stays in my mind in slow motion. Everything was starkly etched in the late afternoon, livid with light. So when I turned into the archway of UCG, porter Pádraig Ó Flathartaigh's answer to my query about directions to Arás de Brún sounded equally bewitching.

I couldn't really believe my luck. Only a precarious few weeks earlier, I had been stared at and finger-pointed and had taken foolish risks in the increasingly manic belief that Belfast was still an open city. My pal and I had been followed to our little flat in east Belfast. Loyalist para-militaries had called to the door, 'They're only collecting money, right?' I had worked my notice as a library assistant in the Fine Arts depart-ment of the Central Library in Belfast's Royal Avenue – bombs to the left of us, bombs to the right, scotch-taped windows left open wide, evacuation procedures, the bomb-disposal officer's hectoring voice on the megaphone, the resigned faces of we poor Joe Soaps standing waiting before we could resume our lives, 'after the bomb goes off'. Now, I was walking towards the Arts Block, with the heavenly Corrib flowing by, my feet barely touching the ground.

As for Professor Reynolds, she was sitting behind her desk, a tall spindly woman, wearing a Virginia-Woolf-like hat, with an accent I couldn't quite locate. Cool but kind, formal yet interested, she asked how my journey had gone, if I found myself suitable accommodation, recommended I check out the Hardiman Library for its holdings in nineteenth-century journals, newspapers, historical and literary texts, and that I should 'proceed to Kenny's' and see what I might find there.

A brief courtesy call with Professor Heavey, a smiling adorable woman tending to plants in her office, and I was off again, skirting the canal, the cathedral and into Nun's Island, past the imagined home of Joyce's Gretta in 'The Dead', past Dominick Street, over O'Brien's Bridge and into High Street, where, on a corner, stood Tom Kenny's map shop, next door to Sonny Molloy's, which faced the double doors of Kenny's Bookshop, the front shop of which I entered with the jangle of a bell. From then on, for the next twenty years that is, Kenny's became home from home, with all its transformations and expansions – upstairs, downstairs, next door, towards Middle Street, the recall of the Abbeygate Street premises, the gallery in Salthill – all these developments were logged alongside my own vague journey – from hotel to rented room in Spiddal, to half a house in Knocknacarra, to a flat in Abbeygate Street, to a bungalow in Ballindooley on the Headford Road and, finally, to our home in Glenrevagh in Corrandula. Kenny's was the backdrop; the fulcrum.

My first and subsequent books were launched there, numbers of magazines edited were sent on their way; the walls of our different homes had paintings bought from Kenny's. Older artists were rediscovered, new friends made and met, strangers introduced, interviews conducted, photographs taken, luggage and messages left, drink consumed, rumours heard, first editions bought, borrowed, lost and found; afternoons spent 'perusing', evenings begun, weekends brokered, highlights installed in the memory, guests entertained, lives lived. 'Would you like some tea?' I turned from the bookshelves, William Carleton's *Traits and Stories of the Irish Peasantry* (two volumes, illustrations by Phiz) in my hand.

'Tea?'

'Yes, I always have a cup of tea around this time. Lemon tea. And you can borrow that if you like.' A rare edition.

It was Mrs Kenny, a conductor, behind her bureau. A rare moment. A total stranger. Hooked for life. 'Yes, thanks,' I said. 'Thanks,' and told her briefly my story.

A ROYAL COURT AT KILLALOE

Aubrey Flegg

In the 1860s, Queens were sold for £2 2 shillings a ton, while Princesses twenty-four inches long and twelve wide were reckoned in thousands at 10 guineas, Duchesses, Countesses, Ladies, Doubles, Mosses, Quarters and mere Commons, cost from 10 guineas to 8 shillings a thousand. And good value too as these were the titles and prices of the roofing slates being raised in the area around Killaloe during the nineteenth century, and still keeping many a house warm and dry today.

If you are travelling on the road from Dublin to Limerick, take time to follow the lake drive from Nenagh to Killaloe. After a pleasant few miles skirting the northern slopes of the Arra Mountains, the road rises sharply into the village of Portroe. From here your eyes will be drawn northward up the great sweep of Lough Derg with the contrasting browns of Slieve Aughty to the west and the lush greens of the limestone pastures on the eastern shore. Below you, hidden in the trees, is the tiny lake port of Garrykennedy where, for 150 years and more, the courtly slates of Killaloe took ship for Athlone, Dublin and anywhere else along the thriving canal ways of Ireland.

Each slate shipped out, however, represented a success story, because for every slate finished, six failed to make the grade and were cast aside to form the spectacular tips characteristic of slate workings worldwide. Turn your back on the lake for a moment and you will catch glimpses of these tips spilling out about the numerous workings on the hillside above. When, as a geologist, I began to explore these quarries, I suffered a tinge of guilt at the desecration of these lovely hillsides, but the slates are beautiful themselves. The slater's hammer is silent now, banks of heavy-scented gorse bristle on the quarry rims, wild strawberries ripen on the sun-warmed stone and foxes look apprehensively over their shoulders as they clatter over the sliding slates. In the silence, however, one can hear the echoes of industry past.

We know that slate was being raised about here in the time of Brian Boru, because, according to the Four Masters, slate was used to roof the buildings in his fortress in Kincora just north of Killaloe. It was in the nineteenth century, however, that the working of slate reached its climax. It was a time of contrasts: of wealth and poverty. Great estates extended hungrily over the fatter lands along the lakeshore, but the hills were crowded with the smallholdings of impoverished local farmers who tilled small fields to feed many mouths. The growth of the slate industry must, to them, have seemed like manna from heaven. Writing in 1845, George Wilkinson wrote how the quarries 'gave employment and food to many hundreds by converting what was the wild uncultivated mountain, on which goats and coarse cattle alone found poor subsistence, into the busy scene of labour, improving the habitations of the country, and, in endless ramifications, distributing wealth around'.

When I was working there in the early 1970s, there were still hale men who had worked in the quarries up to the time of their closing in the 1950s the pit at Corbally was then 350 feet deep. They told me about their work, speaking of red-ends, slants and soles, a remembered hammer danced in their hands again. They told stories of strikes and disasters and how the wild goats, who still inhabit the bushy margins of the quarries, would feel the rock slipping under their feet and warn the men in the pit of an incipient rock fall by taking themselves off, out of danger up the mountainside.

So when you see the grey tips on the mountain sides or watch the rain bouncing off a slated roof, bear a thought for the royal slates of Killaloe and the men who gave them their tiles and earned a welcome wage in return.

AMARILLO ON MY MIND

Mick Ransford

The graphic on the road sign is immediately recognisable: that piano-shaped state fills me with an inexplicable sense of achievement. Driving across the States, through Texas in particular, gives you some under-standing of rural America's attachment to gas-guzzlers. Towns are great distances apart; vehicles need to be roomy to haul groceries alone.

By the time we hit Amarillo, Gerry's in no mood to tackle down town. I'm the cook on this trip, but I feel no more like rustling up supper than he does driving. Gerry's boys, hoping to spot another Wal-Mart, suggest heading out on foot for something to eat. Amarillo has grown in recent years. We walk along a highway that not long ago was a country road.

Sunburned prairie to our left, fenced-off commercial premises on our right. There's no footpath. Just a bumpy strip of grass, pockmarked every yard or so with what I insist are gopher holes – though I would-n't know a gopher hole from a hole in the ground.

Mexican workers glare at us from a battered Ford. I am the colour of buttermilk and strawberries, I am luminescent. I tell Gerry to take off that stupid hat. This straw yoke he bought back in Missouri that prompted the boys to nickname him Hucklegerry Finn.

We've been pointed towards a block of bars and restaurants; having walked for half an hour they seem no closer. The sun is merciless. General Phil Sheridan said if he owned Texas and Hell, he'd live in Hell and rent out Texas.

We fall to quarrelling. Gerry wants to turn around, wants me to make use of that trolley-load of groceries we bought in Oklahoma. 'I'm doing all the driving,' he says.

I put my head down, slog forward, keeping an eye out for more gopher holes.

Gerry and Aengus begin to lag behind. Soon myself and Fionn are yards ahead. Passing a parcel office, I decide to confirm the existence of these fabled eateries. I'm in the middle of asking a retiree, who's in the middle of slipping into a vintage Lincoln, when this blocky guy with a swallow tattooed on his neck offers us a ride.

I glance into the bed of his pick-up — no duct tape or rusty hand-cuffs. It's his turn to flinch when I point to Gerry. All six-foot-four of him, lurching up the road, in that straw hat.

The breeze created speeding along the highway is as good as a cold drink. I feel like an Okie, sprawled out in the back of this truck. There are handshakes all round when our Good Samaritan pulls up outside a roadhouse. A ranchy-looking affair. Big, with lots of varnished wood. Chuck Berry booms out of a jukebox. Peanut shells carpet the floor, snapping and crackling under our feet.

We're served by a drawling waitress, so bubbly she must do this job for something other than money. I'm starting to come round. I grin apologetically at Gerry; he hesitates then grins back. Waiting for my steak, I recall impressions of Texas thus far.

Suddenly, there are more black and Hispanic faces. Suddenly, there are cattle everywhere. Hundreds of steers mill in pens all along our route, mucking up the dry grass underneath them. Cotton candy clouds sweep immense shadows over the rumpled prairie, like quivering pools of oil. Eighteen-wheelers roll up yellow dust on roads that branch off the Interstate in horizontal lines. Legions of telephone poles stand sentinel against CinemaScope-skies. Road signs offer seventeen ounce steaks free to anyone capable of finishing them in one sitting. Others warn motorists not to stop for hitchhikers in the vicinity of state prisons. One we passed advertised 'Road Kill Apparel'.

Before I know it, I'm recalling something I'd buried for over thirty years. It's a sunny, Saturday morning. I'm in my father's Beetle, beetling through my hometown. My father has escaped domesticity for the day. He's looking forward to a cool bottle of McArdle's with his brothers in Allenwood. He flicks the radio on with a flourish: Tony Christie, his voice full of sunshine, belting out 'Is This the Way to Amarillo'.

EGGS AND PASSOVER

Judith Mok

I love eggs. Boiled eggs especially. Even when the egg white has turned blue or red or any other colour of the Easter rainbow because the dye has seeped through the shell.

In Holland, I always knew when Easter was approaching because our neighbour's Belgian workhorse would be seen going down the steep road past our house to the sea, dragging wicker chairs down to the beach for the summer season. They were the kind of chairs that keep out the wind, as they were shaped in the form of a beehive sawn in half. There were double and single ones and we, all eight of the village children, used to sit in them during weekdays after school and have pretend tea parties. There were also big piles of straw that we could bounce off until we would be chased away by the beach guards. But best of all was the trip to the shops to buy egg dye for the chocolate bunnies and the tiny lambs made out of butter that we'd put on the table at Easter for decoration.

Easter meant eggs. We drew faces, birds or butterflies on them and when they were ready we put them in a basket so the Easter Bunny could hide them. Our house was built on a large sand dune covered in helm grass, dune roses and wild gorse, so it can't have been easy for our parents to find places to hide the eggs. On Easter morning, we ate a special kind of cake with lots of butter and I devoured at least three boiled eggs before running outside with my friends to look for more. Egg parties: I loved them.

It so happens that the Jewish Passover is often in the same period as Easter. The only ritual of *Pesach*, as it is called in Hebrew, that my parents thought we should celebrate, was the first night, the Seder. This is when the people around the table ask the youngest person in the room four questions about the history of the Jews. In the Haggadah, it says that the purpose of this feast is to feed the children's curiosity.

One year, we went to Haarlem where a friendly Jewish family had invited us for the Seder. Mr Meyer was supposedly a wise and learned man. When we walked into the dining room, the first thing I noticed on the table was a bowl of boiled eggs. I must have been about only five years old but my delight at food was already well established. They could fire away any questions now that this new egg party was on the way. We sat down and Mr Meyer started a monotonous chant that seemed to go on forever. I decided to take a small bite out of an egg, with just a piece of matzoth, unleavened bread, on the side.

'Why do we eat *matzoth*?' Suddenly, the chanting had stopped and everybody looked in my direction. My mouth was full but I managed an answer. The Jewish people were slaves and fled into the desert with unleavened bread because they hadn't had time to bake it. And we eat bitter herbs with it because our fate was cruel and bitter, and those chopped up apples and nuts remind us of the bricks of the pyramids we had to build for the Pharaoh. 'Stop!,' all the adults exclaimed at the same time. I had decided that I didn't want to stop and have my meal interrupted again so I added boldly that the parsley on the table was a symbol for spring and the salt symbolised our tears. My parents started to laugh but the Meyers were not amused. In their eyes, I was a badly behaved child. The idea was that you wait for the questions to be asked. I leaned back in my cushions and attacked my second egg. The monotonous chant had started again. It took a while for the last question to erupt from Mr Meyer's mouth. 'Why could we lean back in comfortable cushions the way we did?' I meekly answered that we were free and therefore allowed to relax. But then I added, 'Could I ask a question?' The adults nodded in eager expectation of my question. 'If I am free,' I said, 'can I say that I really prefer Easter eggs to *Pesach* eggs?' We left that Seder quite early and when I later went for a walk around our house I was delighted to stumble on a hidden egg that nobody had been able to find.

Recently, I took my grandfather's *tallith*, his black and white prayer shawl, out of the cupboard and spread it over a chair in my study. My grandfather died in a concentration camp but my father managed to hang on to this garment all through the war, hiding it from the Nazi regime. Today, I am free to recline on it as I wish, and to enjoy any egg party I like, even a free-range Irish one ...

KALO PASKA

Fionnuala Brennan

Only sometimes do the Western Christian and Orthodox Easters coincide; this year, 2008, there is a difference of over a month. Greek Easter is on 27 April and the next time that we celebrate Easter together will be on 4 April 2010.

The reason for the difference in the timing of Easter in the Western and Eastern traditions lies in different church calendars. We go by the Gregorian calendar, while our Greek and Russian Orthodox brethren follow the Julian calendar. In both traditions, Easter must be celebrated one month after the Jewish Passover, which is on the first Sunday after the first full moon after the Spring Equinox, not earlier than 21 March. As for calculating in either tradition when Easter will fall on any particular year, one would need a degree in higher maths or the like to work out such mysterious factors as the Golden Number and something called an 'epact' which apparently is to do with the age of the moon at certain times of the year. I am happy to leave such calculations to whomever it concerns.

A new method for calculating the date of Easter, discussed by the World Council of Churches and the Middle East Council of Churches in Aleppo, Syria in 1997, could have resolved the differences had it been put into practice in 2001 when the Julian and Gregorian Easters coincided, but the Russian Orthodox Church especially was reluctant to change, having already experienced a schism caused by the calendar issue.

Another difference between the Eastern and Western practices of Christianity is the fact that Easter, not Christmas, is the major feast in the Orthodox rite. We will not be in Greece this year to celebrate *Paska* with our friends, but we will be with them in spirit. We will be thinking of our old friends, Maria and Arsenia, who for the duration of Lent, do not eat meat, fish, dairy or poultry, nor does Maria cook with olive oil. They enjoy the end of the fast all the more.

As usual this year, they will attend all the great preparations during *Megali Evdomada* – Holy Week. Maria, who is a sprightly ninety, will go to the magnificent fifth-century Byzantine Church of the *Ekatonapiliani*, the Church of the Hundred Doors, as it is colloquially called, with her daughter Arsenia and her many grandchildren on *Megali Pempti* – Holy Thursday. They will be back for the Good Friday ceremonies when the icon of Christ is taken down from the cross, wrapped in linen and placed in a flower-covered casket symbolising the tomb of Christ. With the rest of the congregation, they will follow the bier through the village streets lamenting the death of Jesus.

They will, of course, stay up for the midnight Mass on Easter Saturday. On that night, the great church is in darkness until the Pascal candle is lit by the priests and the flame passed from candle to candle throughout the congregation until the church is ablaze with flickering gold. The priest sings out, '*Christos Anesti*' – Christ is risen – to which the audience replies in one voice '*Alethios Anesti*' – truly, He is risen.

Fireworks explode in the church courtyard and the congregation files out into the night, shielding the flames of their candles in the hope they will make it home before they are snuffed so that they can mark the sign of the cross over their door to protect the house for another year.

Then Maria and her family will sit down at a laden table to break their fast with *mageritsa* – a wholesome soup made with lamb sweetmeats and egg and lemon sauce. Later that day, the family will enjoy *kokoretsi* – lamb cooked over a spit. Maria will have baked the traditional Easter bread *tsoureki* in which she will have embedded *paskalina avga* – red-coloured hard-boiled eggs. The family will crack these with those sitting beside them at the table, and the one who holds the last uncracked egg will be the lucky one for the next year. The feasting will go on all day. The sun will be shining and the wild flowers will be blooming. I wish we were there to wish them all *Kalo Paska*.

FRIDAY NIGHT TREAT

Clodagh O'Donoghue

When I was a little girl – we're talking six or seven here – my bedtime was at 7.30 p.m., the same as my younger brother. I was acutely aware of the injustice of this because, at two and a half years his senior, I should have commanded a later bedtime – eight o'clock, say. However, my little brother was what was commonly known back then as a 'holy terror' and the idea that he would go to bed quietly while I was still up and about was simply laughable. In contrast, as the rule-abiding and biddable eldest child, I could be prevailed upon to overlook my seniority and go up at 7.30 p.m. I may have been a goody-goody and I may have done as requested without making a fuss, but it didn't mean I was happy about it; it didn't mean I didn't see the unfairness of it. My parents, recognising this and appreciative of my obliging nature, devised a form of compensation. And it was this: on Friday nights, if my little brother could be got to sleep by ten o'clock, then I could sneak downstairs in my jimjams and watch *Come Dancing*.

And so it was that from Sunday to Thursday (Saturdays operated differently again), I submitted to an embarrassingly early bedtime with as much grace as I could muster. My brother and I shared a room at that time and I would retreat behind an Enid Blyton paperback and endeavour to ignore his antics as he fought sleep manfully. These included jumping on the bed, badgering me to have a feet fight, and trying to tunnel out of the house through the wall with the aid of a dessert spoon. All of this I endured in stony silence with an air of long-suffering martyrdom. However, on Friday nights, I became a different person. I became a caring and solicitous big sister. I was all sweetness and light. I plumped his pillow; I listened to his prattle; I read to him until I was hoarse; I may even have sung to him – anything to get him to sleep before *Come Dancing* kicked off.

Of course, probably if I'd done nothing at all he would still have been asleep by ten o'clock, as being a holy terror is tiring work – but I was not prepared to leave it to chance.

And so, at the witching hour, my mammy or daddy would creep upstairs, help me into my dressing gown and slippers, and bring me down in time for the theme music.

In those days, the show was presented by the elegant Judith Chalmers, and regional teams from various parts of the UK would compete for the final. As a young man, my daddy had been a keen ballroom dancer and so he could pronounce authoritatively on the technique of the couples as they glided across the floor. I would nod sagely to indicate my agreement with his assessments but, really, I was there for the dresses.

There were two distinct sections in the competition – oldtime and Latin – and the dresses worn for the Latin dances were frankly alarming. The female contestants – all of whom had implausibly orange tans considering they hailed from such locations as Bristol and Leeds – seemed to have eschewed frocks in favour of spraying a few bits of glitter in strategic places and hoping for the best. At age seven, I was something of a prude – my most fervent wish back then was that crinolines would be back in fashion by the time I was a teenager and that discos would have been replaced by formal balls complete with dancing cards. So, you can imagine that the skimpy Latin creations, made up of a lot of flesh-coloured nylon and a few sequins, were not my cup of tea.

No, it was the old-time dresses that excited me. Yards and yards of floaty material made up layers and layers of petticoats that stood out almost at right angles to the body. The men in their white tie and tails had to somehow negotiate these voluminous skirts and engage with a fight with the fabric to get close to their partners. Even more than the dresses' shapes, I loved their colours – the peacock blues, the deep pinks, the sherbet lemons – and all with high-heeled court shoes of the same shade for a perfectly co-ordinated look.

I notice that there as been a recent revival and rejuvenation of ballroom dancing as an early evening Saturday family television entertainment. Only now, of course, in keeping with the television practices of today, there must be celebrities involved – however minor or obscure – who are partnered with professionals and sent on a crash course to learn the foxtrot or the samba or whatever. And there has to be an elimination process in which the public have their say and get to vote for their favourite.

Although it is interesting to see how the ballroom dancing genre has been reinvented for today's TV audiences, for me, it has lost a lot of its magic. Maybe it is because it lacks that staying-up-late thrill or maybe it is because my sleeping holy terror of a brother is not upstairs oblivious to his big sister's secret. But it does serve as a pleasant reminder of an almost-forgotten Friday night treat. And I still like the dresses.

EMPTY ORCHESTRA

Lorraine Griffin

My knowledge and experience of karaoke spans student summers in the Canaries, dodgy pubs around Ireland and, most recently, a Chinese restaurant on Parnell Street. From the highs of a boisterous micro-phone-swinging, crowd-chanting 'Wild Thing' to the lows of a tumble-weed-inspiring 'Nothing Compares 2 U', I've seen it all.

Now, before you start thinking you're dealing with some sort of *X-Factor* wannabe or Billie-Barrie-the-Grown-up-Kid, let me set you straight. As an Irish punter in her early thirties, I've a certain amount of boozed-up singing under my belt. I'm not saying I'm proud of it, but this is the reality. Our motivation in brandishing a mic and squinting at those speedy neon songwords is no different from our ancestors belting on their bodhráns and sean-nósing into the night.

The Germans have their lederhosen and beer. The Swedes have good-looking people. Italians have their cheesy chat-up lines. The Irish? We have an Aul Singsong. Karaoke is merely an expression of this. Without it, we're adrift, wobbly launching into the 'Fields of Athenry' or tearfully lamenting Molly, Maggie and Danny. This wonderous Japanese invention simply gives structure to our crazed repertoire.

Working as a euphemistically-titled PR exec in Playa del Ingles, the job entailed getting rowdy blokes and gals into The Harp Bar with the promise of two-for-one and free paella and chips. The karaoke machine was key to this operation. It was the USP of this otherwise soulless, formica-tabled Oirish bar. See the theory rings true: when people have had a few drinks, they either want to dance, sing or eat chips. In my capacity as PR exec, I could offer them all three and, what's more, all three at once if that's what they wanted! 'Harp Bar. Free karaoke inside! Go as many times as you like. Sing your heart out!' And so they piled in, Madonna was murdered and I got paid.

At the end of a tough college year, and in need of intense partying, I was lured deep outside the Pale to a karaoke night in the snazzily named 'LA' bar. I threw on the early 1990s ensemble of Barratts black boots (with chunky lego-style high heels), obligatory Morgan top and orange-lined bomber jacket. Good to go, I was revved up to enjoy the Californian-style delights that awaited. Unfortunately the 'LA' didn't quite match our expectations and my perky rendition of 'Like a Virgin' was greeted with a chilling community-style death stare from the regulars.

Most recently, I was invited to a karaoke dinner with Chinese friends in Parnell Street. This one topped the lot, you could call it the pinnacle of my karaoke existence. These guys are hardcore; not for them the obligatory five pints and two shots. For them, this is a sober art. In fact, they can select a song, pack a dumpling and belt out an epic tune without so much as missing a note. Impressive. So when the mic was handed to me, it was a matter of national pride that I took the floor. No matter that the only English song turned out to be 'Happy Birthday'. I sang that bad boy with gusto, infusing years of sweaty, oops-missed-that-line ... hope-the-chorus-comes-soon ... is-that-really-my-voice? enthusiasm. Why? Because I was singing for Ireland, singing for all of our collective cringes and next-day flashbacks, our Sweet Carolines and Proud Marys. And as the last note died in the shaky amps, I handed back my mic, downed a Green tea and strode happily into the night.

AN OPEN LETTER
TO GEORGIA O'KEEFFE

Sharon Hogan

My dearest Georgia – I hope you can hear me.

You once said about your beloved New Mexico mountain, the Pedernal, that God told you if you painted it enough, you could have it. Well, it's yours, Georgia. Juan Hamilton scattered your ashes at its foot. Mind you, your paintbrush had already swept its sandstone shoulders – caressed its ochres and russets and rose pinks – so sensuously, so 'equivalently', that no other painter goes near them without thinking of you. You also said that what you regretted about dying was that you would see no more the stark colours and the vast beauty of 'the Faraway' – as you called the landscape you loved. Your Native American friends only smiled and told you your spirit would walk there after you were gone. They were right. I sensed you there.

The Museum of Modern Art here in Ireland is currently showing paintings spanning sixty years of your work life. Of course, your sumptuous, luminous flowers are there, and fluid abstracts from as early as 1918 and as recently as the late 1970s. But your tender rendering of the rust-red Abiquiu Hills returned me to where I'd sensed your presence. I'd been part of a company of actors visiting New Mexico for research: we wanted to make a theatre piece about you. So uncertain were we about how to call up your immense spirit – your lively humour, your uncompromising dedication, your formidable womanhood – that we'd begun playing, like – tourists.

First, we'd tramped up to the White Place – it figured so fantastically in your work – and were stunned by the pale, strange columns of sixty-million-year-old volcanic ash. Then we'd visited your adobe-house at Ghost Ranch, explored your bedroom and your studio – its blank canvasses, white bones and weathered desert flowers precisely preserved as if you'd only just stepped out. Finally, in your shadowy stone yard, surrounded by pink sandstone hills, we paid quiet respect to the great American artist you'd been for nearly a century: in 1946 you were the first woman ever to have had a retrospective exhibition at the Museum of Modern Art in New York; in 1997 you became the first woman to have an American Museum dedicated entirely to her work; you were the muse of groundbreaking photographers throughout the twentieth century, including your husband and collaborator, the visionary Alfred Stieglitz.

But – it was when I held your paintbrushes that I finally comprehended you. From the moment the curator at the Santa Fe Institute set the trays of brushes on the table, thought swept clear out of my head – my heart felt as if it'd been sliced wide open. So clean, your brushes were, so stark and spare, elegant as bleached bones, purposeful as surgical instruments – some had been in daily contact use for decades, and yet there wasn't a paint splatter or a splayed edge on any of them. 'Yes,' the curator nodded, 'yes, you may touch them.'

And then they were in my hand, cool on my palm, weighty and light in the same moment, and as viscerally as if I'd been shocked. I heard you whisper: 'Be brave.' I remembered reading that you had never let it stop you. And I remembered how you'd told a friend that it wasn't just talent that made an artist. 'You have to have something else,' you'd said. 'It's mostly a lot of *nerve* – and a lot of very, very hard work.'

And I remembered – when after years of painting in vivid colours, you decided one October that you would only paint in black and white until you understood every nuance of light and shade – and then – only when there was something you simply couldn't do with charcoal or black paint – would you touch a colour. Eight months later – following your mother's death – you finally reached for blue. And the master of colour you became! Such seriousness in your study, such exuberance in your execution!

Holding your paintbrushes that afternoon stirred my seriousness. Standing before your vibrant paintings still has that effect. 'I want to love as hard as I can,' you once wrote to a friend, and 'filling space in a beautiful way – that's what Art means to me' – what gorgeous ambitions! Can you hear me, Georgia, if I thank you for being so vital while you lived that you still inspire those who remain behind?

When macular degeneration eventually robbed you of your precious eyesight, a friend pointed you in the direction of your beloved Pedernal and asked if you could still see it. 'No,' you answered, 'but I know it's there.' I can't see you, dear Georgia. But I know you're there.

THE NORTHWEST PASSAGE TO TALLAGHT

Joe Kearney

Economic necessity made John Franklin an expert on the merits of baked beans. However, it was not the contents but the tin itself that engaged his interest. These were the years of the mid-1970s and John recycled the empty container to repair a leaking exhaust system on his old Fiat 124.

John had much in common with his Victorian namesake, the famous Lord John Franklin, who perished, together with three shiploads of men, whilst attempting to locate the elusive Northwest Passage at the top of Canada. Both men hated the cold, were curious about the geography of their world and found alternative uses for food tins.

Our John arrived amongst us during the bitterest of winters. In our new suburban caves, we had gone into a form of hibernation. Home to work, work to home, heads down with just the briefest of nods to the neighbours. Amongst the cul-de-sacs of identical semi-ds, there was little concern for neighbourliness. We were preoccupied with spiralling inflation, mortgage rates and high levels of unemployment. Ours was a diverse assemblage in a new housing estate, 'nestling' as the brochure told us 'in the foothills of the Dublin Mountains'.

John had undertaken a long trek to arrive here. Together with his new wife, he had fled the country of his birth, Rhodesia. When they left, they carried little more than a pocketful of hope for a safer life. Their country was then engaged in a bitter war for independence and the prospect of ongoing conscription forced them out. The young couple selected Ireland on a map of the world and that was how they became our neighbours.

That grey winter eventually weakened and gave way to watery sunshine and it was about this time that we noticed the man who sported shorts and sandals while we were clinging to our woolly jumpers and cords. We also became aware of exotic cooking smells and fragrant smoke leaking over the breezeblock garden walls. The Franklins back garden soon became the focal point for an entire neighbourhood. He introduced us to his home-made beer, home-built BBQ (an oil drum cut in half), as well as his DIY philosophy. The latter always involved clothes-hanger-wire and empty tins of beans. Soon, we began to forget the economic depression; the neighbours were becoming our friends.

During the course of one such gathering, John introduced us to his notion of barter. He observed that we all had individual skills and proposed that we should pool these on a non-financial exchange basis. Thus, a plumber could assist a house painter and visa versa. In our cash-strapped-lives, this seemed an inspirational arrangement.

It was through this trade that the Franklins ended up with a spanking new hi-fi system in their otherwise under-furnished front room. John had traded his tax accountancy skills with a man who struggled to manage his electrical store.

John loved rock music but his record collection was painfully scant. Like his namesake of old, he was curious to map the lesser byways of his adopted home and on one such excursion, he made a discovery. On a dusty roadside beyond Tallaght, he saw a lad displaying a home-made sign that offered a solution to his musical deficit. The sign read: Rush, Queens, Records £1.99, three for a fiver. As John reversed back through a cloud of oily exhaust, he was already extracting a £5 note from his all-too-slender wallet. Never ones to be dented by a setback, potatoes featured prominently on the Franklin's BBQ for many weeks afterwards.

The land of John's birth altered. It changed its name to Zimbabwe. The cold Irish winters weighed heavily on the Franklins and they returned eventually to the land of the sun. New planting softened the concrete of our housing estates and the economy finally improved. The neighbours shifted to new addresses and we lost contact with the man who encouraged us to wear shorts on inappropriate occasions and to light BBQs in the snow. We remember him now that his country is once again in the news.

Back in 1845, the British admiralty found the remains of three of Lord Franklin's crewmen. They were buried in a cairn composed of 700 food tins filled with stones. The original contents had spoiled and the ice proved too resistant to the starving mariners when they attempted to dig graves for their companions. I know our John Franklin would have approved of the imaginative recycling involved.

A DAY IN TIPPERARY

Mae Leonard

My mother is humming a tune as we drive past Limerick Junction on our way to Tipperary. 'Oh ... that's nice,' I say, what is it?' She sings louder, '"And I'll never more roam to my own native home Tipperary so far away." Connie Foley used to sing that.'

'Oh ... Who's Connie Foley?' She doesn't reply, but there's no time for further discussion as we arrive in Tipperary town in a matter of seconds. There, we pick up my daughter with the intention of treating her to lunch and maybe we would be introduced to the new boyfriend. When we take a turn right in the middle of the town, the majestic Galtees are there in front of us. Mother points at the middle peak. 'Galtymore,' she says with a sort of reverent smile in her voice 'We climbed it on my twenty-first birthday, your dad and I. That's where he proposed to me on the very top of Galtymore.'

Oh?

I would question her further but decide to allow her the silent pleasure of that happy memory. She herself breaks the silence after a little while still using the same sounding voice, 'This is Dan Breen country. I read his book to ye years ago, remember? *My Fight for Irish Freedom*. I made tea for him once y'know – for Ernie O'Malley too.'

Oh.

I hold my breath waiting for the rest of the story and, in that pause, I see a road sign for Mount Mellary – perhaps we could have lunch there? Even my ever-hungry daughter agrees – so we take the road up to and through the Knockmaoldowns with Mother casting aside her memories to watch out for the famous scenic V-Gap.

And then what happens? Rain. Not exactly what you could call rain but a thick mist engulfs us and we never get to see the V-Gap in all its glory and it's the hunger, rather than religious fervour drives us on to Mount Mellary.

The car crunches up the gravel drive and there it is looking very bleak and unwelcoming in the rain. We enter the church to the chanting of the monks and emerge sometime later to seek out the restaurant but a sign tells us it's too early in the season and there are no hot meals today.

A chorus of Ooooooh.

We backtrack down the mist-obliterated V-Gap, each of us gripped by massive hunger pangs. The daughter is practically growling on the back seat.

Ballylooby is just a bend on the road but there's a pub with a great big sign – luncheons our speciality. There the lady proprietor looks askance at us. We're too late. Lunch is finished.

Oh.

We're about to traipse back to the car when this angel says, 'Hold on, I'll see what I can do for ye.' And, minutes later, she produces three plates of bacon and cabbage with a bowl of potatoes that are bursting balls of flour. She apologises for the lack of white sauce but puts a dish of butter on the table instead. She apologises again when she comes with jelly and custard, the only dessert left. Apologise?

Oooooooh. This is food fit for a king or even three very hungry travelling companions. Ballylooby. We'll never ever forget Ballylooby.

Eventually, back in Tipperary, we meet the boyfriend. Mother sizes him up and I see her eyeing his long hair disapprovingly – until he turns to her saying – 'Would you like to see the house where Dan Breen lived? In fact I could take you to his graveyard – he's buried right beside my grandfather.'

It's Mother's turn to say, 'Oh.' And he gets an immediate stamp of approval in Tipperary.

TRASNA NA dTONNTA

Joe O'Toole

From Kilmore Quay Westward via Kinsale had been a pure pleasure.

In Crookhaven, we met music, merriment and mighty *comhluadar* late into the night but there was no early morning life around O'Sullivan's pub as we slipped moorings and left the idyllicly sheltered harbour at five thirty.

Sarda, making barely three knots, quietly nosed her way through the moored boats with their snoring crews. Among them were sore heads soon to be nursed and cured, so we kept our wash to a sympathetic minimum leaving them undisturbed.

We rounded the Alderney Rocks and headed parallel to the shoreline towards Mizen Head passing the beautiful Barley Cove along the way.

Approaching the Mizen, almost directly underneath the spectacular lighthouse, the most southerly building on the island of Ireland, the sea was uneasy in itself and well agitated. The chart warned us of rips and currents. Be careful! It was exactly here that then Taoiseach Charlie Haughey came to grief, losing his boat and almost his life.

Not wanting any of that, and being cowards at heart anyway, we held course for another clear mile southeast before helming westward, leaving the infamous and spectacular Mizen Head behind us convinced, once again, that the more stunning and dramatic the coastline, the more dangerous it also is.

Crossing the wide expanse of Bantry Bay without shelter, we were at the mercy of a strong westerly which hammered us, uncomfortably, on the beam.

None of your 'Trasna na dTonnta' here, but a sea of white horses with every wave crest foaming. A sea which would have been perfect for a sailing yacht, but not so for *Sarda*, who was pitching and rolling down the sides of the waves and yearning for the calmer waters of river or estuary.

Leeward of Dursey Island, the sea settled but we were stymied once more trying to find the entrance to Dursey Sound.

Landlubbers won't understand this, but it is notoriously difficult to differentiate between island and mainland as they appear to merge into one over the horizon.

Which one of those bumps is Crow Head?

Back to the chart, painstakingly and manually rechecking, recalculating the position. It seemed right. Eventually, we had to make a choice. We inched ahead. There was an opening. But was it a blind inlet or Dursey Sound? Plenty of water under us but would it swing northwest?

At sea, at times like that, it is easy to feel stupid. Joan relieved the anxiety, 'There's the cable car!' and we were into the Sound.

And what a splendid sight it was. This magnificently beautiful fjord-like passage between Dursey Island on our port side and mainland Cork to starboard connected and framed by the overhead cable car. Just sublime, but we were refocused by the pilot book's instruction: 'Keep to the western side but beware submerged Flag Rock west of the centre.' Hugging the island, we avoided that sneaky rock.

Then, without warning, we shot out into the Atlantic again, into a dirty northerly wind and lumpy sea directly on our nose.

An uncomfortable welcome to the Kingdom of Kerry.

Continuing north, those aptly-named but dislocated ruminants, the Bull, Cow and Calf rocks broke the western horizon.

Away to our starboard was the fine bay of Kenmare, fraudulently misnamed Kenmare River by a greedy landlord who got Westminster Parliament to declare it a river and so purloined the salmon-fishing rights.

But our anger calmed as we saluted the Liberator's Derrynane and soon the jagged point of Sceilig Mhichil stabbed through the horizon. Remote and godforsaken until St Michael and his fellow monks brought God to it, it rises majestically out of the sea imperious and challenging. No monks now but a haven for archaeologists and historians, though still a retreat for gannets and puffins.

Next up over the horizon is Valentia Island, where the transatlantic telephone and telegraphic cable snaked out of the seabed, making

Valentia cable station the crucial fulcrum of Western European communications for almost a century.

But, we now entered Dingle Bay and how 'the savage loves his native shore'.

I love these waters and was reminded of a time when I was younger, lighter and fitter and spent happy days subaqua diving around here. Even eighty feet down, the sun's rays sparkled like theatre floodlights. There was colour, life and vividness everywhere. Those were the days.

Ahead of us was the mighty reach of Corca Dhuibhne, its mood always changing with the light. Today it is sombre, serene and broody, stretching westwards, through Cruach Bhréanainn and charging into the Atlantic at Slea Head. There paddled its offspring, the renowned Blaskets, source of more literary output per square yard than any place on earth.

We set course for ten degrees and 15.48 minutes west. It should leave us clear of the Crow Rock, between the Tuairín Bán and the lighthouse at the mouth of Dingle Harbour.

It was spot on. We were past the lighthouse. There was Slaudeen where I had learned to swim but any reverie about the past was cut short by having to give way suddenly to a boat chock full of tourists coming straight at me. I gestured at the skipper, whom I could see in the wheelhouse. He stuck his head out and shouted, 'Welcome home, Joseph.' It was John Francis, an old school classmate.

Just then, Fungi, the Dingle dolphin, leapt in a perfect parabola across our wake.

It was simply the best of welcomes home.

OH ME, OH MY

Cyril Kelly

Memory can be capricious. But my memory is that, along with forty-nine other scruffy, huffy, guffy High Infants, I began to bark at print as Bean Uí Chruaillí wrote hieroglyphic symbols on the blackboard. I can still get the limey whiff of chalk dust. I can still feel the sensation of water in my teeth when a flinty fragment in the chalk squealed on the time-shined surface. Bean Uí Chruaillí, blessed with demonic energy, would rasp the chalk against a leg of the easel, tighten the pegs supporting the board, grasp the frame and resume. And as she wrote, fifty scruffy, huffy, guffy High Infants bayed, 'At ... Bat ... Cat ... Fat.'

Then, one day, Bean Uí Chruaillí wrote in large letters L O O K. Taking a stick of blue chalk, she squiggled a round blue spot in the middle of each O. Standing back she spoke just one word, 'Look.' And, lo, two eyes were staring at me from the board. That was around the time when the configuration of words began to intrigue. The *g* in 'pig' had two plump porcine ovals, with a piggy's curly tail; 'horse' could rear up on the hind legs of the *h*. Soon after that, I discovered that words not alone had, but could also engender, feelings. And as *at* plus an *e* became 'ate' and the drill led to 'date' and 'gate', 'hate' turned into our cat, Tibs, arching her vicious back, hissing, 'hate'.

And it was around this time, too, that language presented me with my first metaphysical dilemma. It concerned my curiosity over the two letter word 'me'. I puzzled endlessly, struggling to define the essence of 'me'. If I lost my voice, like The Balk, would I still be me? What if I came back from the war without my legs like Veteran Vinny? Say if I lost my hands and my legs and my eyes? Like, what exactly was *me*? Was there some secret, inviolable place in my heart or in my head that contained and defined the essence of *me*?

After the excitement of learning to read came the adventure of reading to learn when metaphysical dilemmas were left behind. And so I witnessed Nial na Naoi nGiallaigh capturing Patrick, I saw longships crammed with marauding Norsemen tacking into the mouth of the Shannon, attacking Scattery Island and the round tower at Rattoo, nine miles outside Listowel. After that it was the Normans and, finally, 'See who comes over the red-blossomed heather, Their green banners kissing the pure mountain air, Heads erect, eyes to front, stepping proudly together, Sure freedom sits throned on each proud spirit there ... The Bold Fenian Men', in the same key as the rebel hand that set the heather blazing at Boulavogue.

By then I was ready for that local seat of learning, St Michael's College, where I was the doubtful beneficiary of a classical education, doing Latin and ancient Greek. What I didn't realise at the time was that such a grounding would be part of a future fascination with words. Slowly, I began to discover that words could influence words around them not alone with feeling and meaning and colour and music but they had a derivation which gave them gravitas, where the root could trace a semantic seam down through layers of usage back to a classical bedrock.

And now I've arrived at a time in life where I am beset once more by metaphysical musings, all because of another word, another two letter word, to whit 'my'. Not the vocative 'my' as in 'My Dear' or 'My Lord'. But the possessive adjective 'my'! Celtic Tiger Ireland seems to have spawned a spurious, privileged *my* status. As in people now frequently refer to *My* dentist; *My* surgeon; *My* Filipina cleaner, and so on. I have to admit that I can scarcely say *my* house, *my* garden, *my* child without chiding myself for such possessive presumption.

These ramblings have been rendered as a result of reading Seamus Heaney's recent essay, 'Human Rights, Poetic Redress', an essay to mark the sixtieth anniversary of the Declaration of Human Rights. In the course of a beautifully written and cogently persuasive piece, Heaney argues that artistic endeavour is part of the redress which maintains an equilibrium between right and wrong. But there, at the end of the essay, the word *my* lay in wait to ambush me.

Outlining the genesis of his spare provocative poem 'From The Republic Of Conscience', Heaney refers to 'my writing students in Harvard'. And suddenly, reading this most pacific of poets, flashpoint images erupt in my brain. As if marching down through history, come rabid ranks of *My! My!* The long slant of each *y* is a spear slung from a short Sam Brown. And all the colonial regiments of *My! My! My!* converge at various times in history; as Norsemen; as Normans. They plunder as Saxon hordes, all the Third Reich *My! My!* goose-stepping through Europe, swelling into battalions, brigades, divisions. *Hate,* my long-ago word, stalking Middle and Far East. *My! My! My!* milling together, advancing to the rapacious battle cry of *Our! Our! Our!* To rhyme with *Power! Power!* And its corollary; *Cower! Cower! Cower!*

The brainstorm passes as quickly as it came and Heaney's vision asserts itself once more; from the detritus of battlefields springs a frail perennial hope, which the artist must fashion into a flower of redemption, a flower that will illumine the garland that is the Universal Declaration of Human Rights.

MAY

WILD FLOWER WOMEN

Michael Fewer

The first wild flowers I can remember noticing and getting to know were the bluebell – that Keats so well described as 'sapphire Queen of the mid-May' – and the delicate primrose, that herald of spring, probably because these were the earliest blooms to appear in abundance after the long Irish winter. At the first taste of mild weather, we had family expeditions to a favourite place we called Bluebell Valley, to pick bunches of powder blue and pale yellow blossoms for our little May altar. While I never became expert in any way on botany, I have always remained a devotee, and have found endless pleasure during walks discovering species that were new to me, and later seeking to identify them and searching for what folklore had to say about them.

My mother showed me that even common wild flowers, dare I say weeds, have a wealth of history behind them. Who would have thought, for instance, that the dandelion, named from the French '*dent de lion*' recalling the golden teeth of the heraldic lion, was richly praised by many seventeenth and eighteenth century poets, that its roots were used by poor peasants in Germany as a substitute for coffee and that it is a proven medicinal remedy for liver complaints? Even the little daisy that suburban gardeners abhor in their lawns was Chaucer's favourite flower, and had its unique uses. It was said to encourage pleasant dreams of loved and absent ones when placed under the pillow, to provide a readily available salve for soldiers' wounds on the battlefield, and in the days of chivalry the little much-maligned flower was a symbol of romance: a knight had a daisy tattooed on his arm to signal to all that he was in love.

In those days, when plants were used for medicinal purposes, their accurate identification was all the more important. I no longer have my mother to name the unfamiliar plants I find, and although nowadays bookshops have whole shelves devoted to publications that show a myriad species in perfect, sharp images, even they can sometimes let us down.

Years ago, on a May morning on Carlingford Mountain in County Louth, I came across a tiny plant with a purple flower I had never noticed before and on returning home, I consulted my wild flower books, poring over many photographic illustrations to try to identify what I had found, without success. I finally turned to an old, much treasured book and in a short time found a clear image of what I had seen: its name was the common butterwort. A penned note under the illustration stated that the book's original owner had come across the plant 'near Carlingford, Co Louth, on the 25th May 1927'. The feeling this little discovery gave me, the sense of communicating across all those years with Annette, was exhilarating.

The book concerned, the 1924 edition of Hooker's *Illustrations of British Flora*, contains over 1,300 black and white line drawings of plants, and I had bought it for £1 at a jumble sale some years before. The inscription penned inside the cover reads: 'Annette J. Spence, from her loving pupil Iris Ainsworth, 9th of August 1926.' I wonder, had Annette retired from teaching? The volume had been lovingly bound with stitched canvas for use out-of-doors, and it seems that, for the next few years, as Annette explored the countryside around Dublin, she delicately and accurately coloured in the line drawings of plants she found with water colours. Under each little masterpiece she noted where and when she found it: at a glance it can be seen that she came across wild strawberries at Abbotstown in September 1926, and the fragrant orchid near the Dodder River in the Dublin Mountains in July 1927. Only a small proportion of the plants in the book are so coloured, and the last 'entry' noted is the water dropwort she found beside the canal near Castleknock on 31 July 1928. I often wondered what became of Annette and her love of wild flowers, seemingly enjoyed for such a short time, but since that Carlingford day, as I wander in perfumed boreens, I somehow know she has joined my mother at my shoulder.

THE FLASK

Alison Wells

The main advantage of moving to Ireland, according to my eight-year-old self, was that I would be able to bring a flask to school. I was making a list of pros and cons. We would soon be moving back to my mother's birthplace in Kerry from the flat landscape and the singsong accents of the East Midlands. I would miss my friends, but would make new ones. I would be living in the countryside instead of on a redbrick estate, would take a bus to school instead of walking. I knew that there would be a lunch box, rather than school dinners — and, of course, the all-important flask. That tipped me in favour of the move.

There was a notice in the *Gainsborough News*. It was the first time Barnes and Wentworth removals would be making a trip outside the country. I wonder now at the contrast they must have experienced from the beginning of their journey — with its neat rows of houses along wide pavements — to the end — a rickety farmhouse laneway, potholes filled in with stones and cement.

We travelled in tandem to Swansea and from there to Cork on the Sealink ferry. For much of the journey, my sisters and I sang a modified version of a Rod Stewart song 'We are sailing, to see Granny'. At the ferry port, we were delayed gaining entry because of our family pets and watched the lorry trundle ahead. We caught up with them in Killorglin — three small children in the back of the Ford Escort Estate pointing excitedly as the lorry struggled up the steep hill to the town.

Beyond Glenbeigh, we reached the coast road. Still narrow then before tourist improvements, we tottered precariously upon the cliff edge. An expanse of sea below us, thrilling and frightening, Dingle and the Iveragh Peninsulas jutting out to our right and left. In front of us, the removal lorry seemed to sway. We willed it to stay close to the wall of rock above which traversed the tracks of the spectacular but now unused Farranfore to Valentia branch line. Somehow we made it, full of wonder and that fresh bright feeling of novelty. The removal lorry unloaded, our parents young and hopeful, cramming their hard-won possessions into Gran's house where we would live before we built our own home.

In early May, we started school. In the mornings, we would take Tom Cournane's bus as it wound its way down side roads and tracks to the doors of farmhouses. The route from the bottom of Gran's road headed then down to Kells Bay, on a road not made for the passing of two cars. Then back up again, hairpin turns, stops and starts until we reached the school a good half an hour later.

Now nine, I had a crash course in Irish, skipping quickly from *Tá Teidí ag siúl* up to *Pól agus Síle* and their madra Bran. In the playground, the children were playing a strange game, a sort of piggy in the middle but with five participants. They tried to explain the rules but my ears had not yet attuned to the heavy accents. I couldn't understand them, so I stepped back, just looking, feeling foolish. It was still an alien world. We wore pretty dresses and long hair; they wore practical trousers, T-shirts and crew cuts. We needed time to adjust to one another.

In the course of events, I joined in their games, made new friends — although four of the five in my class were my first or second cousins anyway. I played tag and football and spies, and used the outdoor toilets, with the leaves drifting in under the door. I danced the 'Sweets of May' and 'The Walls of Limerick' and swapped my recorder for a tin whistle. I collected flowers for the May altar and, in the summer, had adventures on bog castles, among rushes and rocks and on windy hillsides. Imaginary horses were saved from burning barns, adversities overcome. When September came, I brought cheese and jam sandwiches to school in a lunchbox. The reality of the move was, inevitably, a step sideways from what I had originally imagined. That winter, I ate bread from John O'Donnell's van with vegetable soup which was cooked in a vat and handed out in tin mugs. Consequently, I never did experience the anticipated glamour of bringing my own flask to school.

ANNA AKHMATOVA AND THE MULLINGAR CONNECTION

Joseph Woods

What could possibly connect the great Russian poet Anna Akhmatova with Mullingar and its Renaissance-style Cathedral? The Cathedral of Christ the King was built relatively recently – begun in 1936 and consecrated in 1939 on the day the Second World War was declared.

The cathedral's connection with Akhmatova I discovered during the course of a conversation I had with the Russian poet and translator Grigory Krushkov in Milan. When I mentioned in passing that I had lived in Mullingar, Grigory's eyes lit up as if I had mentioned a mythical place, and he asked had I ever seen the Boris Anrep mosaics in the church there.

The cathedral possesses a rich interior of mosaics, the most treasured of which form the backdrop to two adjacent chapels at the top of the church, across from the sanctuary steps in front of the altar. Both mosaics depict scenes from the lives of St Patrick and St Anne. They are the work of Boris Anrep, a Russian Mosaicist who led a colourful life.

He was born in Russia in 1883 and came from aristocratic stock whose family tree connected him to mediaeval knights, Swedish King Charles XII and Catherine the Great. Anrep was, by all accounts, a romantic and charming man who lived life as a bohemian. As a young man, he married in 1908 and went to Paris to study art and then to England where he became part of the Bloomsbury set.

At the outbreak of the First World War, he returned to Russia where he took a commission as an officer in the army. It was during this period in Russia that he met and fell in love with the poet Anna Akhmatova. She had only recently separated from her husband the poet Nikolai Gumilev and was waiting to be divorced; meanwhile Anrep's wife was conveniently in England. A passionate relationship between the two ensued during 1915 and, despite the war, they dined out frequently and went sleighing together that winter. Akhmatova began writing passionate poems about Anrep as if she had waited all her life for him and would continue writing poems about him – critics have counted thirty-four – and talking about him until the end of her life.

Anrep, fearing what would come from a Soviet government, fled Russia in 1917. He asked Akhmatova to come with him but she refused and saw his departure as treachery to herself, to the Orthodox Church and to Russia. When they parted, Akhmatova famously gave him a black ring, which her Tartar grandmother had given her in the belief that it would protect her. Anrep wore the ring on a chain around his neck as a talisman for many years.

They would not see each other for fifty years. Anrep never wrote, perhaps fearing what would happen to Akhmatova if letters arrived from abroad. But she kept writing about him as if absence increased the power he had over her and her imagination. Anrep would subsequently lose the black ring she gave him during a Nazi air raid in Paris, during the war in which he took an active part in the French Resistance.

In 1965, a year before her death and at the age of seventy-six, Anna Akhmatova was allowed out of the Soviet Union to receive an honorary degree from Oxford University. At the award ceremony, in which Siegfried Sassoon was also honoured, she was disappointed that Anrep didn't show up or make the journey from Paris. She decided to go to Paris on her return journey to Moscow to see him instead.

Anrep was apprehensive about meeting up since he had lost the black ring and since he wanted to remember her as young and beautiful, the woman whom Modigliani had once painted. They had both grown old and much fatter as Akhmatova later commented. Her disappointment on meeting him was intense; he was a portly old man, no longer the handsome and dashing aristocratic officer of 1917. He had only a few more years to live. It's been suggested that she had wanted from him some sort of confession or expression of regret for having abandoned her, but neither was forthcoming.

One of Anrep's finest works are a series of allegorical mosaics he made for the National Gallery in London where he cast famous people or people he knew as gods or muses; so Virginia Woolf was cast as Clio, Muse of History, Greta Garbo as Melpomene, Muse of Tragedy, and Akhmatova appeared in a composition entitled *The Awakening of the Muses*. Later in another commission, the *Modern Virtues*, Anrep included the face of Akhmatova as the face of Compassion.

Some years later, in the Marion year of 1954, Anrep was commissioned to create two mosaics for the cathedral in Mullingar. The subject of the first was of St Patrick, and the second was of St Anne depicting the Blessed Virgin Mary being presented in the temple by her parents, saints Joachim and Anne.

The subject of the Virgin Mary being presented in the temple is hardly a surprising one, given that 1954 was a Marion year. But what is surprising and a little remarkable is the arrangement of the mosaic. The figure of the tall, slim and gaunt St Anne dominates the mosaic, takes centre stage and bears more than an uncanny resemblance to the young Anna Akhmatova as depicted by artists and photographers.

This emphasis on St Anne in the mosaic is reinforced, as her name is spelt out in capitals in the centre of the picture beside her halo. She is the only named saint and furthermore, St Anne's name is spelt unconventionally as Anna, like the poet, Anna.

Anrep, it seems, had once again characteristically cast someone he knew as an immortal; the immortal poet Anna Akhmatova as the immortal St Anne. But it also declares something of Anrep, despite the gulf between these once lovers and the fact that there had been no contact between them for fifty years; she was present throughout his own creative life as a muse who haunted his imagination.

PILGRIMAGE TO CHARTRES

Cathleen Brindley

One of the ambitions of my early life was to become a student in Paris and when that ambition became a reality, I was determined to get the most out of the experience. So, come the Pentecost weekend, or Whit as we all used to call it, I hurried to sign up to take part in the annual pilgrimage of the Sorbonne students to Chartres. The Cathedral of Notre Dame de Chartres had always been the focus of pilgrimage since mediaeval times and what better way, I thought, to see this great wonder than to arrive on foot, following history's path.

This latter-day pilgrimage had been started in the 1930s by some Sorbonne students at a time when Charles Peguy, poet, socialist, essayist and philosopher, was much admired. Peguy, who was born in Orleans in 1873 and killed at the Front in 1915, left the Catholic Church for a period of his life and then returned to the faith but not to the Church. When, in 1911, his son Pierre became seriously ill, Peguy made his first pilgrimage to Chartres and so revived the tradition of making the journey on foot. He spoke in a poem of quitting the meagre Sorbonne and its poor little ones. I was now one of these poor little ones, although I didn't feel so except in the usual way students feel poor.

By the time I came to join my fellow students, well after the Second World War, the pilgrimage was a well-organised event — it had to be as, the year I did it, 6,000 students took part. On Whit Saturday, a train took us southwest to the edge of the city and then we were on the road, rucksack on back for the long march. The immense crowd was divided into chapters which were subdivided into teams, each chapter having its own chaplain. We set off cheerfully singing but soon the murderous sun, which blazed down on us throughout the whole three days, began to take its toll on backs and feet. We had to take enough food for the three days as it was not allowed to buy anything in the little villages en route — understandably as it would have been as if a swarm of locusts had passed through. France recovered slowly from wartime food shortages and if you were twenty-one and fit, very little in the way of food rations came your way. I was greatly excited by the availability of a tin of 'thon' — tuna — not many of us knew tuna then, but carried in a hot knapsack it was not an ideal food.

Every now and then, the march stopped and we all sat down to meditate and discuss spiritual matters. The theme that year was the Mystical Body of Christ ... I greatly admired my French friends' ability to discuss abstract and philosophical matters at the drop of a hat. Things may well be different now, but, in my day, the Irish were not in the same class at all and, as there were several Irish in my *équipe*, we did not shine in theological discussion. In any case, being bad at meditation myself, I got my spiritual kicks from the pleasure of looking at the great plain of La Beauce with its waving sea of wheat and in listening to the larks singing overhead.

Nights were spent in the big barns belonging to farms along the way. A former pilgrim advised me to grab some straw as the nights were surprisingly cold, but I never found any straw, so wrapped in my rather ratty blanket, rucksack under my head, I slept the sleep of exhaustion on the earthen floor. Washing was a primitive exercise, face and hands under the farmyard pump, and then back on the road at dawn.

Whit Sunday saw us seated on the grass in front of a mediaeval chateau while the chaplains concelebrated mass. After the mass, the owner of the chateau sent around pails of a Bovril-like *bouillon* which disappeared rapidly when we discovered it was laced with rum. The hymn singing was loud and jolly as we marched on. Our food was getting more unattractive as time passed — stone-hard bread, squashy fruit and the now hated tuna.

At dawn on Whit Monday, we were on the last leg of the journey. Suddenly, across the plain the spires of the cathedral appeared like match sticks on the horizon. Now the long procession marched along in complete silence until it reached the cathedral. After High Mass and the wonders of the twelfth-century cathedral, we all sat down on the ground in front of the Royal Portal to watch the performance of a thirteenth-century Miracle play – the *Miracle of Théophile* – an early Faust-like story where a restless and ambitious cleric signs a pact selling his soul to the Devil. Repenting, he seeks help from Our Lady who snatches the document from the Devil and restores it to Theophile. While waiting for the play to start, there was a moment of comic relief. To amuse themselves a group of students started chanting '*de l'eau, de l'eau*' – water, water. The good citizens of Chartres from the balconies of their houses looking down on us, started to sprinkle us with water. I was in the direct line of fire and was soaked to the skin, a relief in the circumstances.

Then, from the cathedral the actors filed all dressed in stone-coloured robes as if they had stepped down from among the statues. It was truly uncanny.

To my surprise, I found that the pilgrimage still takes place, though not perhaps in the form I knew it. No, we didn't have to walk back to Paris. Trains took us to the city. When I looked in the mirror in my lodgings a blackened face stared back at me, hair stiff with dust. I felt like a true pilgrim.

FROM LEUVEN TO DROMORE

Tadhg Ó Dúshláine

Today, 20 May, in what is now known as The Louvain Institute for Ireland in Europe, in Leuven, Belgium, the founding of the Irish Franciscan College by Florence Conroy, 400 years ago in 1607, is being celebrated.

Conroy, by birth a member of the learned Connacht Ó Maolchonaire family was, by vocation, a distinguished theologian and recognised authority on the works of St Augustine, and had considerable influence with Ferdinand and Isabella of Spain. Not only did he acquire the funding for the establishment of an Irish College, but he also had the vision to set up the first Irish printing press for the Catholic *émigrés* at Leuven. Of all the colleges of the Irish Diaspora from Bordeaux to Brussels, from Paris to Prague, that of the Franciscans at Leuven is by far the most famous — not just for the catechetical and devotional works produced there for the home mission, but particularly for the great work of the Four Masters in compiling the *Annals of the Kingdom of Ireland* and the *Lives of the Irish Saints*.

Conroy's Irish version of the classic *Desiderius*, first written in Catalan, a type of *Pilgrim's Progress*, for the wandering Irish of the time, was the first book off the new printing press in 1616. In his inspiring introduction, he tells us that this bestseller was translated into all the great modern languages and asks why the Irish shouldn't have it too:

> This book appealed so much to the people of Europe that
> it was translated into Spanish, Italian, French, German and
> English. It appeared to us and to that it would be beneficial

to translate it into Irish, to bring the light of understanding of the holy things it teaches to that part of our homeland that does not understand any other language.

For the great paradox of the fall of Gaelic Ireland at Kinsale in 1601, and the emigration of the earls in 1607, was that both political failures were a blessing in disguise, allowing us to avail of all that was best in the post-Renaissance, Baroque Europe of the time. And the great achievement of the Irish *émigrés* of that age, were not political, academic or religious, but above all literary in their mastery of the great baroque themes of the time – flux and fragility and the vulnerability of the human condition.

Two years after Conroy's *Desiderius*, what many scholars now consider the finest literary achievement of the period came from the Franciscan press at Leuven. Ostensibly a treatise on the sacrament of confession, Hugh McCavill's *Speculum Confessionis* is as dramatic and impressive in its description as the painting of Caravaggio or Bernini's sculpture. His version of a contemporary tale in order to impress the danger of dying in sin has all the vigour and vitality, localisation and dramatic effect of Caravaggio's *Supper at Emmaus*:

> Not too long ago an example of what we are discussing happened right here in Brussels. It concerns a certain army officer, intelligent but reckless. His friends were forever advising him to mend his ways, but this wise guy always replied that one quarter of an hour would be enough for him to put things right with God at the end. Wait till you hear what happened to him: while he was having dinner, with a group most unlike the twelve apostles, just as he put a bite to his mouth, the life and soul leapt out of him, and he went to a place where he received his just reward, and that isn't considered to be a very nice place.

McCavill's skill as a scholar, preacher and missionary was recognised and he was ordained Archbishop of Armagh in Rome in June 1626 but died in September that same year, is buried in St Isadore's, and never got a chance to visit his native Downpatrick. But in the dispensation that now obtains on this island, there is something singularly appropriate in the fact that, after the Restoration in 1661, Jeremy Taylor, known as 'The Shakespeare of Divinity', was appointed Protestant Bishop of Down and Connor and lies buried in Dromore Cathedral. And how fitting it is that Taylor's classic on the art of dying should echo McCavill's earlier work in Irish, for both borrow from the same classical and biblical sources. Meditations on life and death helped both these bishops put things in perspective in the troubled times of the seventeenth century. 'Homer calls man "a leaf",' Taylor says,

> the smallest, the weakest piece of a short-lived plant; Pindar calls him "the dream of a shadow"; St James says our life is but smoke, tossed by every wind, lifted up on high, or left below, according as it pleases the sun. It is less than a mist or a shower, and not substantial enough to make a cloud. It ends after a short time, like the shadow that departs, or like a tale that is told, or like a dream when one awakes. The sum of it all is this: you are but human, and consequently your life is a series of heights and lows, of lights and shadows, of misery and folly, of laughter and tears, of groans and death.

There is much to admire in the writing of these two humble bishops, McCavill and Taylor, whose words of wisdom lead to that peace that passes all understanding, when the political spites and squabbles of the time have been long forgotten.

GREENE'S BOOKSHOP

John Boland

The first genuine books I ever read — not *The Secret Seven*, not *Biggles Sweeps the Desert*, not even *The Wind in the Willows*, but real books with adult thoughts and feelings — came courtesy of Rathmines Public Library, where I spent too many evenings of my teenage years. Yet even though a library is a fine and private place, for real lovers of literature, there is nothing to compare with a shop that sells second-hand books, and the first such shop I ever entered was Greene's on Clare Street, which closes its doors next Friday after 164 years in existence.

Samuel Beckett, who lived across the street from it above his father's business premises, frequented it often, as did his mentor James Joyce, and not just when he was waiting for Nora Barnacle to finish her working day at Finn's Hotel almost opposite. I used to imagine, as I was poring over dusty volumes on its stairway shelves, that the ghosts of these men were brushing by me. We wouldn't, of course, have talked because there's something about the atmosphere of a second-hand bookshop that invites the willing silence which libraries famously demand — an atmosphere that says that reading is a serious business and that we who are perusing these books are serious people, searching for something with which to provide solace for our solitary hours.

Part of the pleasure of this quest — a large part, I would say — is its uncertainty. You enter a second-hand bookshop usually having no idea what you are looking for or, indeed, if you are looking for anything at all, and suddenly there on the shelf in front of you is an old Everyman's

Library edition of George Herbert's poems or Montaigne's essays and, years later, you look at these volumes on your own shelves and realise that, for a few pence or a few shillings or a few euro, you discovered in these bookshops writers who were to become your companions for life.

Or, but this is rare (though it's the rarity that gives the thrill), you suddenly find yourself face to face with a book you've been seeking all your life and you stand for a few seconds with giddy disbelief at your amazing good fortune before hurriedly seizing the treasured object just in case anyone else suddenly snatches it out of your grasp — even though it's been standing, forlorn and forgotten, on these shelves for months or years. I had that sensation when, after twenty years scouring through bookshops in various cities, I found myself in Los Angeles and happened upon a book that had been my bible as a teenager in Rathmines Library — Kenneth Tynan's 1961 book of theatre reviews, *Curtains* — now miraculously there before my eyes in mint condition and for a mere $10 in this rambling warehouse of a bookstore on the edge of the world.

Nowadays, I can go onto the internet, where this week on the Abebooks site I found forty-four other first editions of Tynan's book at prices ranging from a ridiculous $1 dollar to a more daunting $167, but though this is a wonderful online service and I use it regularly, somehow it's not the same — you don't experience the delirium of discovery or the feel of the spine of the book or of the smell of its pages or of the whole inimitable ritual of entering the shop, the proprietor nodding at you, the other customers glancing round from their silent reveries at the shelves to size up the demeanour and perhaps the moral character of this newcomer, this fellow explorer who has decided to embark on the same voyage of discovery.

I went back to Greene's last week to say farewell to it and to imagine it soon sharing some Valhalla with Webb's on the quays and the Dublin Bookshop on Bachelor's Walk and those other irreplaceable emporiums that no longer exist in this supposedly literary town of ours. While I was there, I browsed among the depleted shelves on the stairs, leafing through old Reprint Society editions of Neville Shute and Nigel Balchin and Elizabeth Jane Howard and all those other writers who, like Greene's itself, have had their day.

I finally came across and bought, for a mere €2.50, a lovely compendium called *The Musical Companion*. The scrawl in fountain pen on the flyleaf informed me that it was once the property of Dorothy Beattie, who acquired it at Christmas in 1946. Years later, she or her family, for whatever reason, banal or heartbreaking, felt obliged to dispense with it. Was she one of the ghosts I sensed as I walked back down the stairs of Greene's for the last time?

THE BOY SOPRANO

Bernard Farrell

When I was growing up in Sandycove, the back garden of our house backed onto the bigger houses and bigger back gardens of Spencer Villas. In these houses lived richer people, more aloof people, people we seldom saw and, when we did, we silently and respectfully passed them by. The house at the end of our garden was owned by Mrs Brennan who, despite her Irish name, was a most aristocratic lady – 'Like the Queen of England,' my father would whisper whenever we saw her, as she promenaded down Adelaide Road with an air of majesty and entitlement. She spoke to no one, ever – but all that changed the year that my sister began to take singing lessons, the year when I turned twelve.

In our family, my sister Margaret had an exceptionally beautiful singing voice and, in her early teens, she was already taking lessons in operatic interpretation, vocal training and choral work. And every afternoon, in that last summer of my pre-teen years, she would be out in our back garden, practising her scales, rehearsing her exam pieces and occasionally, with so little effort, soaring into something by Puccini or Offenbach.

And this was the time that Mrs Brennan and I first met and spoke.

I remember I was walking up Adelaide Road when suddenly she was standing in front of me, saying loudly and firmly: 'Good morning, Bernard.' I stopped in wordless amazement but now, more like Lady Bracknell than the Queen, she was continuing, 'I was in my back garden yesterday and I heard you singing and I must say that you have the most beautiful boy-soprano voice I have ever heard.'

I looked at her, knowing that I should immediately explain that she was listening to my sister, not to me but, at that time of my life, I was so starved of compliments that I suddenly heard myself humbly saying, 'Thank you very much, Mrs Brennan.'

And so began our relationship as, in the weeks that followed, whenever she appeared, she consistently praised me, encouraged me and assured me of how gifted I was. As I accepted these compliments, my youthful confidence continued to grow and grow, as weeks turned into months and the seasons changed, and winter drove us indoors, and spring reunited us, and then we were into a new summer. And it was at this time, with my confidence at its zenith that my voice broke.

Suddenly, I was speaking hoarser and harsher and in a tone lower than I thought possible. But as I self-consciously monitored these adolescent changes, I never once questioned the effect they would have on my relationship with Mrs Brennan – until, quite suddenly, I met her again.

She greeted me with her usual enthusiasm and it was only when I replied, 'Good Morning, Mrs Brennan', that she stopped and asked what had happened to my voice. I politely told her that, over the past few weeks, my voice had begun to break and this was now how it would be for the rest of my life. She looked puzzled. 'But,' she said, 'I heard you singing yesterday, in your back garden.' I was trapped. I had to think quickly – and I did. I said, 'Ah yes, Mrs Brennan – what has happened is that I have had to stop singing – but my sister, Margaret, has now started and it was probably her you heard.' She looked at me for a moment and then said, 'Well, she does sing quite well – but she will never be as good as you.'

In the years that followed, I saw less and less of Mrs Brennan – she no longer promenaded along Adelaide Road – and then I heard of her illness and, soon after, that she had passed away. By then, my sister's singing career had begun to blossom and, for many years, she revelled in the appreciation and the applause, until she relinquished it all for love, parenthood and family. And some months ago, at too young an age, she too died. At her funeral, as I remembered her, I also remembered Mrs Brennan and I wondered if they were now together, speaking to each other at long last. And I smiled at the thought of Margaret telling her who was really singing in our back garden all those years ago – and Mrs Brennan now knowing that the boy soprano never really existed, that he was just a young, insecure impostor who had once tried to live in the shadow of his much more gifted sister.

GOING TO GRACELAND

Conor Bowman

I had expected to be travelling with a friend of mine but he couldn't get the time off, and so I found myself flying to Nashville on my own. I rented a car, contemplated the hazards of driving on the wrong side of the road, then headed west on Interstate 40 with the Country Music Hall of Fame in the rear-view mirror.

When he died I was twelve. By the age of seventeen, I had a huge record collection. It only covered the works of two artists; I had a single called 'Jeans On' by David Dundas and everything else was by Elvis Presley. I had posters, T-shirts, badges, stickers and, of course, the music. I wore enough Brylcream in my hair to lubricate a fairly large lawnmower. I had a pair of drainpipe trousers and blue Gola runners instead of suede shoes. More than just a fan, I was the only Teddy-boy in Galway. I knew the addresses of his houses, Belugia Ave in LA, Audubon Drive, the Circle G. Ranch in Mississippi. I knew that he'd had a pet chimpanzee called Scatter, that he loved Mario Lanza; I even tracked down a man in Westport while on holidays who'd served with him in the army in Germany. I was obsessed.

The miles disappeared under me and I was passed out by dozens of huge shiny chrome trucks but eventually, I reached Memphis. A very precise set of instructions from the car-hire firm got me to Elvis Presley Boulevard. There wasn't a single sign anywhere along the way which would have helped me otherwise. A four-lane highway runs past the house and visitors park on the other side of the road in the commercial complex of souvenir shops, museums and the Heartbreak Motel. A shuttle bus carries twenty fans at a time up to the most famous celebrity house on the planet.

Set on fourteen acres in a pretty dodgy area of a dodgy-to-begin-with city, think Áras an Uachtaráin in a run-down industrial estate and that's Graceland. Once you pass through the gates, though, it's out of this world. It's tranquil and calming and you can't hear the cars on the road below. The house is smaller than you'd imagine and, because of that, it's intimate and somehow more real. Seeing his piano, the dining room, kitchen and Jungle Room, as they were thirty years ago, made my heart race. I knew every bit from the photographs I'd been gazing at for decades. There's the spot where they had the Christmas tree each year. For an instant, I could see Elvis and Lisa Marie laughing together as she unwrapped presents. There are buildings behind the house, a converted indoor go-kart track and a racquetball court, where every available inch of wall-space is covered in gold and platinum records. There are clothes, including the Eagle suit from the Hawaii concert and *that* leather outfit from the comeback TV special in 1968. I saw memorabilia from almost every palm-tree-filled, Acupulco-based, girl-laden movie he ever made. His musical achievements are absolutely staggering. One award marks 400 million sales.

The tour finishes in the Meditation Garden, where Elvis, his parents and paternal grandmother are buried. There is a memorial to his twin brother, Jesse Garon, who died at birth. My favourite Elvis song, 'If I Can Dream', began to play on the headset you get for the tour, just as I stood and looked down at the grave of my hero. Suddenly, I was crying uncontrollably and not caring who saw me. A lifetime of devotion to someone I'd never even met was set free among the rhodedendrons and the stained glass windows. In that moment, I was a child again and felt as though two distant parts of me were connecting for the first time ever.

As I waited for the shuttle bus back to my own life, I heard the faint clamour of grown men racing golf-carts over the lawns, of them having fireworks fights near the swimming pool and the lonely sound of someone playing gospel songs on the piano and asking the Lord to help him make some sense of it all.

FATHER CHARLES (1821–1893)

Vivien Igoe

Father Charles is among the many characters in Dublin mentioned in James Joyce's novel *Ulysses*. Joyce's close friend J. F. Byrne, whom he first met in 1893 when both were pupils at Belvedere College, recalls suffering with eye problems as a very young child. At the time, Byrne was attending the Infants School run by the Holy Faith nuns in Clarendon Street. His cousin, Mary Fleming, brought him to St Vincent's Hospital where his eyes were treated, but not cured. She then took him to two eye specialists on Merrion Square, but that too proved unsuccessful. Then someone suggested that he be brought to Fr Charles, the Passionist at Harold's Cross.

Byrne recounts in his memoirs entitled *Silent Years*, that he had heard, of course, about Fr Charles, for you couldn't have lived in Dublin of these years without hearing of his sanctity and his miraculous good works. Indeed, he was the uncanonised saint of the city of Dublin.

So Mary brought her young cousin to Harold's Cross. As they approached along the avenue and neared the church, Mary pointed out Fr Charles to him. He was strolling with another priest in the grounds; the sight of Fr Charles left a huge impression on the child. The priest was aged, frail and thin and they both understood immediately from his face and appearance why everybody referred to him as a saint.

They entered the church where other people were waiting for his touch. Soon he entered, and began his prayerful ministration. Byrne recounts how he beheld a vision of unutterable holiness. As he felt the emaciated fingertips of Fr Charles over his closed eyes he was in a state of near ecstasy. The following day Byrne's eyes were completely cured and he never suffered from them again. No doubt Byrne related his story of his cure to Joyce.

Blessed Charles of Mount Argus was born on 11 December 1821 in Holland, the fourth of a family of eleven children. He was christened John Andrew. The family lived a simple life and worked in a flour mill owned by an uncle. John Andrew served as a conscript in the army. When he was twenty-four, he joined the noviciate of the Passionists in Belgium where he was given the name Charles. He was ordained in Tournai on 21 December 1850.

Two years later, Fr Charles went to St Wilfrid's Retreat in Staffordshire, England. It was here that he met the famous Fr Paul Packenham, son of the Earl of Longford and a nephew of the Duke of Wellington. Packenham who had converted to Catholicism had been a captain in the Grenadier Guards before becoming a Passionist, so they shared a military background. Packenham helped Fr Charles by giving him English lessons. It was during this period that Fr Charles first came in contact with the Irish people, many of whom had immigrated to various places in England seeking work in the coalfields and factories after the Great Famine of 1845. He was greatly moved by their dreadful living conditions.

In July 1857, Fr Charles came to Ireland to the newly-founded monastery at Mount Argus. Father Packenham was its first rector and superior but, sadly, had died two months before Fr Charles arrived. Father Charles spent the next nine years at the monastery before returning to England. He was recalled to Mount Argus in early 1874 where he remained for the last nineteen years of his life.

During his years at Mount Argus, a steady stream of people called to be blessed by him, sometimes up to 300 a day. They travelled from all parts of Ireland, England, Scotland and America. Many cures were attributed to him and his fame spread rapidly. Even when his health deteriorated, Fr Charles continued to work tirelessly and went out to visit and comfort the sick in atrocious weather conditions at all hours of the night.

Father Charles died on 5 January 1893, and was buried in the community cemetery. His funeral was said to have attracted more mourners than that of Parnell. His grave became a place of pilgrimage, where people came daily to pray. In November 1949, by order of the Holy See, his body was transferred from the cemetery to the church at Mount Argus. He was beatified by Pope John Paul II on 16 October 1988.

Blessed Charles of Mount Argus, whom J. F. Byrne termed as 'the uncanonised saint of the city of Dublin' so many years ago, is to be officially canonised this May by Pope Benedict in Rome.

HOGARTH'S
GENERAL ELECTION

Catherine Marshall

Before the euphoria of the May 2007 general election victory goes to anyone's head, the newly-elected candidates would do well to look at Hogarth's print *Chairing the Member* from the Election Series which has just gone on show at the Irish Museum of Modern Art. Clearly, Hogarth thought the pitfalls facing the victorious candidates exceeded anything they had overcome to gain the seat. The dangers all stem from the member's own enthusiastic supporters who, drunk with the joy of winning, are about to topple him from his throne to land among the pigs at their feet, or worse, to tip him into the river. The unfortunate man stares desperately ahead, only to be confronted with a skull and crossbones cheekily held up for his attention by a monkey and a grimy little chimney sweep. They are far more in control of their destiny than their new parliamentary representative.

Chairing the Member is the final one of four prints that make up the Election Series, based on a group of paintings of the same name. The first three prints, *Canvassing for Votes, An Election Entertainment* and *The Polling*, take us through every kind of electoral corruption and debauchery imaginable. The three different drinking houses that provide the back-drop to the canvassing are familiar enough today, but money for votes and debauched election entertainments? Surely not! Certainly in our general election, the polling officers did not leave the candidates to

supervise the procedure while they slept on the job. The prints antici-
pate troubled times ahead for the country also; the politicians look after
their own interests while the coach Britannia (representing the nation)
is being driven off the rails by the driver and his friends, who gamble
and cheat at cards instead of attending to their responsibilities.

Hogarth, of course, was referring to a notorious election in Oxfordshire
in 1754, the first in fifty years, in which the campaign ran for a full two
years, only to return the same Tory incumbent. Artists are supposed to be
ahead of their time, but he couldn't possibly have been thinking ahead to
the Irish elections ... or could he? The rotten boroughs of eighteenth-
century Oxford may have disappeared but the political dynasty is every bit
as important today as it was then. And while the absence of political
posters is refreshing to our eyes, the pre-election banquet anticipates tents
at the races. Perhaps we should be grateful that election campaigns now are
limited to three or four weeks.

Hogarth's take on the manners and morals of his society is always
refreshing. Clearly there was much to be learned as a child in his father's
Latin-speaking coffee house, a paradigm for Georgian vice if ever there
was one, where coffee loosened the tongue and facilitated uncensored
discussion about politics, poetry, the theatre and God knows what else.
It is to this and, above all, to his outstanding skills as a painter and
printmaker that we owe his many other great series – *Marriage a la Mode*,
The Rake's and Harlot's Progresses and his incisive attacks on social preten-
sion and self-interest.

Human nature doesn't change and print-making lends itself to social
satire more than any other art form prior to the media revolution in the
late twentieth century. The Madden Arnholz print collection at the
Irish Museum of Modern Art, from which the Hogarths are taken,
abounds in good examples. Consider the tiny, almost postage-stamp-
sized images of peasants in sixteenth-century Nurenberg by Hans
Sebald Beham where the peasants dance merrily to the right while
vomiting their excess alcohol, with equal energy, to the left, or skip a
hundred years and feast your eyes on the foppish pirouetting of the
courtiers in Jacques Callot's work, or skip forward again to the later and
larger prints of Goya and Daumier, where the humour becomes both
savage and, in Goya's case, nightmarish.

Satire in prints is certainly not unusual, but Hogarth was more
catholic in his targets than many of the others. Everyone from innkeep-

ers and brothel managers to property developers, clerics and aristocrats fall in for their share of his venom. Or is venom the right word? You get the feeling, looking at the prints in the Madden Arnholz collection, that Hogarth, like Dickens, really loves his rascals or, more likely, enjoys finding the right framework for exposing their many weaknesses.

THE BURIAL OF PATRICK IRELAND

Gemma Tipton

It's quite a thing to arrange your own funeral, but not entirely unheard of. People select the music, the readings, sometimes even the coffin. It's quite another to arrange your funeral with the intention of attending it – and of walking away, hale and hearty afterwards. But this is the achievement that Brian O'Doherty is adding to an already lengthy list of rather great things he has done. I think if O'Doherty, who was born in Balahadreen in 1928, were a historical figure, he'd probably be on every-one's list to have dinner with – when you're playing those imagining games, inventing meals where you're sitting down to a feast of food and conversation with James Joyce, Beckett, maybe Leonardo, possibly Einstein, Marie Curie, and one of the Brontës.

So where do you start with this man? Describing someone, describing anyone, is a tricky business. Do you say he's a charming man? An artist? A writer? A husband? Do you describe how he looks? Blue eyes … Well, maybe, but you'd be missing plenty. In O'Doherty's case, you'd need to add: qualified medical doctor, experimental psychologist, broad-caster, critic, film maker and novelist. And you still wouldn't quite be there. This is a problem for some, especially in this era, when we like to classify people, put them in handy boxes for easier understanding. And it's not just that he does and has done all these things, it's that he has done them so well.

Take the medicine part – he studied at University College Dublin, then went to Cambridge. Then Jack Yeats helped him to get a scholarship to Harvard. But, at the same time, he was writing poetry and making art. So take the art. Well, he's had exhibitions at the Dublin City Gallery, The Hugh Lane and the Douglas Hyde Gallery in Ireland, and is in collections at the Pompidou in Paris and in MoMA and the Metropolitan Museum in New York. In New York, he became friends with Marcel Duchamp. In fact, he made one of the last portraits ever of Duchamp by taking his electrocardiogram one evening when Duchamp came to dinner (while we're at it, by the way, I think I'll add Duchamp to the list of guests for my imaginary feast). Anyway, Barbara Novak, who is married to O'Doherty, tells the story of meeting Duchamp on the street a while later, and being asked – 'Well, how am I? Is my heart still beating?' Yes it was, and it still is, in the specially constructed light box that O'Doherty made for it.

In other aspects of his art, he creates shapes and spaces in galleries with lines of rope and colour, making you think about the place you're in, in a different way. He makes paintings filled with the whispering abstract shapes of Ogham and gorgeous sculpture (again from Ogham) which would be in my top ten list of Art Works I Would Consider Stealing (another imaginary game I have been known to play).

And the novels? Well, the first was optioned by Mick Jagger for a film, though he never made it, and the second, *The Deposition of Father McGreevey*, all full of lovely lyrical language, cruel west of Ireland winters and plenty of sheep, was shortlisted for the Booker Prize. Another one is on the way. I asked him once whether it all came easily to him. 'I'm more like a pig on a track,' he said, 'determinedly truffling my way up a hill.'

In 1972, Brian O'Doherty became Patrick Ireland – after Bloody Sunday. He staged a performance at the Project Arts Centre in Dublin, and said he'd keep the name as an artist until the British military withdrew from the North. Back then, no one seriously thought that could happen. Lee Krasner told him he'd never get his name back. But that's all changed now – and that's what this funeral is all about. After thirty-six years, Brian O'Doherty is coming home from New York, where he now lives, to bury an 'other' self.

As I think about all this, I start to wonder whether I have a case of hero worship. Would that be wrong? It seems it's fine to consider David Beckham a god, and his wife something to which to aspire. Or that it's good to scream and throw our knickers at sundry pop stars, but not at anyone who has any real substance. I'm not planning (I have to say) to throw my knickers, but I am planning to attend Patrick Ireland's funeral. Suitably attired for the occasion, too.

Patrick Ireland is to be buried in a ceremony at the Irish Museum of Modern Art, in the old Pauper's Graveyard in the grounds of the museum. It's happening on the 20 May 2008. And maybe once he's buried, we'll dream of having dinner with him too. But it would be far better to celebrate Brian O'Doherty properly while we still have him here.

YOU'LL NEVER WALK ALONE

John O'Donnell

Like many others of his age, my son had no choice. His news that day was a burden he had to share. 'Dad,' he said awkwardly, as if confessing to a fatal illness or life changing desire, 'I'm Liverpool.' His fate had been decided not by virus of rogue gene but by a cocky classmate. When my son's turn came to choose which football team to support, this knowing nine-year-old loftily declared, 'We've enough United. Tell you what: you can be Liverpool.'

What was I supposed to do? Should I persuade him of the virtues of a local team rather than some foreign legion? Should I cajole him to switch allegiance to the dodgy East End London team I'd supported through thick and — mostly — thin for over thirty years? I did what anyone would do. Heading for the nearest sports shop, I forked out a succession of notes in exchange for the official shirt, shorts and socks. On the shop floor, my son twirled, demanding to wear his new kit on the way home.

I could have said that in choosing Liverpool he was following a long tradition of Irish supporters and Irish players: Heighway, Lawrenson, Aldridge, Houghton. So what if some of these were, as it were, 'adopted' Irishmen? Liverpool had long supported us. In the thirteenth century, King John had used the port as base for his Irish campaigns, but by 1885, the city had elected an Irish nationalist MP to Westminster and, in 1918, a Sinn Féin candidate won a seat. Sometimes, Liverpudlians seemed more Irish than the Irish: spirited, contrary, resourceful and brimming with ironic, self-lacerating humour. Like us, Scousers have been accused of wallowing in 'victim' status; they've certainly had their share of it in recent years: Toxteth, Hysel, Hillsborough. When the city mourned the execution of Ken Bigley in Iraq, Conservative MP Boris Johnson drew howls of protest as he told them they were hooked on grief.

If it was grief my son was looking for, he'd come to the right place. Being a football fan is far more about the agony than the ecstasy, no matter who you support. How could I explain to him that in signing up for this, he was signing up for a lifetime of affliction; days and nights of groans and tears, and only the occasional trophy? But as it happened, that season 2004–2005, Liverpool was in the hunt for one trophy; the Champions League, the greatest football prize in Europe. After we watched Liverpool's first match, my son insisted we make a pact: we would watch every European game the team played in, on TV, together.

How could I say no? Aside from naked self-interest, wasn't this a perfect opportunity for father and son to bond together? Two dents began appearing in the couch. I told myself this was education in action, a practical way of learning the geography of Europe; like watching Eurovision. We toured Europe from our living room, gazing at games in Austria and Monaco, Greece and Spain and Germany. In the quarter-finals, they knocked out favourites Juventus of Turin; in the semi-finals, they disposed of Chelsea, thanks to a single flukey (perhaps illegal) goal. Somehow, against many predictions, Liverpool made it to the final, against AC Milan in May in Istanbul.

Perhaps this was as good a time as any for my son to learn a lesson: that in life there are very few happy endings. I tried to explain. Milan were the aristocrats, flashy, suave sophisticates; Liverpool were grunt and honest effort. Of course, I hoped they'd win, but really it was piano-players against piano-shifters. We took up our positions and waited.

A goal in the first minute for Milan seemed ominous; two further goals were the last nails in the coffin. An optimist by nature, my son enquired, 'Dad, do you think they could still win?' I shook my head, preparing to comfort the afflicted. At half-time, 3-nil up, Milan's squad were already celebrating. Should I send him to bed now, or allow him to endure and thereby learn from what was certain to be a long night of the soul? Resigned, we watched on.

A goal by Liverpool ten minutes into the second half: 'What do you think now, Dad?' More head-shaking; a consolation prize. Then, a minute later, another. 'Well, Dad?' I sighed knowing coming close would only make the pain of losing worse. Five minutes further on, a Liverpool penalty was parried by the keeper, but a red shirt stuck the rebound into the roof of the net. Three all. Liverpool fans who'd left the stadium at half-time begged taxis to turn back. In our house, a small red shirted figure danced around the furniture, 'Well Dad ... what do you think *now*?' Elder lemon to the last, I soberly assured him. 'Even if they make it to the end, they've got no chance on penalties.'

One of the milestones in a child's life is the moment when he learns his parents are not infallible; perhaps a milestone in the parent's life as well. Astonishingly, they survived a barrage on their goal in extra time. Thanks to their rubbery-legged Polish goalkeeper and three coolly-taken spot-kicks later, Liverpool won the Champions League – on penalties – in a match which has been described even by non-Liverpool fans as the greatest-ever game.

We sat joyously together as the screen filled with pictures from the far-off Turkish night of delirious fans singing their team's anthem, 'You'll Never Walk Alone'. Incandescent with delight, my son crowed and whooped; not only had his team won, but his dad had been proved wrong. It's hard to know which mattered to him more. In the future, there would be days when things did not go right; days when we would both be wrong. But, for now, we cheered for happy endings; for how in the most unlikely places the lost innocence of childhood is sometimes rediscovered.

ALL OF A SUDDEN OR
GO TOBANN

Gerard Corrigan

All of a sudden, or as we would have said in our essays *as Gaeilge, go tobann*, in 1978 Nott's Forest scarves and bags appeared out of nowhere. They were red leatherette bags, all festooned in hand-written graffiti with the names of popular bands at the time. Blondie and AC/DC sat scribbled comfortably with Gina, Dale Haze and the Champions. Nott's Forest had just won the league under the management of Brian Clough. A team of journeymen had come from what seemed like nowhere and were now revered by many of Ireland's teenagers; this reverence manifested itself in the form of scarves and bags.

Our religion teacher was a quintessentially 1970s folk mass, guitar-playing, be-clogged stereotype. This image had meandered its way from the California of the late 1960s and eventually hit Ireland in the late 1970s. He had soup stains on his tie for the three years he taught us religion. He had the same sports coat for three years with leather patches on the elbows. His winter jumper also had leather patches on the elbows. I imagined that he probably had leather patches on the heels of his socks. He brought in LPs and played us selected tracks. I remember him playing Kevin Johnson's 'Rock & Roll I Gave you the Best Years of My Life'. I forget what he said that the message in that song was. He was always looking for messages in things. The message that we sent back through our disinterest was that we would have preferred to hear Rory Gallagher.

At lunchtime, we would walk downtown and watch the culchies eating steaming bags of chips. We would admire the girls from the convent. The ultimate compliment for a girl was to be designated a 'fine thing'. Outside the café, a queue formed daily. This was a queue to watch the select few who could master the one Space Invaders machine in the town. Only a handful of the older lads had control of this machine. They were high-scoring legends and their ability and prowess inspired awe amongst us first years. They were school celebrities and any interaction with one of them brought one great street cred. No matter who got to the machine first when one of the Space Invaders legends walked in, the machine was freed up for them. They played that machine like a concert pianist. They concentrated like a brain surgeon and their eventual defeat was greeted with real disappointment that stopped short of tears.

A few people in our class had already got RTÉ 2 aerials and the pilot broadcasts of the *Streets of San Francisco* had started in advance of the launch date. Having a second aerial was a real status symbol in 1978. As we entered a world of choice, of two television channels, we could enjoy more than the wholesome diet of *Féach, Outlook, Amuigh Faoin Spéir, Radharc* and *The Riordans*. Now we would have *Top of the Pops* and all sorts of TV exotica. Imagine you could be watching something and then by getting up and pressing a button you could watch something else.

Every Friday, my copy of *Spotlight* would arrive at the local news-agents. I'd study the Irish charts, albums and singles. It seemed that 'Bat Out of Hell' would never leave the charts. One week, there might be a feature on The Rolling Stones and the next week an exclusive interview with Big Tom. Surreal. *Spotlight* would publish song lyrics every week, but it was a real genre lucky dip. It might be Brendan Shine or Philomena Begley or it could be Santana. The uncertainty was alluring. The showbiz news seemed dated, more deep-frozen off the presses than hot off the presses. The bizarre juxtaposition of country and Irish and heavy metal on the same pages was superb. What other publication in the world could feature Dana and Ozzy Osbourne on the same page?

Not long afterwards, the Pope came and told us all he loved us. Nott's Forest bags started to disappear. Liverpool bags were back.

1968 AND ALL THAT

John Boland

I was in UCD in May 1968 but I was no college radical. For one thing, I was far too busy belatedly cramming for my finals in English language and literature to bother my barney about the state of the world or the nation or even the academic injustices that were so exercising my fellow undergraduates in the self-styled Students for Democratic Action, otherwise known as the SDA – protesters love acronyms.

Anyway, temperamentally, I wasn't suited to the physical and psychological rigours of student protest – all that marching, all that shouting, all that self-righteousness. Or as the horrified aristocrat said when he arrived in the trenches, 'The noise! The people!' Of course I was aware of what was happening beyond the pampered purlieus of Earlsfort Terrace. Martin Luther King had been assassinated a few weeks earlier (Robert Kennedy was to be murdered a few weeks later) and Paris was in uproar.

But what struck me most about events in that city, which I hadn't yet visited and thus hadn't yet fallen in love with, were the protests over the attempted sacking by French culture minister André Malraux of Henri Langlois, legendary director of the Cinémathèque Française and revered mentor to such dazzling New Wave directors as François Truffaut, Jean-Luc Godard and Jacques Rivette, who were men I revered.

So my response to 1968 was almost entirely cultural and, when I look back on it now, what I recall most are the books of the year, the movies I was seeing and the music I was hearing. Not so much the books, perhaps, because I still had those bloody finals to do and was frantically ploughing my way through *King Lear*, *Paradise Lost*, the Metaphysical poets, the Augustans, the Victorians and late Yeats.

But it was about that time that I came upon *Kiss Kiss Bang Bang*, the second book of movie reviews by New Yorker critic Pauline Kael and became hooked on her writings (*Hooked*, in fact, was the name of a later collection by her). I thought her the most sassy and provocative of critics, with none of the solemnity of most other critics, and I didn't notice then the hectoring and bullying tone that later began to weary me somewhat in her writings.

I read, too, Norman Mailer's *Armies of the Night*, a terrific piece of extended reportage about unrest in America over the Vietnam War – and still, I think, one of Mailer's least flabby and self-indulgent efforts. But the book that has stayed with me longest from that year is Joan Didion's *Slouching Towards Bethlehem*, a collection of wonderfully observed and beautifully written essays about the fag-end of the hippie era in San Francisco, about sad marriages and silly self-awareness groups, about all those dreamers of the golden dream and also about her meeting with one of her oddest heroes, John Wayne, a film star she had adored from childhood. I thought her book a classic then and I think so even more now.

Then there were the movies of the year – not a vintage year, actually, but we did get to marvel at that sardonic sultan of cool, Steve McQueen, as he fought political corruption and criminal villainy in *Bullitt*. Everyone loved the bouncing cars in that famous chase scene, but I thought the airport ending the real bee's knees, both thrilling and somehow existential as McQueen did what he had to do, then shruggingly walked away.

Elsewhere, I wasn't as wowed by Mel Brooks's *The Producers* as my fellow students seemed to be (it just wasn't that funny, I thought), while I was left entirely cold by *2001: A Space Odyssey*, the ponderous and interminably slow movie in which Stanley Kubrick first decided he was a Serious Artist, with a capital S and a capital A. It was downhill all the way from there.

But it's the music that, forty years later, most evokes the year for me, and if you need convincing that those twelve months marked a vintage time, all I really have to do is list the albums – *John Wesley Harding* by Dylan, *Beggars' Banquet* by the Stones, *Cheap Thrills* by Big Brother and the Holding Company, *Electric Ladyland* by Jimi Hendrix, *Sweetheart of the Rodeo* by the Byrds, *Bookends* by Simon and Garfunkel, the *White Album* by the

Beatles, *Dusty in Memphis*, *Wheels of Fire* by Cream, Pink Floyd's *Saucerful of Secrets*, *Music from Big Pink* by the Band and last, though certainly not least, Van Morrison's *Astral Weeks*. They don't make them like those anymore.

But forget about the albums – how about the singles? 'Hey Jude', 'Lady Madonna', 'Hello Goodbye', 'Jumpin' Jack Flash', 'The Weight', 'Piece of My Heart', 'Do You Know the Way to San Jose', 'All Along the Watchtower', 'Dock of the Bay', 'Young Girl' and, of course, 'I Heard It Through the Grapevine'. There you had it – the world was in turmoil, but Marvin couldn't get over the fact that his girlfriend was cheating with some other guy and was making him blue. That's called getting your priorities right ...

JUNE

LUCKY

Enda Wyley

Lucky the man
who listens
to Monteverdi,
who walks
out the quiet lane
'Lamento della ninfa'
in his head and finds
the hedgerow yellow
with wild primrose,
the stones a maze
for the spider, the fields
undulating with ewes
and their soot-faced
soot-eared young.

Lucky the man who
hears the pheasant rising
high over Hunt's field
and is startled as much by it
as the tenor he's just heard
singing in soprano
the poem of another man
writing as a woman

in the seventeenth century —
contradictions
complex and beautiful
like dust-mites he sees
falling down now
through the sun's rays.

TRAVELLING WEST

Anne Enright

It is easier, they say, to travel west, and I believe them. I have just been around the world, quite literally. Last week, I was around the world. I took a plane to Heathrow and I took a plane that stopped over in Hong Kong, then I got back on it and flew to Auckland, New Zealand, home of the writer Witi Ihimaera, whom I met the last time I dropped into Hong Kong – in March when it was just as smoggy as this time, in May. I was travelling east, the plane was ploughing through the night, and then through another night – you could see it on the little video screen, the plane was overtaking the spin of the earth beneath it. At least I think it was. But I might be wrong, I have little enough grasp of relativity.

I had a lovely time in New Zealand, blinking in the wrong light, at the wrong time of day, waking up bellowing with hunger at 4 a.m. and then fasting through dinner time. A few kilometres outside Auckland, they told me, is the point on the globe that is farthest away from London. I tried to think where the farthest point from Dublin would be, the farthest point from my house in County Wicklow – had I already crossed it? But God knows I can't tell even my left from my right, which is no help at all when you are on the other side of the world, watching a fat moon rise over Auckland and wondering if your children see the same moon, or a new moon, and how can you be so stupid about the world and how it spins and tilts? How can you miss this essential *tendency*: living meanwhile in the silence that happens when everyone you love is fast asleep, an electronic silence when you lift the phone and put it down again, because you can not figure out the hours until they wake. You are mathematically lonely. You are, in your brute ignorance of time and tide, all at sea. You can not tell your North Star from your Southern Cross, despite which, they have let you go off to circumnavigate the globe.

I nipped back west to Australia for a while and then got on another plane east to Auckland and from there east again, crossing the international dateline on the way – and please don't try to explain the international dateline to me, whether I lost a day or gained a day – and why it was, for so many, many hours, still Saturday. I have no idea what has happened to my time in the past couple of weeks; am I younger now than I should be, or older?

Auckland to LA where I got off the plane, queued for an hour to be fingerprinted by the American Department of Homeland Security, and just had enough time to dash up to departures and back on to the same plane, same seat, to go to Heathrow. This time, although I might be wrong about this, we stayed in daylight. We seemed to do this by flying towards the North Pole, where light is plentiful at this time of year. The map said that we were skirting the night – there was the shadow of night, in a curve, just south of us – at least there it was on the map, I looked out the window to see where night began, but I could not tell where dusk edged into dark – I could not see the night that tried to approach as we flew away from it, up over Nova Scotia clipping Greenland, and falling with the curve of the earth towards home.

A long-haul flight is a very emotional space. I had a little cry at *Chariots of Fire* and the person in the next seat thought maybe someone had died, maybe that was why I was on this plane home. In fact, I was just avoiding the film *I Am Legend* which featured a vampire race in Manhattan: creatures who were afraid of the light, as I in my jet lag – you know it's easier if you travel west – flinch and blink when the sun shines in the middle of the night, even when I am home. In which state – full of alarms, little flickering lights in the corner of my eye – I sit and write this, and wait for my soul to catch up with me, so I can scoop it up and take it with me, west, at last, west to County Kerry.

SATISFACTION

Hugo Hamilton

In 1972, there were said to be thirty-five pubs in Listowel. That was the figure we were given, at least, when we got there. We tried counting them all. Tried to go into each one of them, but then lost count soon enough. And there was one we couldn't get into, where the door was always locked. We had to knock. Somebody came out, took one look at us and told us to go away each time.

We probably didn't have the right dress code. A small group of musicians and singers, all around nineteen or twenty years of age, gathered together along the way, from Dublin, Newbridge, Kilkenny. Bearded. Long hair. Deliberately shabby. One of us with an inspired Lazarus look, wearing a torn fur coat and a pair of canvas tennis shoes that were falling apart as he stood. Bits of us were being left behind everywhere we went.

We were just out of school, full of rebellion and an almighty thirst. The idea was to play a few tunes in each pub, make a collection, then move on. The money would finance our journey around the west. It would take us to Miltown Malbay and Lahinch and Lisdoonvarna. Then, on to a folk festival somewhere near Ballyvaughan.

We sang a song or two. Played a few requests, usually a slow air called 'The Cualann' which brought silence to any bar. We ended with a masterful version of 'Finnegan's Wake' and occasionally, on demand, did 'Satisfaction' or 'Stairway to Heaven' as an encore, but then we were already out the door, on to the next bar.

Funny, that word 'Satisfaction'. It had never been expressed with such feeling before, as if the concept itself had only just been discovered. Up to then, the pursuit of pleasure was seen as a vulgarity. The word had no relevance in our lives, employed mostly at school with the slap of authority.

'I can get no satisfaction out of him,' you heard Christian Brothers say. Your exam results were always unsatisfactory. Nobody was ever satisfied. Except for those who drank pints of stout or bought brands of ready-rub pipe tobacco. They had satisfaction guaranteed. Or did they?

Now, the word had real meaning. It was out, so to speak, like an untethered ram. A naked word, revealing everything. Examined and elongated in the mouth in order to extract everything out of life that had been denied up till then.

Sa-tis-fac-tion.

We trawled through the pubs of Listowel looking for it. And if there were thirty-five pubs in a town, then we didn't see why we could not have a pint in each one of them.

The pub we wanted to get into belonged to the well-known writer John B. Keane. And because we were turned away so often, we kept coming back. We drew up a plan. We narrowed it down to one person, the most respectable one among us, hoping that he would get past the door and then secretly let the rest of us inside.

This Trojan Horse principle had worked a million times before, at parties, in dance halls, late-night bar extensions, rock festivals, but, unfortunately, not in John B. Keane's pub. It was a literary fortress.

But then the man himself came to the door and I can remember the humour in his eyes as he told us to go away and choose any one of the other thirty-four pubs in Listowel apart from his.

'You'll get no satisfaction here,' he might as well have said.

At one point, he stood back, almost inviting us in, just to see how packed the place was. A heavy cloud of smoke and sweat and perfume blew towards us. You couldn't move in or out, he indicated. An entire bar full of men and women slow dancing with pints in their hands.

'There's all of Croke Park in there,' he said, as though he had fought his way to the door himself to get out of the place.

We agreed with him and moved on. It was no place for us. Lazarus – in his fur coat and tennis shoes – said he wouldn't be seen dead in there.

FILLING IN THE BLANKS

Joe Kearney

Outside, it was summer in the city. Lombard Street East was a long, darkened canyon that gave way to a view of exuberant sunshine tap-dancing upon the waters of the Liffey. However, on this particular morning, I was not there for the view; instead, I waited with a shuffle of others at the counter of the Registry of Births and Deaths. I needed a copy of my birth certificate in order to fulfil some bureaucratic obligation or other.

When my turn came, the lady behind the desk leaned towards me and sympathised sotto voce, 'Ahh!' she said 'No daddy.' She was referring to the blank space, as obvious as a gap-toothed smile, that beamed out from the copied certificate. 'No Daddy.' What could I do but just nod back to her? I mean, how could she have been expected to know about the man with the sticky-out ears, who liked *The Mikado* and smelled of greyhounds?

I was in my early teens when he arrived into my life. Looking back, he must have loved my mother greatly to take me on as part of the package. I was going through an early teenage awkwardness that involved sullen posturing and much angst. Nietzsche, Dylan and existentialism were, then, my passions. I played, very loudly, my 45s of Julie Driscoll, The Brian Auger Trinity and The Band. I played them until they were reduced to scratched, vinyl crackles and, all the while, the man with the sticky-out ears waited patiently to put on his selected highlights of the D'Oily Carte Opera Company.

When I wanted to talk postmodernist literature, he chatted me through the nuances of inter-club hurling; how the John Lockes might fare out against Muckalee. The Christmas I bought myself a copy of Jean Paul Sartre's *Nausea*, he gave me a present of *Eddie Keher's Hurling Life*.

But you can't suffer angst when you fish for smart trout in slow waters and it was there, on our infrequent trips to the bank of the Avonree, that we somehow drifted together. It was as if with rod and line, we became tangled up in each other.

A brief connection was forged between the awkward teen and the man who smelled of greyhounds.

But back at home, while he grew spuds and onions, I grew my hair and attitude. When I read Buddhist philosophy, he cycled into the Big Chapel to do the First Fridays. It was his passion for the annual coursing meetings in Clonmel that, eventually, brought us into open warfare. While I ranted and pontificated about the barbarism involved in the blood sport, he patiently explained the thrill of coursing and how the odds were always stacked against the greyhound ever killing the hare. And when we could no longer agree, he invariably switched the topic to something safe; whether or not he should switch from carrots to parsnips, so as to avoid the predation of the dreaded root fly or, if that failed, he'd revert back again to his favourite topic ... club hurling.

Our lives together became a kind of delicate choreography as we sidestepped, tiptoed and shadowboxed through the minefields of our cultural differences.

One autumn, when the swallows departed, I joined them. Throughout the years that followed, it began to dawn on me how much I missed him, and how greatly he had influenced me in his own quiet way. It was as if, through osmosis, he had eased himself into my heart.

He is a part of my life that can never be forgotten. Today, Eddie Keher sits comfortably with Nietzsche on my bookshelf. They lean towards one another as if offering support. Particularly on days like today, I recall those troubled years and wish that I could have them back, so as to make life easier for that very gentlest of gentlemen. But all I could do at the finish was hold his hand as the intravenous morphine pump did the easing of his final pain.

The lady in the Registry of Births and Deaths got it wrong. It takes more than blood or ink to fill in the blank spot on a birth certificate. And, for me, it took someone with sticky-out ears, who liked *The Mikado* and who smelled of greyhounds.

THE SCHOLAR

John F. Deane

I remember walking home from the monastery school in Bunnacurry, Achill Island, one afternoon. I must have been in third or fourth class, I suppose, for I had already developed a certain boldness and nonchalance as if I had learned everything there is to know about this earth of ours. My schoolbag with its second-hand readers, its book of tables, its catechism, also contained a great treasure, a tiny lead cannon on tiny wheels that would shoot real matches to a distance of almost two feet. I had swapped my new fountain pen for it and I was in a rush home to show it off.

John Gallagher, a near-neighbour, was in his shirt-sleeves, labouring on the road, shovelling stones into a hole, then back out of the hole and into another hole; at least that's what the gentle labours looked like to me. On his head, he wore a white handkerchief, its corners knotted so that it fitted his skull and saved him from the worst effects of a weak sunshine. I remember how the thick grey hairs of his chest peered from his open shirt like feathers, and how the muscles of his arms seemed to thrust out powerfully under the heavily stained rolled-up sleeves of his shirt. He stopped, fitted his big hands on the handle of the shovel, leaned on it and watched us as we passed, keeping our distance.

'Well, well, well,' he said, in a mocking tone of voice, 'here's the scholars, their heads a-burstin' with knowledge an' I bet not one a yez'll tell me what's the Irish word for tar.'

He was correct, of course. We scholars deciding we hadn't got that far yet in the book, but, of course, we declined to let ourselves down and passed along, preserving a dignified silence, our scholarly eyes diverted. I never will forget his loud chuckling that followed me like a swarm of wasps all the way home. Dear Mr Gallagher, slow-moving, heavy-soldered John James Gallagher.

I was back recently to see the old monastery school, now little more than naked walls, without roof or window or door, open to the skies, with weeds and grasses now for floor. The island winds have become the masters, moving through the empty spaces with complete authority; thistle-dust instead of chalk-dust blows in the air; the only lesson to be learned here now is the lesson of time, and its corollaries. I stood a long while, in wonder and admiration, with the weight of nostalgia pressing down on me. And in my mind I made a small roll-call of the scholars: morning time, we small boys settling, and I hear my name called out, hear my own answering call, *anseo*, present, here I am, but that call was yesterday's call and yesterday was half a century ago. That scholar, that child and innocent, is absent now, *as láthair*, flown. And then I whisper to the dead in their ordered rows: Seamus, Thady, Seán, *anseo*, I say, here I am, still willing, still learning, still studying the difficult art of living. Only the breezes answer, only the cries of curlews echoing from the distant shore.

I was reminded of all of those boys, those years, and of John James Gallagher and his call – 'Here's the scholars, their heads a-burstin' with knowledge' – when I stepped into the Burns Library at Boston College, bearing the burden of the title 'visiting scholar'. Here I am to stay for some five months and give a course to freshmen and sophomores, true scholars, in the writing of poetry. I have to teach for two hours every week, and the rest of the time is my own. Oh yes, can't you hear John James Gallagher, labouring man, his incredulous, his mocking chuckles. Isn't it strange how far a person may wander from the sources of his or her first lessons, and there before me, in the plush and daunting furnishings of the Irish Room in the Burns Library, I am actually calling names out in a genuine taking of the rolls, strange names, names that betoken the many immigrants from so many lands, Jessica Hincapie, Jay Lin Lang, Heather Bourke Polanczyuck, and all these bright and eager students gazing up at me as if I, scholar from the tiny monastery school of Bunnacurry, Achill Island, can dare to tell them how poetry occurs, how to catch the wonders of this creation in magical words and forms. And tonight I will give a public reading, in what appears to be an Aula Maxima, to an audience of professors, masters, doctors of philosophy and medal-winners, offering them poems on the crumbling of the monastery in Bunnacurry, on the harbour at Cloughmore, on the current at Bullsmouth. I shall stand before them, a-tremble, far from home, trying to hold my scholar's head on high. *Anseo*, I will whisper to myself, here I am, still learning, still ignorant of the Irish word for tar.

OFT IN THE STILLY NIGHT

Pat Boran

Growing up in a prison town like Portlaoise, we were always aware of the presence, the threat, of the largest building in the town. Though we were too young to grapple with the political situation that had given rise to it, as we headed off on summer evening escapades, the prison was always there somewhere behind us, the dark, perhaps even invisible matter at the centre of our galaxy.

The tug-of-war between motion and stillness, between always going somewhere and simply staying put, while part of any youngster's life was, for us, amplified, made concrete, as it were, by the castellated walls and look-out posts of a building that had been erected to restrain, to contain, to imprison.

In truth, I wonder now if all sorts of apparently unconnected things might not, after all, derive some of their importance for me, at least in part, from the existence of the prison.

There is, for example, the issue of my two favourite songs from my pre-teen years. The first was about the joys and almost gravitational pull of movement. The second about its opposite.

'The Happy Wanderer' by British bandsman Frank Weir had been a hit in the 1950s, ten years or so before I was born. No doubt the fact that it was almost bursting with optimism endeared it to a generation of parents and teachers for whom the gloom of the post-War years was still a recent memory. And had they, or we, known that the song derived from a German folk song, an unofficial anthem at one point for the

Hitler Youth, it would hardly have lessened its appeal. For in the early 1970s, nothing pleased us more than when our singing teacher Mary 'Nana' Claffey weekly lined us up, like so many scouts or soldiers — smaller boys to the front, long drinks of water like myself to the rear — and had us belt it out, staccato, for all we were worth while Nana tested her ancient piano in the middle of the room with a similarly thorough musical workout.

> I love to go a-wandering along the mountain track,
> And as I go, I love to sing, my knapsack on my back.

This was in the Old Woodwork Room in CBS Tower Hill, Portlaoise, a dusty, half-lit panelled space, more like the hold of a nineteenth-century transportation ship than the concert hall Nana seemed determined to transform it into. But even here, or especially here, that song uprooted us, lifted us, freed us from our individual selves and set us collectively in motion, the sprightly movement of Nana's hands on the ivories, or beating time in the air, a rhythm a deaf child might have followed.

But there was another song, too. At the other end of the scale. Thomas Moore's 'Oft in the Stilly Night'. One of those songs that adults used to sing, and always wanted children to sing, but which children were rightly suspicious of.

For one thing, it was too slow, certainly too slow for three bench-loads of country boys and country-town boys struggling for balance while at the same time trying their best to topple the bench-load of singers in front.

The second thing was that it was almost impossible to understand. Even if you somehow worked out what the individual words meant — 'oft' meaning 'often'; 'stilly' meaning 'still'; 'slumber' meaning 'sleep' — there was still that chain in the second line ('like the prison in the background') or 'fond memory bringing the light', which always made me think of the usher in the Coliseum Cinema, shining her torch beam into our faces ...

Yet every week, after throwing us the raw meat or the pure sugar that was 'The Happy Wanderer', Nana would move quickly on to 'Oft in the

Stilly Night' as if leading her classroom of happy wanderers into an enchanted, half-lit forest and abandoning them there.

And then, one day, my preference for the first song over the second changed. It was one of those bright, early-summer schoolday afternoons when you don't even bother to take off your uniform, just run into the house, drink a glass of milk with a biscuit, and hit the road again – off on some mysterious adventure or just off, out, away.

Whether that particular day's wanderings had taken me out on my bicycle to the Rock of Dunamaise, or just on a circuit of the town, I don't remember, but suddenly it was almost dark, everyone was heading home, and we wheeled our bikes up the slow incline of Main Street from the Bridge Street end, in the doorway of a pub on the corner a man was singing. And, passing him, I was shocked to recognise the song.

For here, again, were slumber's chain, the eyes that shone now dimmed and gone, the cheerful hearts now broken. But from the way he was singing – almost to himself, eyes shut, shoulder against the door jamb – it was clear he'd been singing it for many years.

Though it was early summer, here was a man singing of chains and darkness, of fallen leaves and wintry weather. Here was a man, like a cartoon character under a cloud, stood in a doorway, half crying into his beer, but somehow rescued by a melody that barely caused his lips to move or breast to swell.

Were prisoners ever released? Did they go home, come home, back to their lives? Did people recognise them? Did they still love them? I knew nothing of the answers then, and have learned little since. But in the last thirty years or so, I've heard Moore's song in a great many places: often in churches and concert halls, once at a funeral, maybe half a dozen times on the radio. But I often hear it in my head, coming home late at night, especially on all-too-rare overnight visits to Portlaoise. And every time I see again that man in the doorway, prisoner or prison warder, or very likely neither of the above, but either way his happy wandering done, the laughter and bar sounds distant now behind him, above him the open sweep of a star-flecked sky.

DÉANTA IN JAPAN

Micheline Egan

I met my father on an Italian train when I was eighteen. We connected with each other in a strange way. Inter-railing across Europe with one's father is unusual enough but unwrapping his whole personality away from home was simply wonderful. As his eighth daughter, I was invisible at the bottom of our family of nine. On the rolling stock of France, Austria and Italy, I had him all to myself. Sure, we got the 'Sugar Daddy' stares and the Italians, in particular, did hiss a bit. But for those four weeks, I felt the luxury of being an only child and we remained devoted to each other until we reached the goal of his journey – Vatican City.

Don't get me wrong, now. My father always lived at home. But somehow, through forty-three years of marriage, he managed a life of beautiful bachelorhood.

Dada hijacked my inter-rail trip. I wanted to roam and wander on my own. As my father, he was concerned that I would meet undesirables in isolated train stations, so he just came along. Soon into the journey, the tables were flipped and I ended up minding him, running back to train compartments for his left-behind hats and walking stick. The deal was he paid for the big things and I made the odd contribution from my puny wages as a provincial newspaper reporter.

In Rome, he walked me into the grand foyer of the Excelsior Hotel. We weren't stopping for lunch. I could use the loos and sit on the squashy couch in reception, people-watch and steal the peanuts from the beaten silver dish.

Dada taught me how to live an interesting life. At home in Castlebar, he loved his life as a country solicitor. He was passionate about astrology, psychics, numerology and St Anthony. He put an eight in every deal he did – even if it was in the other person's favour. He enjoyed Mrs Bucket of *Keeping Up Appearances* and always carried a bar of Cadbury's in his pockets.

After a hard day at the office, he would cross the yard into the kitchen and lean against the Aga. Dressed in Cavalry Twill trousers, a yellow shirt and thin tweed tie, he would tell his daily news. I'd often spot that his Church shoes were filthy. A giveaway that he had walked the land with a local farmer to inspect a boundary dispute. When I commented on the dirt, he would just pause, walk to the press, take down the Jacob's biscuit tin full of brushes and polishes and say, 'Light a candle …' I quickly learned my job was to take action and get polishing.

He loved people, their stories and the intricacies of their lives as they presented in his Oval Office. His two favourite expressions were 'Is that so?' and 'Really' in his soft Mayo accent. He also enjoyed mixing with the ascendancy and was Lord Lucan's land agent. Every year, the phone in our hallway rang when British reporters had heard of another sighting of 'Lucky Lucan'. They thought Michael Joe Egan knew of his whereabouts.

His deepest love after Mama and us and Castlebar and his faith was travel. And at eighty he got his wish. He died in his sleep on a trip to Toyko. Mama woke to find him dead beside her. He was listening to his shortwave wireless on his Walkman.

The Japanese embalmers made him up like a Geisha and sealed him hermetically in what looked like a tuna fish tin. Dada travelled out to Japan a wandering tourist. He came back with his very own airway bill as a piece of cargo. When we got him home, my sisters and I took out our compact makeup and lipstick to bring his face back to Ireland, removed the layers of Percale Cotton sheets that he was swaddled in and put colour back in his cheeks. As a last touch, I lined his coffin with the *RTÉ Guide* and some hand-made chocolates. Just in case he'd be caught between worlds and wanted to tune in from the other side. I wondered who'd be there to let him in. Would he bump into Nehru, Gandhi, de Valera or would he just keep in with his own people?

And in the end when I kissed him and lifted my head up from the plain deal coffin, I knew the trace of his lipstick on my lips was a mark of his love and of his faith in me.

My father had taught *me* how to fly.

THE BEARD

Conor O'Callaghan

The great joy of teaching, apart of course from the pleasure of impart-
ing pearls of wisdom to teenage minds, are the extended holidays. As a
result of those three free months, I have long surmised that summer is
a time for taking the scenic route around your regular life, for doing
things and being something that the nine-to-five of those other damp
nine months seldom allows. Two years ago, for example, I became a vegetarian on the first of June. I survived three weeks of nut roast, then my
wife cooked a stuffed chicken and those doubts I had been experiencing
about the whole vegetarian ethos called my bluff. Last year, I put our
TV in the bedroom wardrobe. Ours was to be a TV-free house for as
long as the sun shone. Unfortunately, the sun seldom did what it's
supposed to in summer. I knew I'd failed when, four days later, me and
the kids watched *Chitty Chitty Bang Bang* in its entirety while perched on
the edge of the spare bed.

This year, I decided not to impose my beliefs on the rest of the crew,
to go it alone. This year, I grew a beard. It's one of those things I've
always wondered about but never actually tried. It's true, there were a few
times in my late teens and early twenties when it may have seemed to
reasonable bystanders as if indeed a beard was my chosen facial appearance. Truth is, those whiskers were the results of unemployment, late
mornings and something that might be termed loosely as laziness. They
were never planned. Once, I cultivated sideburns that drifted perilously

close to my mouth. I thought they looked cool. Then my first cousin Suki, bless her soul, told me they looked stupid and ugly. They vanished soon after.

This year's whim was prompted by a student in my writing class. All semester, Rob's chin was coated in a generous tuft of brown. Last class but one he trundled in late and shaven.

'Rob,' I interrupted his implausible excuse, 'what happened to the beard?'

'I hated it,' Rob shrugged.

'If you hated it so much,' I asked, 'why didn't you just shave it off months ago?'

His response shook me to the core.

'I thought it was expected of me,' he said. 'Almost everyone else in the English department seems to have a beard.'

Rob was right. Soon after, I did a private tally of those male colleagues, permanent and temporary, who enjoy some bristle about their chops. The results were startling: out of twenty-three, seventeen have either beard or moustache or both. One of a minority of six, I resolved there and then to switch allegiance. I began correcting end-of-terms on three days' growth. I posted grades two weeks later, feeling and looking like a new man.

All the while, I wondered what made beards attractive to intellectu-als, and why so few sportsmen have them. At least glasses suggest erudition, reading. Is it that they provide a mask? Or is it that mere shaving distracts the life of the mind from higher things?

Academic life, it occurred to me, is not the only context in which beards are de rigueur. A couple of years ago, our all-conquering pub quiz team went along to a night hosted by the local branch of the Green Party. At times, it seemed there were more beards being scratched than pints being sipped. What, I wondered for days after, was the link between environmental politics and facial hair? The invisible thread that bound whiskers and gluten-free produce? I remain in the dark.

June turned hot and humid, and my face itched 24/7. Added to that was the bitter fact that, however much I trimmed, my own beard refused to adhere to the colour of the rest of my hair. It was an alarming shade of carrot, mottled with swathes of pure white. Some mornings, it looked as if a Siberian tiger had lodged itself indefinitely on my lower jaw. Still I clung on, if only because I knew without it, I could never be a true organic egghead. Then one Saturday half a jam croissant got side-tracked en route to my hungry mouth and my wife, between giggles, politely enquired, 'Still love the beard?'

It was her discreet way of telling her husband that the fuzz on his face looked, well, stupid and ugly. I boiled the kettle, lathered the brush, clipped on a fresh blade and began, at long last, to shave.

MY FIRST BASQUE VILLAGE

Paddy Woodworth

Itziar was the first Basque village I ever saw.

Its enormous church swung abruptly into view, set high on a hill above the road, as I was hitch-hiking from San Sebastián to Bilbao on my very first day in Basque country.

Those were stirring times. The old dictator, General Franco, lay dying in Madrid, still signing death warrants as if the execution of his enemies might somehow further postpone his own wretched and lingering departure. A great wave of democracy was waiting to break over Spain, but the heavily-armed police at checkpoints I had passed along the road were a reminder that change would not come easily.

The noisy and overheated political side of my brain suddenly went silent, however, when I was dropped off on the old main road, which ran between Itziar and the sea. I thought the great Gothic church above me was like a stone ship anchored to the steep green hillside. I thought that this was an original thought until I found, years later, that it was a commonplace in Basque writing.

That day, other images seduced me: a brace of oxen, their chunky wooden yoke blazing with woollen decorations in primary colours, and the wiry man in blue overalls and a black beret urging them on, almost pushing them up the slope; the tang of freshly-cut young bracken, the sweeter smell of mown grass; and, everywhere and yet nowhere in particular, the echoing of sheep bells. Itziar became my image of a Basque pastoral Eden.

Two years passed before I returned to the same spot. It was an exceptionally bright June day when I turned off the main road and took the long sweeping S-bends up to the village. The great white farmhouses with their sloping red roofs gleamed like another country, more north African than Basque. And it was Sunday lunchtime, so not a soul was stirring outside the family home. But it was far from silent in the shimmering heat.

From one of these centennial farmsteads, someone was playing Pink Floyd's drug-fuelled *Wish You Were Here* at full volume. Oddly, it did not seem inappropriate to the setting. Wandering off through the woods which dipped up and down towards the townland of Lastur, I saw a little bull, a very little bull. I thought the bull was funny when he started tossing his head aggressively, but I stopped laughing when he charged. I climbed a tree very fast. It gave me a glance of bored contempt and abruptly dashed off again.

Looking back, I wondered if the whole day had been a dream, some bizarre mixture of nostalgia for student psychedelia and a childhood fear of cattle. Itziar remained as remote and desirable as ever.

About ten years later, I began reading Joseba Zulaika's landmark book about ETA's social roots, *Basque Violence: Metaphor and Sacrament*. I was amazed and disturbed to find that Itziar, of all places, was the object of a masterpiece of anthropological fieldwork. The book also tells the story of the author's youth at a time of great crisis – which happened to be precisely the time I had first seen the village. It contained much stranger, more wonderful and more terrible things than I had imagined in my idle fantasies about Itziar.

Zulaika made vivid the nearby caves, with their masterpieces of Neolithic cave painting hinting at ancient Basque ancestors. His mother had seen the Basque goddess Mari flying like a ball of fire through the sky. The old ways were fading in Zulaika's youth, but, even as an adult, he could still interview someone who saw a witch sitting beside his tape-recorder, quite clearly in broad daylight.

The social world of Itziar in the 1970s was equally strange, and more tangibly dangerous. Zulaika's youthful companions had included an active service unit from the armed Basque separatist group ETA. This is a much more secretive group even than the IRA. Many people in Itziar admired ETA at this time for giving the dictatorship a bloody nose, yet they were deeply shocked to find that it was local teenagers who had made the headlines for several weeks by kidnapping a businessman. After sharing many sociable meals with him in an isolated farmhouse in the townland around Itziar, they had shot him in the head.

The village, Zulaika wrote, encompassed both a rich tradition of Basque oral poetry and distinctive rural sports including rock-lifting, and a disco where the callow sex-and-drugs lifestyle was much the same as in Mullingar or Madrid.

When I finally met Zulaika, I told him about my dream day in Itziar. He could explain it all. His brother Xalbador, who has sadly since died, was a big Pink Floyd fan, and always played their music very loud. And Lastur, it turned out, is famous for its puny but pugnacious bulls.

Today, another of Zulaika's brothers, Bixente, is struggling to bring Lastur back to life. Its tiny scattering of houses now forms an extended restaurant and hostel, which enclose two sides of an earth arena. Here, the little bulls again do battle with youths, in the Basque style, on Saturday afternoons. This is a kind of burlesque bull-fighting, in which the animals are taunted but rarely harmed physically. It's very popular with stag parties from nearby towns.

Bixente jealously guards the authenticity of the old rituals. He knows the intimate history behind every faded photograph in his restaurant: the bohemian-tragic life of the itinerant accordion players; the brilliant but alcoholic folk healer who lost his daughters to typhus; the rock-lifter whose record has never been broken. Leading poets come to 'sing' spontaneous verses in bersolari style at the communal meals Bixente organises; champion rock-lifters and lumber cutters perform at fiestas.

Itziar and its townlands today, and yesterday, are a far cry from the garden of Eden I had once imagined them to be, but somehow I feel at home there, and perhaps that makes it a kind of paradise.

LEARNING TO DIVE

Pat Boran

The boy who is learning to dive
has a lot on his mind:

how to place
his unfamiliar, disobeying feet
on the wet rungs of the ladder;

how to straighten himself and walk
the length of the glossy board
without looking down;

how to stand
and extend his arms straight out, straight ahead
as the other boys do, without wavering;

how to cancel the height,
the shake in his legs;
how, once again, to breathe.

But while he stands there, and the water stills,
on a board higher than his
from out of nowhere a kid half his size
and age comes charging out

like some cartoon character
to pedal pedal pedal in thin air

and then, to the cheers of all his friends,
drops right through, right down,
into the target of his own reflection;

upon which the terrified boy gives up,
gives in, surrenders himself
to gravity, stepping clear

to fall, in slow motion,

into the rapturous applause
of water, each glistening drop
a medal freshly struck for him,
to honour his bravery, his offering,
the triumph of his letting go.

PARADISE

Julia Kelly

They arrive early, as the elderly do, in a minibus fusty with talcum powder and TCP, stiff with their sticks, dickey hips, plastic bags of medicines and swimming togs in Delta Airlines bags or sausage-rolled under arms. Once they've paid the off-season rate of $3 for the day, they organise themselves pool-side, positioning Zimmer frames and oxygen tanks within safe reach of the water, wedging towels between the plastic slats of rickety loungers, which immediately flap themselves free.

They undress with the insouciance of old age – flat posteriors in the air, egg-bellied paunches hanging loose over elastic, armbands on, hair tucked into caps, togs pulled into place around soft-skinned thighs – and lower themselves into the water with trepidation, groaning, exhaling, faces as textured as elephant hide, disconcertingly uniform teeth. Their gashed knees and bandaged ankles a testament to limbs they can no longer trust.

At the foot of the snow-capped San Bernardino Mountains, above the San Andreas fault line, the mineral water destined for Desert Hot Springs percolates beneath the surface at 140 degrees but is tempered to bath-water warm. A hunkered-down motel that was fashionable in the 1950s, it's twenty miles on the wrong, dusty side of Palm Springs. Monkey-brown Buicks and Lincolns are parked in carports of a cement block that's home to vast palms, mocking birds, sandstone, spirals and swirls, pea green carpets, panel-effect beauty-board. There's a forest of wind farms on the horizon; tumbleweed blows through the high street.

If the Salton Sea is where people go to get lost, Desert Hot Springs is where the elderly idle their final days. The water in the mineral pools is not just the perfect temperature; it's soft, unchlorinated and textured with ripples from the wind. Once immersed, faded beauties, bit-part players, former good-time girls are eased from their arthritis, lumbago and all those other ailments of the aged. In the water, they are free and graceful; their limbs fluid in movement again.

'Hallo, cutie,' says a man with a baseball cap and a moustache that's flour white against a freckled Californian tan. He squeezes lemon into a hip-flask of tequila, takes a slug and sidles up to an octogenarian, on her back, arms outstretched on the tiles behind her, kicking her legs vigorously, like a child. He asks her if she's in showbiz. They chat, words lost in bubbles under water, others not heard or misunderstood. Another man joins them – he claims he can yodel, a chuckle becomes a choke and conversation comes back, as it always does, to where it began – the temperature of the water.

A damaged man-child in a hooded wetsuit and a spittle-flecked goatee screeches and flaps as he lopes from pool to pool, loose-hinged feet like paddles, his father or nurse behind him, in polo shirt and slacks, holding a towel in the air like a matador trying to tame. As the palm trees bend in the breeze, a Japanese man searches for his wife. He has the sort of face that looks as if he's permanently searching for something. His wife sits in the sauna watching him, without gesturing, through the one-way window. 'Are you sure you're not a film star?' says the baseball-capped man to the cutie. She smiles with flattery but doesn't reply. 'I was Alfalfa in *The Little Rascals*.'

The handyman is in the Sunshine Café, swinging on a naugahyde stool. He fingers the swizzle stick in his Jack Daniels as he chats up the waitress who's sexy in a tired way. He tells her about the darndest thing he saw in LA: a hobo who'd worked his way into the window display of a home-furnishing store on Third Street and sat there unchallenged for an afternoon, counting his change on a chaise-longue.

She lifts the hatch, a J-cloth in her fist, and wipes tables, half-listening. Through the window, the handyman watches an ancient woman, supine and floating towards the deep end of the Olympic-sized pool. Water wings keep her buoyant, her bathing cap of white roses sits high on her head; her waxen feet are flexed and afloat. She hums loudly and tunelessly as she goes, eyes shut against the sun.

No one needs to be anywhere else. The day meanders into dusk: filters at pool edges gurgle and suck, the rhythmic clink of a flag stay against a pole, clouds charge silently across a vast sky, a chambermaid billows a sheet over a balcony, a radio plays somewhere.

'This is about as darned close as we're going to get to Heaven on Earth, right here,' says the handyman aloud to himself.

BALLYBUNION

Colm Tóibín

My mother's Aunt Molly, Mrs Cullen, the postmistress of Ballyfad in
County Wexford, used to go with her husband every Sunday to
Courtown Harbour. When I was about nine or ten and stayed with
them for a summer, I used to play Pongo in one of the amusement
arcades with them as the afternoon faded. It was a version of Bingo
popular in Courtown at that time and it was my idea of fun.

Courtown was one of the glamorous seaside resorts, full of glitz, early
neon, amusements, ice-cream parlours, transistor radios and general sea-
front excitement. It was like Bray or Tramore or Bundoran or Salthill or
Ballybunnion. Specially created to replace sea air with glamour in a time
of dullness.

By the time I came to Listowel Writers' Week for the first time, I was
fascinated by these left-over places, which once must have seemed most
fashionable and now seemed retro, half-faded and oddly old-fashioned.
The first afternoon I had free, I drove from Listowel, a town full of
writers, to Ballybunnion to walk along the beach there and look then at
the hotels and the shop fronts and get a sense of a different Kerry, so
far from the strange and stark landscapes of the Dingle Peninsula.

It was at the back of a cove that I noticed a sign and a small building. The sign said 'Seaweed Baths'. When I went in, I found a sort of tea
room with tables and a counter with prices written up. This place served
tea and sandwiches and soft drinks, but it also, according to the price
list, offered seaweed baths. I asked the lady behind the counter if I could

inspect a bath and she, in a tone both utterly pleasant and very businesslike, told me that I could. When I looked, I saw that it was nothing out of the ordinary, just a line of small cubicles with baths in them and doors which locked. I had already had a shower that morning, I thought. I did not need a bath.

I was about to go when I asked the woman, 'But what about the seaweed?' She told me that a bucket of seaweed came with each bath and she advised me to try it. It did not cost much. She went down the corridor with a towel which she left for me and she turned on the water in the bath and put in the stopper. As the bath filled up with steaming water, she returned and flung an entire bucket of fresh seaweed into the bath. She nodded at me. 'I hope that does you good, now,' she said and left me there.

I locked the door and, in the steamy cubicle, I took off my clothes and got into the bath. At first, it was nothing. It was like having a bath with a whole lot of weeds. I pushed them towards the taps and thought I had been fooled, wondering what the writers back at Listowel would say if they saw me now. In a bath with no soap or shampoo, just a mass of smelly seaweed. I would leave as soon as I could, I thought, and tell no one.

Slowly, however, things began to change. The seaweed started to ooze a slippery oil and when I gathered the mass of dark yellow and green strands towards me, it oozed even more. Soon, I was not covered in water as much as in a mass of slime that smelled beautifully of the sea. If I lifted my hand from the water, the oily substance clung to it and began to slide down my arm. I turned off the taps and lay there in the slithery silence, running the balm that came from the seaweed all over myself. This was how prawns and lobsters and oysters felt to the tongue when they were fresh, and there was a delicious sense of wallowing in something elemental, closing your eyes, sinking down in the bath, up to your neck in the sea's thickening comfort, ready for anything, sure it was worth the money, more exciting even than Pongo in Courtown and exciting enough not to tell anyone about it when I got back to Writers' Week, keep it as a deep and smelly secret for when I would return the next year.

LISTOWEL CALLING LONDON

Joseph O'Connor

In the winter of 1989, I was living in southeast London, in the not entirely lovely suburb of Lewisham. It was a tough district that had escaped bombing in the Second World War, mainly (so it was said by some of the locals) because the Luftwaffe had looked down from their passing-by airplanes and assumed it had been bombed already.

For some years, I had been trying to write, but it was not going well. Writing was like trying to juggle with mud. I would send out short stories to the literary magazines. They would come back in an unstoppable stream.

I had entered a short-story competition in the *Irish Post* newspaper to win a trip to Listowel for its world-famous Writers' Week. I had not won the competition – nor had I deserved to – but to lose seemed typical enough for any young Irish person of the era. You felt you had emigrated from a country that had failed, and that the last one to leave should turn out the lights.

One evening, I came home to my cheerless bedsit to find there was a message on the answering machine. The voice was familiar, as it would have been to any Irish person. It was the voice of John B. Keane.

Would I come to Listowel for the festival, he was saying. 'What matter you didn't win. We'd love to have you anyway. I hope London is good to you. Kerry's full of O'Connors. You probably own Carrigafoyle.'

John B. Keane had rung my flat. John B. Keane had dialled my number. To me, it was the equivalent of winning the Booker Prize.

In all the great city of London that night, there was no happier soul than mine.

His *Letters of an Irish Parish Priest* and his *Letters of a Matchmaker* were books my grandparents loved. As a young teenager, I had read them, been amazed by their contents. In the parish priest book, the narrator tells a story about two lovers overheard on a Kerry beach. The man utters to his sweetheart, about to plunge into the waves, perhaps the most romantic line in the whole corpus of Irish literature. 'Your buttocks have me intoxicated.' There were clearly other Kerries than the one to be found in the pages of Peig Sayers' autobiography.

But there was loneliness in the books too; there was brokenness and loss. There were people who had taken wrong turnings. Everything about his work was based on one profound insight: that a small place, in a small country, could be the whole round world and all its adventures, if only you had the eyes to see.

For some reason I cannot remember, I didn't go to Listowel. But some years later, after my first book was published, I did go, and I met that genius of storymaking. To say he was kindly would be like saying it sometimes rains in Kerry. The weather in his eyes was always warm. Like many of the greatest writers, he was modest about his work. Not falsely — it was a modesty that came from self-assurance, I always felt — but he never seemed to want to discuss it. He would talk of other matters, with laughter and delight, and a kind of casual wisdom he didn't seem to know he had. He would remember the names of your children, despite never having met them. He would ask to see their photographs. He would tell you they were beautiful. And what were you writing? And would you not give up the smoking? 'Always remember, your family is everything.'

I was privileged to meet him a few times, always in the town of Listowel, a place I can never visit — and never will in my life — without thinking of his kindness and grace. But I never got the chance to say to him what I wanted. That I had seen the Bull McCabe in Lewisham High Street, shaking his stick at the traffic. That I had seen the ghost of Sive in New Cross Gate and the Hiker Lacey in Deptford. That his people walked Piccadilly and the Tottenham Court Road and Archway and Camden and Kentish Town High Street, in those distant days, those unhappier times, when to be Irish in London was to be suspect or a joke, and to be poor was no laughing matter.

Who wrote about them? Few but John B. Keane. Who told their stories? Who saw behind their tears? The quarrels over land, the secrets of families, the wants of young lovers, the memories of old men, the hurts done to these outsiders and the hurts they did themselves. That he had taken all of these and made of them stories that would speak to people all over the world.

A writer's life is punctuated with moments of remembered blessing. One of mine happened on a cold, wintry day, when life was not good and I felt very far from home. On an answering machine in London came the message like sunshine: 'It's John B. Won't you come to Listowel?'

JULY

THE OLD BALL GAME

Tim Carey

To understand America, you should really understand baseball. America is partly defined by its national game and it holds a central position in its cultural life. Pick up any American history textbook and baseball is sure to be listed in the index. It is a game of heroes who form part of the country's collective folklore. Names like Ty Cobb, Babe Ruth, Mickey Mantle, Joe DiMaggio, Yogi Berra, Robin Yount, Carl Yastrimski and Ted Williams are of the household variety. It is part of the glue that has bonded American society from the days of their Civil War, through the depression years, the heyday of the American dream and more recently as a means of providing familiar comforts post September 11.

An enduring baseball tradition linking generations is the '7th inning stretch' when everyone stands and, literally, stretches at a set point during each game. It is a ritual going back to the origins of the game started by no one knows who, for a reason no one knows why. This tradition is mixed with the singing of a gloriously naff 1908 song:

> Take me out to the ball game
> take me out to the crowd,
> buy me peanuts and cracker jack
> I don't care if we never come back
> And its root, root, root for the home team
> If they don't win it's a shame
> And its one-two-three strikes your out
> At the old ball game.

Sport and other forms of culture are not frequent or comfortable bedfellows. But baseball has permeated American culture in a singularly unique way.

Simon & Garfunkel lament the absence of the 1950s New York Yankee Joe DiMaggio in the song 'Mrs Robinson'. Philip Roth's *The Great American Novel* features Word Smith, an ex-sports writer trying to revive the story of a forgotten, homeless baseball team, the Rupert Mundys, during the Second World War. In Robert Coover's *The Universal Baseball Association Inc., J. Henry Waugh, Proprietor*, Waugh invents a whole baseball world whose outcomes are based on the roll of two dice, and he gradually submerges himself into that parallel world. Don Dellilo's *Underworld* begins with one of the most famous games in baseball history – the 1951 league title decider between cross-town rivals New York Giants and the Brooklyn Dodgers at the Polo Grounds. The baseball that was hit for the winning home run plays a central role in the novel.

Robert Malamud's 1952 novel *The Natural* was adapted to a film starring Robert Redford. The film *Eight Men Out* is about the Chicago White Sox, dubbed the 'Black Sox', who fixed the 1919 World series. It features the classic line, 'Say it ain't so, Joe, say it ain't so', spoken by a young boy whose innocence is shattered by 'Shoeless' Joe Jackson. Another baseball movie *Field of Dreams* also features 'Shoeless Joe' who asks a farmer to turn his farm into a baseball diamond so he can come back to play again after his ban from the game. In the same movie, another character comments on the importance of baseball, 'America has rolled by like an army of steamrollers. It's been erased like a blackboard, rebuilt, and erased again. But baseball has marked the time.' For me that has also been somewhat true.

I was born in Milwaukee, Wisconsin. Since coming to Ireland in 1979, my Americanness has been gradually, but irrevocably, receding. The threads of my once American clothes have all but disappeared. But baseball still remains.

The long, hot and humid summer days in the Midwest were filled with baseball. It seemed like my friends and I played baseball every single day. I knew practically every player from every team, collected baseball cards and dreamed baseball dreams. My local team was the Milwaukee Brewers who played a mile from my house. In the back garden, I played out the final scenes of tense games, the radio broadcast mingling with the muffled sound of the crowd rolling down Bluemound Avenue from County Stadium.

One of the players I saw as a boy was African-American Hank Aaron who surpassed Babe Ruth as the greatest home run hitter of all time. In the pantheon of baseball heroes, Aaron was right up there. I saw him hit his second last home run on a blisteringly hot summer day in 1976 to win a game for the Brewers. Over twenty-five years later, my wife and I named our son Aaron – we passed on Hank – in his honour. My Americanness is almost invisible to my children but, in that name, there remains a connection between my son, the place where I was born and some of my best childhood memories.

FINDING JESSE JAMES

Mick Ransford

A barely noticeable sign points me to the farm. Like many before me, though, I'm about to discover that finding the farm isn't the same as finding Jesse James.

The first building I come upon is a large cabin surrounded by a porch. The Stars and Stripes hangs limp from a pole. It's the 4th of July. The flag momentarily surprises me: it would be difficult to imagine a family more opposed to the Star-Spangled Banner than the Jameses. The soda machine on the porch should have been a clue: this cabin isn't original. It's a museum and gift shop. Nothing on this Clay County, Missouri holding is as it seems.

I watch a short film on the history of the James-Younger gang. I study portraits of Jesse and Frank, their friends and relatives, whose activities during the Border War were a savage prelude to that greater slaughter, the American Civil War. Especially compelling are those tools of the trade used to make the gang the most famous train-, stage- and bank-robbing outfit in the old West: a rifle, a revolver, a gleaming saddle.

I find Jesse's boots riveting. They look so small! Reddish-brown. Highly polished. An image flashes through my mind: the boots fix him to a plank floor. The telescopic barrel of a Navy Colt points at a cowering cashier. Jesse's eyes are of such a startling blue they glint like ice, even now, from photographs around the walls.

A guide leads a clutch of visitors across a sunny pasture, along a timbered creek that Jesse and Frank swam in as boys. And there it is — a whitewashed Eastlake cottage with a shingle roof. The house the most famous outlaws in the world were born and raised in! Only it isn't. This extension was added years after Frank and Jesse took to the outlaw trail. It's Frank the guide's talking about now. He points to a horseshoe embedded in a slab. After his favourite mare died, Frank insisted on showing visitors the burial site. As he aged, the old bandit was less inclined to shuffle out to the yard and had the slab moved ever closer to the door.

The original cabin is cramped. Dark inside despite white panelling. I stare at the fireplace, recall the tragic role it played the night Pinkerton agents lobbed a device through one of the low windows. Jesse's stepfather tossed the device into the fireplace where it exploded, killing Jesse's baby brother, shattering his mother, Zerelda's, right arm.

Most of the furniture is genuine. I imagine the old woman riding the rocking chair. Springs creaking rhythmically against the floorboards, cradling her dead boy, her amputated arm, fantasies of bloody vengeance.

There's a reconstructed slave cabin out back.

The unpalatable truth that Jesse and Frank first took up arms in defence of the Confederacy is inescapable. To them, the war was nothing · short of a crusade.

The tour ends with our little group gathered around Jesse's grave. Heaped with faded pebbles, ringed by an iron rail, it's situated in the bottom-left corner of the yard.

The headstone isn't authentic. The first one was chipped out of existence by souvenir-hunters, whose cavalier approach to the dead rivalled Jesse's approach to the living. Apparently, Zerelda sold the pebbles to visitors at five cents apiece, replenishing them from the nearby creek.

The biggest surprise has yet to come. Jesse isn't in the grave anymore. His remains were exhumed in 1902 and removed to the family plot in Kearny. When his body was exhumed again in 1995 to quell the usual rumours attached to famous people who die prematurely, it was found to be lying face down.

Theories abound: a promise secured from Frank that he be buried that way so the whole world could kiss his rear; the custom of burying criminals face down; careless, even vindictive undertakers.

I picture Zerelda, with that stump of an arm, still hearty in the early 1900s. Anyone dumb enough to treat her boy that way wouldn't be long after him to the Promised Land. I'm reminded of something Jesse reportedly said shortly before Bob Ford murdered him. 'I might have to go under eventually but I'll shake the country up once or twice before I do.' He's still at it, it seems.

JAMES BRENDAN CONNOLLY

Mairéad Ní Chonceanainn

Fifty years ago, in 1957, news of his death made the headlines from Boston across the United States. Not many here in Ireland knew about this remarkable man James Brendan Connolly who was outstanding in many fields as fisherman, sportsman, athlete, academic, soldier, journalist and novelist. He had excelled in all and as an athlete was world famous for his blaze of glory at the Olympic Games in 1896.

That year, 1896, marked the revival of the Olymic Games re-instituted after 1,500 years and James Brendan Connolly from Boston was the very first winner when he won the top medal for first place in the Triple Jump contest, which happened to be the first contest listed. In later jumping events, he was also the winner of second and third places.

Only that I lived on the Aran Islands, I would never have heard of this man but for my friend there, the retired doctor James O'Brien, a native islander himself and a book man and book collector. He related with pride to me the life story of this man born in Boston of Irish parents who came from Killeany on the Aran Islands. On the doctor's visits to Boston, he had met the Connolly family and obtained books by Connolly published in the United States. I went on to enjoy his books, *The Seiners, Out of Gloucester, Fisherman of the Banks* and *Head Winds*.

The Aran saga began early in 1868 when Connolly's young parents left Inis Mór for Boston, a grief-stricken couple after an outbreak of smallpox on the island had robbed them of their two small boys.

A further nine sons were born to them in south Boston, James Brendan being the first that year 1868.

Life with such a large family was not easy but their mother was eager to have them educated and established in good positions. Between his work at the desk and play on the sports field, James did very well but he had a love for the sea and was glad to join his uncle on periodic fishing trips out of Gloucester to the Grand Banks. It was as a result of this experience that his vivid writing on the subject became such a literary success. His fishing trips together with office jobs and articles for journals earned him some money while he continued to educate himself. Eventually, he gained acceptance to Harvard University. During his time there, he became aware of the revival of the Olympic Games. Already a champion in athletics and as a national winner of the Triple Jump, he joined the United States Athletics Team and with them headed to Athens. There, at the initial contest in a hop, skip and jump, he landed himself in the annals of history.

Back home in Boston, after all the celebrations, he set to work coaching athletes while he continued to write articles for newspapers and periodicals, but the brine in his veins and Gloucester were calling. Very soon, he was on a schooner again and bound for the Grand Banks. His sea-faring adventures continued with a cattle boat trip to Liverpool a steam trawler voyage from Grimsby bound for the North Sea and then as a sailor-cum-soldier he set out on a warship to Cuba to fight the Spaniards. His writing on this later journey earned him appointments as a war correspondent on battleships all over the world.

Until all this was over, Boston saw little of Connolly and his wife and young daughter had a lonely and anxious life awaiting his return. It was after that that he became a home-bird and set to writing his best-selling novels and short stories. Sadly, he had a lonely old age as his wife and daughter predeceased him. He lived to his eighty-ninth year and died in 1957.

The story continues on to more recent times, although my old friend the doctor was not around to know, as, by then, he had cleared his final high jump too. In 2004, a generous American benefactor in a commemorative gesture presented a collection of Connolly's books to the Aran Library on Inis Mór.

CROMWELL, CALLAN AND COCA-COLA

Gerry Moran

Strange as it may seem but Oliver Cromwell is partially responsible for the success of one of the world's most famous and popular soft drinks: Coca-Cola. We associate Oliver Cromwell with many things — not least cruelty and tyranny — but now we, well I certainly, can add at least one pleasant ingredient to the list: Coca-Cola.

This story begins not a stone's throw from where I live — in the small town of Callan in County Kilkenny, a town that has, for its size, produced more than its fair share of famous people, among them Edmund Ignatius Rice, the founder of the Christian Brothers; the architect James Hoban, who designed the White House in Washington, a design he based on our own Leinster House; and most recently, the renowned artist Tony O'Malley.

As for Callan and Cromwell and the Coca-Cola connection — it all began with an army officer by the name of William Candler who came to Ireland in 1649 with Oliver Cromwell. As a reward for his military successes, Willliam Candler received large tracts of land in counties Wexford, Offaly and Kilkenny, and finally settled in Offaly.

William's second son, Thomas, also an army officer, moved to Callan where he married, settled down and lived in Callan Castle. Thomas and his wife raised a family of six children and it was his fourth son, Daniel, who set the Coca-Cola connection in motion thanks, of course, to

Oliver Cromwell but also to 'that old devil called love'. Daniel fell madly in love with a local Catholic girl, which caused quite a scandal at the time due to their different religions and social standing. Much to his father's annoyance, Daniel refused to give her up and his father duly disowned him. He did, however, give Daniel enough money to emigrate to America where he and his wife, Hanna, who lived to a remarkable age of 105 years, became Quakers. We know this because one of Daniel's sons, William, became an officer in George Washington's army during the American War of Independence and made such an impression that he had a biography written about him.

It was this William Candler's grandson, Asa Candler, a pharmacist by profession, who went on to found the Coca-Cola Company in Atlanta, Georgia, in 1892. Coca-Cola was created by another pharmacist Dr John St Pemberton in 1885 as a tonic for minor ailments. It was Pemberton's book-keeper, however, a man called Frank Robinson, who suggested the name Coca-Cola and penned the now famous trademark in his unique script.

Doctor Pemberton died in 1888 and, over the next two years, Coca-Cola was gradually acquired by the ambitious and dynamic Asa Candler. Three years later, in 1891, he became the sole proprietor of Coca-Cola.

Asa Candler was a brilliant marketing man and, under his guidance, Coca-Cola became one of the world's most famous and most recognised brands. It also made Asa Candler a multimillionaire. In 1916, he retired as president of Coca-Cola and later became Mayor of Atlanta. In 1919, Asa Candler, the pharmacist who had come to Atlanta with $1.50 in his pocket, sold the business for a whopping $25,000,000 – a phenomenal fortune at the time. He died in 1921 and his son, Charles, succeeded him as chairman of the Coca-Cola Company.

Asa and Charles Candler never forgot their Irish roots. As a tribute to their Kilkenny ancestors, they both built mansions in Atlanta – one called Callan Castle and the other Callan Wolde.

Coca-Cola is still one of the most famous and most recognised brands in the world, all thanks to several generations of the Candler family, that old devil called love, the small town of Callan in County Kilkenny and, of course, one Oliver Cromwell.

EVERYTHING HAPPENS FOR A REASON

Deirdre Mulrooney

It was 7 July 2006 and I was heading to Cirque du Soleil's Montreal headquarters, to where they were relocating me to do a stint as an artistic talent scout. How exciting. I think that's what is known as the 'call to adventure'. Well, it's rude not to reply in the affirmative! Plus, I grew up in Canada more or less, until the age of twelve.

The practicalities. My pal Blanaid kindly offered to give me a lift to the airport. I had condensed my whole life into a three-piece set of funky turquoise 1970s pattern luggage — one massive, one large, one smallish.

I had managed to get rid of eight garbage bags of the past — mostly to Wa-Wa charity shop in Ranelagh. I figured, better just open myself to the future, make room for it, and let it in — no matter how left-of-field being spirited away by the circus might seem. More action, less deliberation was the philosophy of the day.

As we neared the airport, however, the radio announced that Dublin airport was being evacuated due to a bomb scare — marking the anniversary of the 2005 London bombings. Maybe this trip, which seemed so far-fetched from the outset, wasn't destined to be after all. Maybe this was it. Maybe I was going to be blown up. Was the universe trying to tell me something?

We found refuge in a pub off the Belfast motorway, where we joined other displaced passengers, drinking watery coffee, all eyes towards the television news. Waiting for the bomb squad.

News filtered through eventually that they arrived and carried out a controlled explosion on the suspicious bag that had us all in a state of chassis. It came out later that it contained some medication, and a copy of the Koran.

As you can imagine, the airport was thrown into absolute chaos by the backlog of flights. So much so that I got away without being charged for my excess baggage.

As we waited and waited for the delayed Air Canada flight, that feeling of solidarity that arises between total strangers in this type of confusion spread across the departure lounge.

The fellow passenger I struck up a conversation with shared in his flat, Dorset accent that he was en route from Siberia to Nunavut, the Canadian Arctic, via his family home in Allihies, County Cork. I was immediately intrigued.

'Wow,' I said. 'Really? My uncle lived in Nunavut, where he worked as a health inspector. Fred O'Brien.'

'Is he a veteran Olympic swimmer?' the stranger replied.

'Yes he is!'

'He worked with my wife, Geraldine, who is medical officer for the region. We actually had him over for dinner last year.'

Curiouser and curiouser!

I asked him a million questions about Nunavut, and the Inuit people, inspired by the fact that my parents taught on Indian reservations in Northern Ontario for ten years, and I had lived there from the age of seven to ten. He told me how his children grew up partly with the Inuit, absolutely loved it up there and never wanted to leave.

'What do you do?' I had to ask, eventually.

'I'm a sculptor.'

'Really – what's your name?'

'Danny Osborne.'

'Didn't you do that Oscar Wilde statue on Merrion Square? Wow! I love that statue and walk by it almost every day, as I live down the road from it.'

It was indeed his statue. I was totally amazed by this coincidence, and the affinties between my rather unusual life experiences in the Canadian north and those of this random stranger.

'You must come up and visit,' he offered later, in the waiting lounge at Shannon airport, 'it would bring you back to your childhood.'

'I would absolutely love to come up there,' I replied. 'I would love nothing more than to write an article about your work up there, but, unfortunately, I am just taking up this trendy job as talent scout with Cirque du Soleil, and can't.'

He told me his current work is inspired by Elizabethan explorer Martin Frobisher, and that he has been painting the Arctic landscape on and off for over thirty years. I asked him to spell out the name for me and, along with his email address, wrote it in my notepad. Frobisher.

Nunavut beckoned to me for many months to come during my stint with Cirque du Soleil. Until, finally, fourteen months later, I found myself on a boat in Frobisher Bay, with Danny Osborne and his Inuit elder friend Seeglook Akeeagok beside me; going clam-digging after the full moon; staying with Danny's wife Geraldine and their two teenage kids, Orla and Oisín, in their house overlooking Frobisher Bay; and gazing again in wonder at the aurora borealis of my childhood from Tom Hesse's boat *Go for Broke*.

Maybe it's true what they say, that everything happens for a reason.

A LARK IN A HOUSE OF OWLS

Orla Murphy

In a house of owls, my father, Séamus, was a lark. Dawn on summer mornings would see him in the kitchen, looking up above the white-washed wall of the back garden to the eyelet of sky beyond the sycamore tree. He could hear the 'Reveille' of the army bugler in the barracks that topped one of the hills out of which the terraces of Cork's northside are carved. He made the breakfast, squeezing oranges, stirring in boiling water and sugar, making toast. It took the ashen-faced intervention of an American visitor, a specialist on Michael Collins and, it seems, on unnecessary risk, to end Séamus' habit of wangling slices of Mother's Pride out of the toaster with the bread knife. While the eggs boiled, he brought marmalade, butter and cereal from the red-painted cupboard in the corner. There was no fridge: houses built into the cliff face had pantries where no sun ever entered, and tiled floors ensured permanent chill. The single window leaked grey light from the yard where meat kept fresh in the safe, a wood-and-mesh box on four tall legs beyond the reach of cats whose unsanctified surplus was donated to the Distillery in Blackpool. Donated, not sold, as Séamus, thinking of Myles na gCopaleen's cautionary tale about the woman who sold kittens, would not risk prosecution by the Vice Squad for living off the immoral earnings of a cat.

After breakfast, he left the house, manoeuvring his bicycle along the hall out across the terrace and, balanced on one pedal, free-wheeled down the hill onto Wellington Road, past the schools, across Patrick's

Hill and down the steep drop to the Watercourse Road where ten minutes' brisk cycling brought him to the big wooden gate that led to his studio.

At that point, Bebhínn, my sister, and I could hear already the sound of chisel on stone from the corrugated-iron shed where Séamus carved statues and inscriptions in daylight, in the open air. On the other side of the yard was the studio proper, where he worked in winter and where he made many portrait-heads in clay to be later cast in bronze, or carved in stone. There, in the veiled light that angled in from the north, it was the silence of that assembly of heads looking at us from various heights, that I remember. And the clean smell of plaster and clay. The Scullery was the name given to the studio by Séamus' friend, the poet Seán Ó Ríordáin. Visitors would spend hours looking, and listening to Séamus but we preferred to watch as he sharpened chisels, heating a coke fire in a barrel, dipping the reddened chisel into water then plunging it back into the fire.

The heat, the hissing of the water as it boiled at the touch of the chisel, the anvil's profile like a knight's helmet: all these were magic. And then the little chisel, in his hand, gliding through stone, leaving only white dust in its wake. Oh it looked so easy, the taming of one element by another, where the chink chink of the chisel sounded the refrain in a game of merry craft over solid mass.

Clay was easier: warm, smooth and malleable. He put an apple-sized lump on the wooden table in the studio and patiently watched as we tinkered. He offered us spatulas or scrapers, and encouragement. We could remember how it was done: we had seen it at home during those long summer evenings; it must have been summer as the attic where he shaped our skulls, or recreated us, was unheated. There was talk but there must also have been silence because we could hear the army band, this time practising marches in the barrack square. Séamus stood about four feet away with his back to the light, and held a lump of clay in his left hand, asking questions about school, or music, or anything he knew to be of interest, as he worked. It was a time of sensations: the intermittent sounds of the band, the flitting of swallows across the skylight, and the cool touch of the calipers ear to ear, forehead to chin, as he checked dimensions.

The surface was built up with tiny pieces of clay, which he rolled between finger and thumb and pressed on with the most elegant of all the tools, a wooden spatula, double-ended, slender and light, polished with age and use. He concentrated all of his effort on the head itself but took care over detail: a bow in Bebhínn's hair, a Cork brooch below the collar for me, saying that the Cork brooch was like the Tara brooch but that the pin was placed vertically.

At last, when the light started to wane, the clay head was wrapped in wet towels. He washed his hands and went down four flights of stairs to the living room to work on a drawing or, at last, to read.

History, biography and poetry filled the shelves of the bookcases. The radiogram played concerts by the symphony orchestra. The sky dimmed beyond the uncurtained windows and seagulls flew down river to their night roosts. As our parents read their books, they could hear far below in the tunnel of sandstone and limestone, the late train, making its way through north Cork to Dublin and to the world beyond.

THE CLOSED SHOP

Mary Morrissy

It was in 1982 that I saw the stage version of Séamus Murphy's memoir, *Stone Mad*, at the Peacock Theatre. Fergus Linehan's adaptation featuring a solo performance by the the late great Eamonn Kelly led me directly to the delights of the book. Set in the Cork stoneyard where Murphy served his apprenticeship in the 1920s, *Stone Mad* is an intimate portrait of the stonies – as the cutters and carvers were known – who trained him in his craft. It eavesdrops with a delicious wickedness on their glorious shop talk and their secret masonic vocabulary. Mallets and skew chisels, crockets and carved bosses, columns and caps, volutes and acanthus leaves. Not to mention the well-travelled stone itself with its sonorous far-flung names – Vermont Granite, Indiana Limestone, Purbeck Marble.

I was working in the *Irish Press* at the time. I little thought reading his lament for the passing of the stone trade that the ancient craft of printing was similarly under threat. It would have been inconceivable then to imagine that the iron-jawed – and seemingly invincible – Linotype machines on Burgh Quay churning out galleys of print, or the metal bogeys on which the finished forms were pushed from stone to printing press, would soon be supplanted by computer keyboards and email connections.

As journalists, we might have fancied ourselves as having masterminded the newspaper and designed the pages to the last detail but it was the printers who magicked them into being. They were like conjurers, slivers of metal like quicksilver in their hands. Theirs might have been considered a heavy industry, but the printers and compositors I knew were champions of grace and invention. And like the stonies, they, too, had their own secret language of delight.

When Séamus Murphy wrote *Stone Mad* in 1950, the closed shop that was the stone trade was in steep decline. Sand-blasting machines had replaced the highly intricate inscription work previously done by hand. 'I do not know how far I have succeeded in giving an idea of how the men engaged in the stone trade worked and lived,' he wrote modestly in the introduction to the book. 'It was not easy for me, I have not the slickness of the craft of writing.' Murphy was being too modest.

He applied the same skills he used as a carver specialising in foliage – a keen appreciation for the smallest detail of nature – the whorl of a tulip, the globe of a cherry – and applied it to human nature. The overlooked curlicues in buildings – often poised several storeys high so that the pedestrian at ground-level missed them – were Séamus Murphy's delight. He recalls a visit to Dublin, immortalised in *Stone Mad*, in which the Granite Fusilier – one of a host of colourful characters with equally vivid nicknames – unveils the hidden gems in the architecture. The carved heads on the Francis Street market building, each depicting a different nationality, the fish, crab and anchor standing in for the Atlantic Ocean over the Ballast Office, the heads carved in Portland stone on the Custom House representing the rivers of Ireland. All of which are still visible today if we care to look up.

But it is the human drolleries and foibles of the men he worked with – Blueskull, the Gargoyle, the Goban, Blackjack, Stun and the Dirty Boy – that endure, revealing Murphy to have been as skilful and precise with the pen as the chisel. *Stone Mad* must be the least ego-driven memoir ever written; the author is like one of those stone caryatids he so admired, a benign presence perched discreetly on a ledge, casting a kind eye on proceedings. Signs on when a new staged version of the book went up at the Everyman Palace Theatre in Cork this year, adapted by playwright Johnny Hanrahan, it was recast as an ensemble piece, where the stonies take centre stage and the figure of Séamus Murphy almost disappears into the dusty set among the blocks of marble and the half-hewn pieces of stone.

Much of Séamus Murphy's public work may, similarly, go unremarked now. It is the fate of public sculpture – it retreats into the background and becomes part of the street furniture. You may think you wouldn't recognise a work of Murphy's. But next time you're strolling through Stephen's Green, you'll pass a bronze bust of Countess Markiewicz near the central fountain which is his. Or when you're on your way through Cork's Bishop Lucey Park at lunchtime, you might notice the gnarled and knotty figure of the Onion Seller. That's his, too.

His work as a stone carver, of course, is everywhere, slyly – and anonymously – inserted into convent chapels and church niches from Kilrush to Tralee, and inscribed on gravestones in cemeteries all over the country. It is that sense of the effaced craftsman that makes *Stone Mad* the literary equivalent of Séamus Murphy's finest work in stone, a door lovingly inched open on the now permanently closed shop.

ANOTHER COUNTRY

Grace Wynne-Jones

I can still vividly remember the delight I felt as that tiny bottle of perfume nestled in my palm. Lily of the Valley it was. My mother had just given it to me for my birthday. The smell was pungent, sweet and clear and feminine. I dabbed it on carefully, not wanting to waste one precious drop.

It was July and I was in my mid-teens. I was home but soon I would be leaving for Switzerland to be an au pair for a month. Au pair ... the words sounded adult and exotic. It was as if I could already taste the scent of it. Savour the French words that would soon be landing, like caresses, on my tongue. Whereas once I had dreaded leaving the precious, rural sanctuary of home, something new was stirring within me. Life had a bouncy seductive feel to it. It suddenly made some kind of sense.

I had been a reluctant teenager. Leaving childhood had meant going to boarding school at twelve and how I missed the lush meadows and tall, sheltering trees of my country home. How I missed my pony, who had left the fold too because I was no longer there to look after him. I missed the fields, the river. I missed myself ... the liberated young girl I had been. Of course I still returned home sometimes, but it wasn't the same.

Glimpses of what it might be like to be a real teenager — one who relished the idea of boys and make-up and giggly chats on the phone — sometimes reached me, but they seemed lacklustre now and somehow connected with studying for exams and dormitories and imperious bells and the absence of truly comfortable chairs. I was kissed occasionally ... the school was co-ed and my classmates were an unusually pleasant bunch of playful cohorts. But these experiences slid off me. I felt as though I had somehow wandered into a small and spartan poky room and dared not remember the rest of the huge, sunbeamed house because I did not know how to return to it. I did not even want to remember the ideas I had once nourished about growing into a woman. The experimentations with make-up, the delicious crushes, my enormous excitement at the prospect of having breasts.

But then fifth year arrived and it had a different feel to it. I was a prefect. I was allowed outside the school grounds on afternoons after classes. I was partially back on civvie street and boys had become more interesting and their kisses more satisfying. Growing up began to offer larger vistas. The door of that poky room opened, oh so gradually.

Lily of the Valley became the scent of that summer, and it seemed its sweetness had found me weeks before I received that small and unexpected bottle. Its tendrils even reached me at a classical concert I had gone to dutifully in my school uniform. I'd attended many similar concerts simply as an excuse to get outside the school gates. Even the ardent music-making of the performers had depressed me. It seemed a lot of fuss about nothing and I felt many of us were involved in some kind of wearisome cultural deceit in which we *pretended* to enjoy classical music because we felt we should. Even the musicians seemed contained in a world of duty and appearances and strictures. I wanted the wildness of Woodstock. I wanted songs of freedom. I wanted the music to speak to my heart. And then, suddenly, it did.

The violinist was a young Korean woman. I gazed at her intent serene expression and glimpsed a sort of love. She loved the notes she was sending flying around the room towards us. They were sweet and free and knew my joys and sorrows and I allowed myself to feel their beckoning. Their soft, improbable shelter. Their possibilities.

It was a good summer. The weeks I spent in Switzerland were nourishing and full of sunshine. I became chestnut brown and acquired a boyfriend called Serge who begged me to sleep with him. He made it sound as though he might explode with passion if I didn't. Somehow I knew not to believe him. However, our discussions about this and other diverse romantic topics probably helped me gain an honour in French in the Leaving. The family I stayed with were delightful, though I discovered their marriage was ending. I heard the details from Madame ... her lover regularly visited when we were by Lake Geneva on our almost daily bikini-clad picnics. I felt sorry for her husband but I am immensely grateful that I did not feel the intense compassion I would have felt now for his circumstances. He was an adult and that was another country. And I was a girl … I knew I was a teenage girl and that was a country in itself. It had taken me so long to find it.

It's complicated being a girl. I knew it before that summer and after it. And I know it now as I recall that country that is still somewhere inside me. My past with its music and scents and meanings. And that small sweet flower, the Lily of the Valley, who first whispered her secrets to me on a summer's day many years ago.

RELIGIOUS PERSUASION

Tommy Sands

There were no Protestants at Mayobridge School, except Harry McGarry. He was different. He didn't come into the catechism class when the rest of us were learning about who made the world and who God is. Instead, Harry kicked a ball about the schoolyard on his own. While we were becoming good Christians, he was becoming a good footballer.

But he told me that he also believed in God, and that he even believed that it was God who made the world. I said I liked football too and we became good friends.

I noticed that he never touched the ball with his hands when he played.

'We're not allowed to,' he said.

'Is it a sin?' I asked.

'I suppose so,' he said.

What a strict religion, I thought.

Later that evening, my father explained that it wasn't really football he was playing, it was a game called soccer and it came from England. Our football game was called Gaelic and it was Irish.

'Is it a sin for a Catholic to play soccer?' I asked.

'If you play for a Gaelic team, then you're not allowed to play for a soccer team,' he said. 'That's rule 27 in the official GAA guide.'

'Would you go to hell if you did?' I asked.

'Not necessarily,' he smiled, 'but you might be told to.'

He explained that, all down the years, England wanted Ireland to become English, but, by playing their own games and singing their own songs, the people here were saying, 'We're Irish.' England didn't want Protestant people here playing Irish games either, in case they would become Irish, for then Ireland would not become English after all.

It all sounded very complicated to me, but I passed it on to Harry as best I could. And we played a mixture of Gaelic and soccer in the schoolyard.

The next day, Harry told me that his da had told him to tell me to tell my da that even if good Protestant policemen wanted to play Gaelic, which they didn't anyway, the narrow Gaelic rules would not allow it, and to 'put that in his pipe and smoke it'.

That night, my father told me to tell Harry to tell his da that the rule only came about because the police force had made an earlier rule banning their own policemen from playing Gaelic games, and to put that in *his* pipe and do what he liked with it.

I don't think either of them even smoked pipes, but I knew they liked whiskey and I wondered why they didn't tell each other all those complicated things while they were drinking together in Hale's pub in Newry on a Saturday night.

Still, some of the messages rubbed off on the messengers and we learned a lot, Harry and me, in that playground of knowledge at the Bridge of Mayo. Sometimes, Harry and I wondered why Catholics and Protestants didn't go to the same school in the first place.

'Tell young Sands to tell his da that Catholics won't go to state schools because the Church of Rome wants to keep control over them, and, while he's at it, would he ask him if he could lend me the loan of the stirrup pump for a few days' whitewashing.'

'Tell young McGarry to tell Big Davy that for years England made it illegal for Catholics to receive any education at all and was it any wonder Catholics built their own schools, and what the hell stirrup pump is he talking about?'

'Tell that wee skitter's get to tell his oul' Fenian da that the Penal days were years ago and there are now lovely schools for everybody to learn in, and there would be one in Mayobridge too, but the Catholics wouldn't go to it, and the stirrup pump is the one he said was great for whitewashing with last Saturday night in Hale's pub.'

'Tell that black-mouthed son of a Presbyterian Orangeman that they can stick their state schools for those schools tell only an English view of Irish history and that I can't lend him the stirrup pump because I lent it to him last summer and he never gave it back, but if I had it, he would get it, for he's a decent man, and if he isn't doing anything next Monday, would he give me a day at the threshing.'

And so it went on until the seemingly insoluble conflicts would be shelved for the time being, for friendships were just as deep as differences and life went on from sowing to mowing and from mowing to threshing.

THE GARDENER

Denis Sampson

I am lying in the pram inside the breakfast-room window, waking up from my afternoon nap. My mother must have positioned the pram here so that she could keep an eye on me from outside, where she is working in her flower garden. Suddenly, I am aware of her on the other side of the window looking in, waving to me and speaking. Something about her suggests urgency, anxiety, and it may be that I have drawn her attention by an effort to get out of the pram, or by rocking it, or perhaps I have cried out. We are separated by the glass of the high window, and it seems as if that prevents me from hearing her.

I know now it is possible to be heard through that window but, in my memory of the scene, I believe she is calling to me and that her voice is lost. I expect she was urging me to stay still while she made her way up the path that ran alongside the house and around and in by the front door. I can remember no more than the expression on my mother's face, and maybe not even that, for the larger, compound memory that really remains is of my mother in her garden every day after she washed up the dinner things and the men went back to work in the fields.

This first image of our separate worlds is of a time so early in my life that I doubt sometimes I do truly remember it. Perhaps it is one of those events remembered by her and recalled to me so that I came to believe it is my own pure memory. Yet, that is unlikely for there is nothing for her to recall, unless I actually leaped from the pram. This was simply a fleeting image of mine, some tremor that touched a nerve inside me, perhaps her tension transplanted into me.

My mother's lost voice is less like a memory than an image from a mysterious or troubling dream, more like a prophecy of my own separation or silencing. Or perhaps the tension transplanted into me is the imprint of her sense of separation and silence, the record of her own exiled life in this surrogate home she had married into, and her desperate attachment to me.

It would take years for me to recognise such inner wells of feeling and begin to examine the tensions that drove her and were transplanted into my own life. The person I thought I knew was always active, a farmer's daughter from ten miles away, a farmer's wife, and she prided herself on her ability to get things done. She moved quickly and decisively, whether it was making her daily loaves of brown bread and white, and once a week – to use the oven while it was hot – fruitcake, queen cakes or spotted dog; washing the clothes on Monday morning, and hanging them out to dry on the line or stretched on the box hedges near the orchard gate, and then watching for signs of rain, and multiple trips in and out to test them, until she could get them dry enough for ironing; and then there were the animals – feeding hens and calves, washing the utensils in the dairy after the milking was done, morning and evening. The jobs were endless each day, each week, each year. 'No rest for the wicked,' she would say, repeating her mother's expression, although I don't think she believed she was in any way wicked. She was a silent worker who took no time to indulge in any sense of estrangement she might feel from where she was.

I came to know her garden well through all the summer days of my childhood: the fuchsia against the wall of the shed at the end, the overwhelming smell of lavender when I brushed against the big plants that overhung the narrow path, the multicoloured dahlias, the sweet william, the phlox, the carnations, the border plants, all mixed up to my mind but pleasing as I walked down the whole length of the garden, for it was a surprise to come upon another dahlia or sweet william but of a different colour than the last one.

My mother seemed to have a plan for the garden, even though it wasn't obvious to me. And she always seemed to have work to do in it, spring, summer and autumn, moving a plant here or there, tidying up those that were dying off, watering, staking the tall ones, pruning and clipping: she never stopped. I knew that is how she wanted it to be, so that the time, her own time, was filled with love until she had to prepare the afternoon tea and the men had to be attended to once more.

Soon, I recognised that her garden was different, essentially different from everything else in her life, the fierce energy and purpose that animated her around the house and in the farmyard, different from the tension that went into the care of her pride and joy. In her garden, she was a supreme artist. There she was far away from the place of her every-day limitations. And now I know that I, too, was her pride and joy, and that, in some way, the creating of her garden and the dream she had for my life are connected.

I am far away from that farm now, and she too left that garden behind. At the age of sixty, she moved to a new house and, for thirty years, she has created an even more magnificent one than the garden of my childhood.

I am lying in the pram inside the breakfast-room window. Early memories come to me, each one finding its silent place in my garden of words.

WELLINGTONS!

Kate E. Foley

What eloquent words would the Duke have uttered as Dame Shirley stepped out, dressed to kill, in her magnificent pink creation complemented by diamante-encrusted footwear costing an estimated £3,000. This was the 'Battle of Glastonbury', summer 2007, where the enemy was thick squelching mud and the most effective armour was the humble wellie. There is little doubt that Arthur Wellesley, First Duke of Wellington, would have been charmed by the spectacle of her grand entrance but perhaps more in awe at what had become of the boot with which he has been synonymous for almost two centuries.

In 1817, with the glory of the Battle of Waterloo firmly under his belt, the duke took a little time out for retail therapy, so to speak, in order to sort out the footwear dilemma posed by a new trend in men's fashion, that from knee breeches to trousers. The popular German Hession boot, which was very much in vogue then, was now considered unsuitable because of its curved, turned-down top and heavy metallic braid and so he instructed his shoemaker, Hoby, to modify it. Having pondered over the long and the short of it, the modified version was made of calfskin with the trim removed and a shorter leg making it more comfortable for both battle and social events and dubbed the 'Wellington'. From calfskin to rubber, wellie to gumboot, the trenches to the catwalk, leisure to industry, the wellington has stood the test of time and is now accepted universally as the most essential piece of protective footwear.

My love–hate relationship with this ever-enduring boot goes back to a time when there wasn't a child in the countryside who didn't own a pair. Indeed, we were truly grateful for their invention when it came to crossing streams, running through the newly-ploughed fields, and coming home rosy-cheeked after endless hours of joy, sleighing on the backhills. But there were those occasions when rain-soaked mornings brightened into warm sunshine and the homeward school trudge in hot rubber was not a pleasure.

Little did we siblings know then, that as we would hurl our black wellies along the soft grassy lanes to feel the cool beneath our feet, we were, in fact, indulging in what was once regarded as the eccentric British pastime of 'wellie wanging' or 'wellie throwing'. Now, it has become a lighthearted sport both here and in many parts of the world, from Finland to New Zealand, with Taihape on the North Island proclaiming itself 'Gumboot Capital of the World'.

Who could have believed that the wellington boot would transcend the world of politics, too, with the role it played during the painful and oppressive Apartheid era. When mining chiefs figured it was cheaper to supply wellingtons or gumboots rather than drain the mines, little did they realise that those same boots would become the inspiration for high-spirited 'wellie dance' and 'gumboot' music so much a part now of the rich culture of South Africa and popularised by Paul Simon's *Graceland*, Ladysmith Black Mambazo and the highly charged musical *Gumboots*.

Meanwhile, Scotland's favourite son, Billy Connolly, was experiencing something of an epiphany when he sat down and penned his seemingly profound but humourous hit 'The Welly Song' in which he extolled the virtues of owning a pair, or rather the dire consequences that would befall us if we didn't. I chose to ignore him. I also chose to ignore the ever-smiling, winking weatherman and still hadn't succumbed to buying a pair for Barbra's concert last July in the firm belief that, it being the eve of St Swithin, surely the gods wouldn't 'rain on her parade … ' Foolish, of course.

But it was neither Billy nor Barbra nor the promise of any other prancing performer in a windswept sea of umbrellas that prompted me to part with my few euros on a recent wet and windy day. As I stood wide-eyed in front of the kaleidoscope of colours, I could feel that gentle tug on my sleeve from my inner child urging me to sink my feet into a pair of blue, green and red spotty ones. The memory of the strong, once offensive smell of the black rubber was long forgotten as I admired my bright, cheerful insulated footwear, and imagined the splash of colour I would add to the russet and amber woodland carpet in the coming months.

Not only that but, as my toes revel in their new-found freedom, I convince myself that all those unseasonable raindrops are not the signs of impending doom but, rather, the result of a little mischievous heavenly collusion between a pious first-century bishop and a famous Dublin-born duke, to ensure that their names remain firmly on our lips as they 'reign supreme' over our summers to come!

WATER

Mary O'Malley

'You never know the worth of water till your well runs dry,' said Thomas Fuller in 1732. Water, cool, crystal pure, muddy or hot. In it, out of it, dying for it or drowning, it bears us up, drags us down, slakes our thirst, washes away our sins. The baby splashes in it, the fish frolic, the great blue whale moves his leviathan shape almost gracefully through it, the shark slices it with killer elegance and the dolphin's unsettling smile suggests something sinister as it shears off westwards, back into the deep from which it came. We are baptized with it and confirmed by it. Some of us shrivel if we spend too long away from it.

Fresh, salt, sweet or bitter, it is earth's loveliest element, and so powerful in its agitation it can rip a city apart in five minutes. From the great flood of the Mississippi in 1927 to the New Orleans floods, there is usually a human element in its great destructions. As a fisherman's daughter, I was raised with the folk memory of the Cleggan disaster, knew that the sea could take as quick as it gave, and give as lavishly as it took. I loved it, needed it, but we were raised to respect it. The well in each village was bailed and limed and treated with a filter of granite and small stones every year. Good drinking water was prized. Even an idiot wouldn't foul the water. Some places have none, some have an embarrassment of it.

Take Galway. It's everywhere in county and city, in little lakes, in rivers, in Lough Corrib, where the oldest stone decorated with a Christian symbol sits beside the monastic remains on Inchagoill, the lake's holy island, where during the pilgrimage mass 'the blackbird is brighter than God's own shadow in the cup now, Patrick ... ', though not Patrick himself but his nephew visited the island. Galway has more than its fair share of water. Added to this, it is built on a swamp by the sea. Its bay is famous, at least in America. It is a merchant city, with a history of commerce going back to its establishment as a safe port for the ships and tax gatherers of a new, foreign administration. The native Irish were banned from its streets by the famous bylaw: 'Ne O ne Mac shall strut ne swagger thro the streets of Galway.' In the minutes of the Corporation, housed in the archives of the University Library, there is evidence, as early as the 1600s, of a sort of primitive Section Four, where one merchant is given a dispensation to build his dwelling a little higher than his fellow corporation members. So you could say there is precedence for the kind of bizarre planning nightmare that has gone unchecked in the town and its surrounds in recent years. Except that, even in the seventeenth century, there were severe penalties for poisoning the drinking water. Turn on the tap today in the most marine city in Ireland, pour a glass and you drink the clear liquid at your peril. It is infested by an organism called cryptosporidium.

Outside the library, the campus retains some of its beauty. The river flows through it. The boats, which used to be available free to us in my student days, have been withdrawn for purposes of 'insurance'. Students no longer row up the river in droves, couples hiding and losing themselves for hours before finding their way back and tying up under the indulgent eye of the groundsman in charge. The old boat club – where we first heard the Boomtown Rats; I decided to forgo hearing some band called Clannad at a venue in the unimaginably distant reaches of Renmore to listen to someone called Bob Geldof – is still there. The river, although visible and open to all, is less used, though you can still see the Jes and the Bish rowing clubs practising in vessels slim as blades, and, under the lower bridges, the canoes shoot out of the overhang like corks from a bottle of champagne. Under the lower bridges, also, the swans are carefully watched, their signets counted. This year, there are eight, two years ago, there were eleven. It is perilously lovely, this water, like Rimbaud's drunken boat, easy to cross and deadly trying to get back from the wrong side, like the Styx.

CLIMBING CROAGH PATRICK

Iggy McGovern

We have things to talk about
man to man, that's why
I'm scrabbling up this stony slope
under a doubtful sky.

Weaned within sound of the bell
of the Protestant church, St Patrick's!
I grew up believing you were
naturally, one, as well:
I had you banishing the snakes
with the same bleak certainty
that pitched the monks in the river
and planted the best of the County.

A rest at the First Station.
For seven-fold penance recall
my seven years' re-education
that you were Catholic, after all.

We'd a great day out on Slemish
for *our* Patrician Ceremonies,
fifteen hapless centuries
of your Mission to The Irish.

Of which I remember only
the Union Jacks all along the route
(reminders that they held you yet)
and sweet, scalding tea.

Hugging the chapel-gable
coveting the tourists'
sandwiches and flasks:
A rain-swept Tower of Babel

Fast-fainting, I now summon
from the vaults of the Old School,
swaddled in cotton-wool,
your One, True Jawbone
that, once, under cover of cleaning,
I closely questioned, slapping
your toothless, brown half-grin:
Whose side were ye really on?

It was all a waste of time.
We saints are trained to say nothing:
Except that on a better day
you must have a great view of Clew Bay.

AUGUST

CULTURAL EXCHANGE

Dympna Murray Fennell

Dublin airport, mid-summer in the mid-1990s, two middle-aged couples meet for the first – and last – time. Over the next few weeks, we get the most intimate view of each others homes and life-styles.

They seemed an ordinary pair from a small town in Alsace, a French version of ourselves. When we arrived at their pleasant little home their adult son was there to show us around; nothing very unusual – the salon, the cuisine, and finally the master bedroom. Nothing ordinary here, opulent Louis Quatorze furniture, a huge four-poster bed, and on the wall a large oil painting of a recumbent nude female.

'Is she an Alsatian Maja?' I asked, wondering if a Goya had been at work here.

But no! 'It is Maman, about twenty years ago,' he replied with pride.

To cover our confusion, we went to the window and admired the landscape; the low forested hills of Alsace with the occasional church spire or castle tower emerging through the cover; in the foreground the Moselle river winding through orchards and vineyards, an idyllic scene. Up the road, the heritage city of Nancy, south of us, Strasbourg, a magic land of history and beauty.

But I couldn't get used to the eyes of Maman watching us from the portrait; I wondered what they thought of my treasured print of the El Greco *Madonna* on our bedroom wall. Maybe we didn't have that much in common after all.

Our next foray into holiday house exchange was deep in the Auvergne. In an almost deserted village, a young couple were lovingly restoring an old manor house. They had tracked down authentic old tiles, old stone, period fittings from similar houses from all over this most unspoiled part of France. Heavy oak doors and thick walls kept the shady interior cool; a mass of bougainvillea and hibiscus sheltered the verandah from the hot sunshine. A pair of lazy cats kept watchful eyes on everything that moved. I felt quite concerned for our partners who were travelling to Ireland on motorbikes, a long trek in the August heat, until we saw a couple of cars in the fine old coachhouse. That and their array of photos from bikers' conventions all over Europe showed that they had other interests far from the world of conservation.

We learned later that they created quite a stir when they arrived in our quiet cul-de-sac back in Ireland; they *vroom-vroomed* in, togged out in black leathers on a pair of magnificent Harley-Davidsons. The neighbours shook their heads and wondered what kind of visitors had now arrived ...

On another exchange in a Swiss village near Lausanne, the neighbours there must have wondered about us when we arrived in the middle of the celebrations for the 800th anniversary of the founding of the Swiss Confederation. Everyone was on the main street for the parade, plump matrons in traditional milkmaid dresses, men in lederhosen and jaunty Tyrolean hats, placid piebald cows with tinkling bells swinging from ornate leather collars, ox-drawn carts piled high with great wheels of cheese; the whole procession urged along by sonorous blasts from the long alpine horns. In the evening, our new neighbours invited us to a traditional Swiss feast; chunks of fresh-baked bread were ready for dunking in bubbling pots of fondue, thick slices of aromatic cheese sizzled on raclette grills, there was even a wood-fired oven cooking huge pizzas, all washed down with copious amounts of cool white wine and tankards of beer.

I stopped thinking about how our partners would adjust to our home and surroundings – How would they manage our temperamental cooker? Would they remember to feed the dog? – Here we were at the foot of the Alps, savouring all the best that Switzerland had to offer, all on quite a modest budget; the only question to be considered was 'where to go for our next exchange', the little flat in a Renaissance building in Rome, or the hacienda in Mexico. What a great way to see the real world, from the inside ...

GENTLE WHITE LIVES

Clare Lynch

She is a lady of late middle age.

Her chin has collapsed into several others.

Under the corrugated rubble of skin is the gleaming gold of a heavy chain. She is the head starter in a conga of many late middle-aged ladies now entering the coffee shop.

It's a coach tour.

Dead giveaway is the dynamic sprint that many of the women encumbered by heavy handbags make towards any architectural possibility that could end in toilets.

They've probably come to photograph Yeats' bones and then move on to check out the toilets. They are hobbling, striding, padding.

Retirees, I guess.

Many women but few men.

One of these few men is bulging with good humour. He must be already cast as the joker in the party pack throughout this tour.

They are from Manchester.

All soft voices cooing like doves over the Celtic knot work cards, Irish jewellery and green ceramics.

There is a man in white.

Completely in white.

Whatever was his wife thinking?

Helping him pack such hard-to-manage clothes on a five-day tour?

I picture one chocolate éclair accident on those impeccable white jeans of his and I shudder internally.

From head to tow, he is dressed in this impossible white, his image bizarrely completed by a large white handbag, its tessellated strap bunched like an untidy rope in his clenched fist.

I'm presuming it belongs to his wife, lost at sea in the Bermuda Triangle of the ladies toilets. But I like the fact the he minds it for her, isn't ashamed.

I see now that the joker of the party pack has a left arm that hangs suspiciously still.

It is as stiff as the branch of a dead tree and I realise that sometime in his life this man has had a stroke.

And from whatever place in his heart, he has come through laughing.

I watch them heave, like a cluster of shuffling emperor penguins, all out through the double doors together.

The joker, laughing, the Hero in White giving his wife her handbag as she excitedly fills him in on the nice hand soap and the tiles she's just seen.

I have enormous affection for them all.

Enormous.

What have they all already come through in their lives? What have each of these weathered and war-torn retirees survived?

Divorces? Widowhood? Childlessness? Survival over strokes? Cancers? Even unimaginably better things?

They are going on to Donegal.

It's a glorious day for it and I am so glad that the Sligo sun shines on them.

For me, the concept of the tour their lives have already brought them on is too much to think about.

Too varied.

Too rough.

Too relentless and long.

Too breathless a view.

I close my notebook on their gentle white lives with a blessing and a wish for their happiness.

GOWLA FARM

Paddy Gavin

When most of Europe was recovering from the Second World War, in the doldrums, and the government of the day was eager to create employment, Comhlucht Siúcra Éireann, the Irish Sugar Company, then a semi-state company, set about the reclamation of bogland at Gowla in north Galway. Lieutenant General Michael J. Costello was the General Manager of the Irish Sugar Company and was advised that bogland treated with balanced artificial fertilizers could be made productive, and he took a personal interest in getting Gowla Farm up and running. This farm was a large expansive bogland of some three thousand acres located between Ahascra and Ballyforan. Initially, deep parallel drains were machine cut from which turf was extracted and surface drainage created. Later, the ground was cultivated and grass seed sown over several acres, a grass meal factory was built which later manufactured dairy nuts and grass meal. A network of railway tracks was laid to convey the cut grass to the turf-powered plant. Other crops, too, like cereals, potatoes, sugar beet and carrots were grown there and, for a period, Gowla was recognised as one of Ireland's biggest industrial farms.

During the school holidays in 1956, I got my first summer job there. I was to assist the agricultural advisor in many of his roles in soil sampling, spraying, tending flowerbeds and cold frames, assisting in crop experiments and several other tasks. My wages were five pounds, twelve shillings and sixpence a week for forty hours' work, about eighteen cents per hour in today's money. There were about two hundred employed there, mostly men, and a few women in the administration office.

That year, 1956, had a particularly beautiful summer, and on the warm days, the tall rye grasses swayed in the breeze, the heat shimmers rose from the warm peatland and the dragon flies moved uneasily as if uncertain of their role in the reclaimed territory.

Our converstaions during meal breaks would range from football to marquee dancing, athletics and several other topics. The top Gaelic players of that era were Christy Ring, the Mackeys and the Rackards in hurling, while in football Sean Purcell, Gerry O'Malley and the youthful Matty McDonagh were household names. In athletics, Roger Bannister was shaving seconds off the mile record while our own Ronnie Delaney was on the verge of world fame, for, later that year, he would win the gold medal in the 1,500 metres at the Olympic Games in Melbourne.

The farm itself was well managed by Captain Michael Grogan, a strict but fair-minded Clare man, who took great pride in his spotless, pale green, Carlow-registered Volkswagon beetle. I cycled to work most days, along the quiet sand roads, by Castle French where laburnum trees overhung the roadway.

In the autumn, the numbers employed there greatly decreased as the part-timers like myself found the outdoor work had become more difficult. In the autumn, too, the loads of grass meal from the plant became fewer and herds of sheep were brought in to eat the root crops grown over the summer. The farm seemed to run well for about ten years. Several young men earned good wages, acquired their first cars, got married, and managed to set up their own homes and farms from their earnings at Gowla Farm. Despite all the liberal dressings of fertilizers and the good management, the bogland's yield never matched that of the upland farms. Then in the early 1960s, the national phosphate subsidies were removed by the government and it became uneconomic to continue farming off bogland, and the company gave notice to all that Gowla Farm was being closed down. The machinery and stock was sold off and the whole bogland sold to Bord na Móna. No more would the local grass cutter's humming be heard from the level expanse of grassland, and no more would the white vapour raise from the tall furnace chimney of the grass meal plant.

There was great sadness over this closure, especially amongst the older workers. Though I had left some years earlier on a different career path, for me Gowla Farm had been my first working base and, these days, when I pass there, I reflect on that noisy industrial farm and on the very fine people I met there.

Today, the bogland is gone back to its original wild state where pink and white heather, rough grass and bog cotton once more abound. Recently, I stopped and climbed over a locked gate and revisited the ruins of the grass meal plant. Wild hares seemed to challenge me as if curious to know my business there. A single piece of galvanised sheeting swung idly from its ruins. It rattled and creaked like a ghost from the past, as if asking to be remembered for the part it had played in what was once Gowla Farm.

SAILING

Mary O'Malley

The last time I sailed from Connemara to Kinvara it was hot enough to make you want to cool down – and I like the heat. People divided into those who complained at the lack of rain and those who felt a drought was overdue. People sunbathed for hours and lay around the beaches.

Those who had booked their fortnight in Fomentera or along one of the overcrowded costas came home feeling cheated. I don't sunbathe. I get bored on the beach. There are better ways of ways of cooling down.

On Friday, I drove to a pier near Carraroe and was given a place on a boat sailing to Kinvara. Polite exchanges were made and then I sat quietly out of the way and listened to the men talking softly. One smoked a pipe. They ignored me, except for the helmsman, who had known my father. I sat listening to their talk as they moved slowly out the bay, then watched the vast sheets of sail fill out against the sky as they caught the first puffs of wind. They were like the wings of some great rusty butterfly, about to lift us into the sky.

These men hunted the wind on calm days, they were alive to its slightest shift and would use it to their advantage for speed. That day they started a friendly race with two other boats, there was some low calling across the water. Farther out, the wind picked up and the sea began to roll. There was a soft-voiced flurry of consultation and they tacked. One of the men I didn't know watched slyly as the boat swung over. I stood up, climbed the slant of the deck to become ballast and breathed in the green glassy air.

'Here, I am happy,' was my single thought.

The helmsman glanced at me and nodded his approval. He lifted an eyebrow towards the other man. The other man looked put out — there would be no fun out of giving me a fright.

They had a good run, the boat far over, sailing close to the wind.

One of the passengers was afraid. I exulted but only because I trusted the men. I leaned against the great wooden gunwale, laughing as the keel seemed about to clear water. The mast was what they called it in Irish, a vast tree above them.

I love this dance of sail and wind, the defiance of gravity, and I love it because it is the only time I am not afraid, though I measured the angle of the jump needed to clear the swinging boom if it tipped that six inches too far as they cut through the sea, balanced on a knife edge, suspended between two transparent elements. Here, I attained my own critical mass, as if everything that was scattered moved into perfect equilibrium. Here, I was entirely myself.

The wind dropped and the sea stilled as we made the shelter of Kinvara and sailed into the bay a couple of hours before dark. I thanked the men, 'That was lovely,' and walked up the quay. The evening was warm. Voices floated across the water, there was some desultory laughter on the quay. The pubs were full of crews and tourists.

About six boats lay at anchor, beautiful creatures that the men I grew up amongst treasured as they could never treasure women. There in the bay were the only females they understood. They talked about their wiles and their caprices and loved them unconditionally. Who could blame them? These females never answered back and they grew lovelier with age.

I was meeting my family for dinner at a house nearby. A couple we knew were renting it for their holidays ... the two families hadn't met since the previous summer.

'So you came from the sea,' the host said. He had a cool voice, slightly mocking.

'Don't be an eejit,' I said and everyone laughed.

The air was still. We could hear the night birds calling down by the water. Somewhere nearby, a fiddle was playing and, behind that, the low hum of several conversations. The teenagers went into the town.

The air was warm, scented with turf smoke and flowers. A heron flapped onto the darkening shore, 'the heron like a tilted italic

Illuminating the gospel of the absurd'. I don't know why I said the lines from Montague's beautiful poem that ends with the twin deities, 'and their dual disciplines of tenderness'.

Both couples were still together then, and I am sure I detected nothing prophetic in the rise and fall of Whitman's wonderful lines with which our host responded: '... On the beach at night alone ...

This vast similitude spans them,
and always has spann'd,
And shall forever span them
and compactly hold and enclose them.'

STONE PEOPLE

Nuala McCann

We are stone people.

Toy donkeys with horsey grins sporting sombreros belonged to another world. Our donkeys were the old Connemara variety, panniers packed with turf on their backs.

T-shirts shrieking: 'I went to Ibiza and all I got was this ... ' were not yet invented back in the 1960s.

Like most small girls, I spent an inordinate amount of time craving a tall Spanish doll in a crimson silk flamenco dress, fluttering a feathery black fan with matching lashes.

She posed on a table in a friend's room for years, a present from an aunt.

And although her skirt sat out in full twirl and she did her best to be noticed, she was invariably brushed past, an ornament, a mere souvenir to the girl who owned her. Only to me, she was exotic.

Now, on holidays, we collect pottery, chalk-white as the small chapel on a hillside in Santorini; necklaces, turquoise blue as only the Greek sea can be.

But back then, in the 1960s, we were always stone people. The beaches of Connemara were ours. And we filled our pockets with razor shells and purple stones from the sands near Letterfrack.

In 1969, our family and our best friends piled up the cars and took off to the wilds. Our destination was an old fishing lodge beside a lake in the middle of nowhere.

There were four adults and ten children. There were bamboos in the garden, windowsills so big you could act out a play on them and old wooden shutters to clank closed and hide behind.

And there were flat slate stones, perfect for skimming. On the first night, after we arrived, the boys took to skimming stones across the lake. But one proved too sharp and my eldest brother sliced open his finger.

He tried to repair the damage privately, but the tell-tale trail of blood from the lake, across the garden to the bathroom, alerted the mothers from frantic bed-making and the fathers from unloading of cars.

They drove far to find a doctor. He was the old style. He pulled out his razor blade and administered a neat set of stitches.

It was perfect weather, that summer of 1969. My aunt donned her costume and her perky bathing cap with its floppy plastic flowers and taught me to swim.

There were no shops, so the adults organised rations of sweets, each day after lunch.

We made up plays and performed them on the big window sills, jumping out from behind the old shutters.

And down at the lake jetty, my father and my uncle chatted to the fishermen. I can still see them, talking and laughing, as one fisherman hands my little brother a small fish that jumps and wriggles in his hand.

Looking back, it was an idyllic holiday. The sun shone and the days were long and lazy.

But sometimes you walked in on an adult conversation that suddenly hushed.

The grown-ups seemed nervous about the return journey. It was 1969. The news was not good from home.

And on the journey north, at the border, I glanced back through the car window and saw a soldier crouched in the ditch, his face smeared, a gun cocked on his shoulder.

These days, the world is off to foreign parts.

But Connemara has a special place in my heart. After all, we are stone people. I keep a small white pebble in my pocket ... a souvenir and a talisman to ward off the world.

At home, our windowsills are filled with stones — purple stones from wild Atlantic shores, sleek black stones like wet seals bobbing in the water, pure white stones that hold the warmth of a fine summer's day in them.

And sharp slate for memories that pierce the heart.

DAYS OF WINE AND ROSES

Anne Sharpe

On that early morning flight back from Milan, I blanketed myself behind a book as my inner reel wound back over the holiday. Steaming cappuccinos within reliable sunshine gave way to cosy piazzas behind winding mediaeval streets. All that national pride in tradition and continuity began to settle on the memory of splendid meals. When, out of the generally elected silence, my companion across the aisle suddenly began, 'Italy ... well, it's a cradle of civilisation, isn't it?'

He was a little sententious. And there was more than a touch of the Ancient Mariner about him, stopping some modern equivalent of the wedding guest within the compellingly confined space of an airline. 'The language of Romans,' he went on, this time wistfully, slowly. But as he launched into his story, mild irritation vanished. For, in a sense, I could not choose but hear.

'The way everyone's spread out over a book ... wrapped up in it. Just brought me back. She was like that.' Then, abruptly, 'Did you ever come across Longman's *Latin Grammar*?'

Doors swung open at once in my head, for Latin had been my favourite subject at school. I'd been intrigued by how its utter clarity had still left room and more for the reservation and qualification of nuance. I loved its sinewy structure, the rolling cadence of those carefully-orchestrated cumulative phrases. And there was always a cold beauty about that inevitable logic. But who would have thought that a casual exchange with a stranger would lead back so deftly and unexpectedly? And anyway, what conscious part could Latin play in the life of any 2000s person now? But he was continuing easily, 'That's what she wanted for her seventy-fifth birthday ... a grammar and dictionary. "The best," she said. Didn't want to mess around with bad teaching.'

'Your mother?' I hazarded. He smiled agreement.

'Those books were never off the table ... so I had to follow what she was learning. One day, the page was opened at something called the "ablative absolute".'

I thought of the ablative absolute, two words, usually noun and verb, closely combined, a pair of succinct precursors. *Roma visa* — Rome having been seen — would be one example. Caesar often used the construction when describing his Gallic campaigns. Having done something, the two words efficiently linked, he prepared to do something else, one eager action following the other. What had just been achieved was a mere stepping stone to some closely connected future activity. Meanwhile, my companion was surging on.

'But it all gave her a new lease of life ... chattier ... her mind opened ... hours every day set aside for grammar and translation. She even began to make shopping lists in Latin.'

Though, by now, he was looking sad. Such a piece of achievement must have somehow reversed.

'How it happened ... the silliest thing ... a needle slipped while she was sewing on a button ... finger turned septic. She neglected it, of course ... and I was away on business. When I saw how it had spread to her wrist, I insisted on hospital. She argued, of course. Refused at first. Hospitals were places to go to die, she said. I scoffed, "What, die of an infected finger?"'

'But she was right, you know. MRSA. Died in a fortnight. So she was right and I was wrong. And you know, her books were still open on the table when I came to clear the house ... still in the middle of learning.'

I thought of the elderly woman eagerly turned to absorb and experience the new, rushing ahead to tackle the next stage in grammar. And I remembered the poem '*Vitae Summa Brevis Spem Nos Vetet Incohare Longam*' by Ernest Dowson, whose title the poet took from an ode by Horace. Within the crammed richness of her last years, maybe she'd had the chance to dwell on such a rendering. Even now, I like to think of her pouring over the original text, translating it slowly in her own way and to her own needs. In my image of it, sunlight glows warmly over the still-potent words laid bare on the table.

> They are not long, the weeping and the laughter,
> Love and Desire and hate:
> I think they have no portion in us after
> We pass the gate.
>
> They are not long, the days of wine and roses:
> Out of a misty dream
> Our path emerges for a while, then closes
> Within a dream.

CHANGING TIMES

Tommy Sands

My father was not, by any stretch of the imagination, a violent man. With one rare lapse, however, in 1960, he managed to cut off all relations between our house and the rest of the world.

In August 1960, he coolly picked up the biggest knife in the kitchen and stabbed our old wet battery wireless in the speaker. He followed this up by throwing a cup of tea in its face, soaking such far-flung stations as Stockholm, Oslo, Frankfurt and London with hot, wet tea leaves. His general target on that occasion was Athlone, the headquarters of Ireland's national radio station, and Micheál O'Hehir, the brilliant sports commentator, in particular.

'Take that, ye karn ye,' he roared. 'And that, you knob-faced knur,' he shouted, delivering a bare-knuckled blow to its hitherto smiling dial.

It was all because of a Gaelic football match. Down was trailing by two points against Offaly. It had been a bruising All-Ireland Senior Championship semi-final. There were just a few minutes left in the game and James McCartan, the dynamic Down centre-half forward, had been downed in the square. Paddy Doherty was getting ready to take the penalty kick. All around Croke Park, you could cut the tension with a knife. Around our table, things were no less fraught and a bread knife that usually cut simple soda farls for quiet country people was lying relaxed and innocent nearby.

O'Hehir was almost hoarse with excitement. 'Paddy Doherty is now standing back to take the penalty. His socks are down around his ankles. The crowd is hushed ...'

At that moment, the whole population of County Down, it seemed, was either in Croke Park or gathered around a wireless like ours, teething prayers and threats alike to saints and other holy people who might have influence on Providence in such times as these.

'Can Doherty score this and save the day for Down and put them into their first-ever All-Ireland final in history?' O'Hehir went on breathlessly. 'He's placing the ball on the fourteen-yard-line ... this could be the most important kick of his life ... the most important kick in the life of County Down ... he's stepping back now ... the crowd are holding their breath ... Here he comes ...', O'Hehir lowered his voice to a whisper. 'He puts his head to one side in that familiar style ... a hush has fallen over the crowd ... here he comes ...'

There was deathly silence. We stopped breathing, waiting for the kick. We waited and waited ... and waited.

But Paddy Doherty never got the ball kicked in our house. Our wireless had stopped breathing too. The wet battery had run out. It needed to be charged again but not in the manner that it was being charged, battered, butted and knifed by my father.

'You dirty, rotten treacherous two-faced son of a bitch's ghost of an excuse for a wireless,' he roared, with lefts and rights to AFN Frankfurt and the BBC Home Service. 'If you were playing that pop rubbitch on Radio Luxembourg, you wouldn't break down. I houl ye, wouldn't ye not!'

Perhaps, we had the volume turned up too loud. Liam Daly told us later that high volume could drain the power out of a battery. Others said that even a wireless could suffer the effects of tension, which, in turn, could have drained the battery. And then there was the weak signal from Radio Éireann. If the game had been broadcast on BBC Northern Ireland, it would have been clearer and less work for the old wireless, but the BBC never broadcast Gaelic games.

As it happened, Paddy Doherty scored that penalty and Down had qualified for its first-ever All-Ireland final, but we wouldn't know that until the next morning when Jack Grant would come with the *Irish Press* and the groceries in Gorman's lorry.

We decided that we would go to Dublin for the final, just to be sure, and hopefully we'd see for the first time a team from the Six Counties win the All-Ireland Senior Championship.

It would be an unforgettable expedition. Josie Shevlin from Armagh said she would take us in her car. We would all go, even my mother. With egg sandwiches, flasks of tea and a red and black flag we had sown together from a dress belonging to my mother and an old soutane belonging to Father Hugh, we headed for the border. All along the way, through the counties of Armagh, Louth, Meath and Dublin, Down flags hung from every tree, in support of the Wee North against the mighty Kingdom of Kerry. We went to the red church in Drumcondra, near Dublin airport, for eight o'clock mass. There were Kerry people in the congregation too, who would be expecting a different result from God. He had already delivered them nineteen All-Irelands. Down had been given none. 'Maybe,' I respectfully suggested to God, 'it is time for a change.'

We were waiting outside the gates of Croke Park from 9.30 a.m., along with thousands of others, singing and swapping sandwiches. At 1.30 p.m., we crushed in and got carried away with the crowd to a heavenly spot, right down beside the wire under the Cusack Stand, and there, in a kind of euphoric trance, we witnessed one of the most memorable spectacles in the history of Irish sport.

Through the two-inch mesh, twelve-foot-high wire fence, we roared, wailed, wept and cheered as these modern-day Cúchulainns leaped in the air like the very grass was on fire and swept up and down the field like waves of myth and magic. At the end, unable to hold back any longer, we scaled that fence like spiders and sped out onto the Croke Park grassland just to touch the hem of a red and black garment.

Down had beaten Kerry and, amid unimaginable celebrations, Kevin Mussen, the captain, carried the Sam Maguire Cup across the border. For a long time, there was no work done on the farms around Ryan, and that victory united Catholic and Protestant for many weeks and the whole of the County Down walked on air.

My father's attack on the wireless that year cut us off from the outside world for many weeks, until Hugh and myself walked the battery two miles up the Crossan Road to Mrs Linden's shop to get it charged. More than thirty years later, her grandson Mickey Linden would lead Down to further All-Ireland victories and I would write a song with my son Fionán as we watched a new generation train in Kilbroney Park, Rostrevor, under the watchful eye of Pete McGrath. Every evening they ran up and down the side of Slieve Martin to Cloch Mór, the big stone thrown there by Fionn Mac Cumhaill to dislodge Benandonner, the icy giant from the wintry north. They seemed to be suffering sweatfully for the very hills that were rising around them, to bring a sparkle of light to a loved homeland in a year of hate and a time of darkness.

> The cheering like thunder rolled
> The flags they flew from every pole
> And we sang and danced the whole way home
> On the day we won the All-Ireland.

When the wireless returned, however, it was never the same again. The newsreader, Charles Mitchell, seemed to be talking through his nose, or like a man who had been shocked by a sudden 'dig in the bake'. But he talked on regardless, and we heard news of John Fitzgerald Kennedy being elected president of the United States and scientists talking about exploring the moon. The whole world was changing.

LAWLESS' GRANNY AND 'HEY JUDE'

Leo Cullen

We were bus conductors in London, Lawless and I, that summer of 1968. Coming off our shifts some evenings we went on to places, without bothering to change out of our uniforms. On recruitment, we had been requisitioned two sets of uniform each, one heavy serge, the other lightweight fatigues. As that summer grew hotter, we favoured the fatigues, khaki-coloured light wear; they were passable we thought, almost trendy. Almost Carnaby Street. After work, with our bus passes, we bussed everywhere in the city for nothing. One afternoon we jumped on the 134 into Oxford Street to see in Studio One Cinema, the matinée of Joseph Strick's film, *Ulysses*. We sat in the midst of a puzzled audience right through the film, recognising our own home city of Dublin. But that was the day that Lawless from Cork fell into an explosion of the titters. He had only been able take so much of Molly's soliloquy and when with embarrassment he couldn't take any more – just as Molly was saying 'yes' for the tenth time – he shouted, 'Let me out of here.' The usherette's light beam searched around for the source of the noise, over all the heads, resting at last upon the rabbit-dazzled faces of two bus conductors unable to conduct themselves. 'Fares please,' Lawless shouted and we bolted into the daylight of the street.

Another afternoon, we found Petticoat Lane and there, amid the hucksters, I bought my first-ever record player, a wee blue box with holes on the side, like in a pepper canister, to let the sound out. We were the canny bargainers that day, having been warned that Petticoat Lane was a nest of cockney crooks and dealers. I took a further gamble and bought a record, my first ever, a Beatles record. Lawless thought I was the last of the big spenders.

But the whole exchange had been done for one purpose. I wanted to hear 'Hey Jude'. I'd heard it on the radio and wanted to hear it again. Its release had prompted a storm, an anti-Beatles storm. And that was something unheard of. Sure weren't The Beatles the 'fab four', the greatest. But now, in *Melody Maker* and the other magazines and on Radio Caroline, there was criticism. 'Hey Jude' was far too long, they said; 'Hey Jude' had stretched Beatle cred to breaking point. 'Hey Jude' as far as I was concerned could go on forever.

We took it back to the bedsit in Finsbury Park. 'Listen to this, Lawless,' I said and lay back in my narrow bed.

'That's useless, boy,' he said when the great symphonic sweep had ended.

'What's useless about it?' I asked.

'It's the same thing over and over.'

Well if Lawless, as well as those Tin Pan Alley hacks, was going to attack my Beatles, I was going to support them.

'What's the same thing over and over?'

'Na', he said, 'how many times do they repeat the same word, 'na'?'

'It's a chorus.'

'How many times?'

So I replayed 'Hey Jude' in my head and I counted. 'Na na na na na na na na na na, Hey Jude' – 'Eleven times.'

'More like a hundred and eleven times.'

'It's a mantra, they got it from the Maharishi Mahesh yogi. It's the universal 'na'.

'Boy, it's more like from my granny. That's the sort of thing she says, dozing over the fire. That's not a song. That's someone losing their marbles.'

It was our first fight ever. I rushed at him and knocked him off his bed. He struck back. It ended in a silent lock of bodies and then, after a while, we went out jogging. It seemed the only thing to do; we'd done it every evening we were off work because, as Lawless said, it kept us out of the pubs. We jogged in our crepe-soled shoes and our GAA togs, for trendy running gear hadn't yet come in. White legged, we tore through the prams of Finsbury Park, first in silence, until the argument took up again.

'Na, like me ould granny.'

'Is she still alive?'

'Just about. In Skib, going "na, na", like The Beatles. She was a great old wan one time. Used to mind me.'

We argued as we jogged. We dodged toddling babies, we dodged bottles thrown from prams, we dodged boys in makeshift Arsenal shirts playing soccer; the mainstream of life was out in the summer evening's sun of that run down park and we dodged it.

But I knew something; 'Hey Jude' had a power and that power proclaimed and praised everything about us and around us. So I said it to Lawless, 'It has power.'

'Do you mean, the power of the revolution?'

'I mean … I don't know … it does good.'

On that note, maybe, we patched up our row and we went back and played the blue box again. But Lawless still wasn't happy. 'Na, na,' he said, 'it was repeated not eleven times but a hundred and eleven times. That's not a song.'

In time, of course, our row healed. I eventually laughed at the comparison of The Beatles and Lawless' granny from Skib. And surely 'Hey Jude' has done good; Na, na, na, na, na, na, na, na, na, na, na … repeated not eleven times but a million and eleven times, a trillion and eleven times, at Christmas and at Easter and at summer, in streets and cities and countries and homes and gypsy camps and battle grounds and field stations and hospitals … in an A & E ward I happened to be in on a recent Saturday night when on the Brit Awards it popped out of a small TV screen high up on a wall and distracted the walking wounded. A symphony. That has brought peace and solace and hope and love and uplifting to a trillion and eleven people.

As did Lawless' granny once upon a time, I'm sure, to Lawless.

THE CANA INN

Gerard Smyth

The law did not like the long hair
of the cider-drinkers, the ones who made the din
on Saturday night in the Cana Inn.

Not the one in Galilee, the Cana
of the wedding feast and the water-to-wine miracle.
But the one they later knocked to rubble

off Grafton Street. It was where we revelled,
carelessly dressed in denim and corduroy,
equipped with copies of Kerouac.

It was the end of summer, the waning
of another decade. The jukebox played
a voice with gravitas: it was Johnny Cash
singing 'Girl from the North Country'.

THE LAST ROSE OF SUMMER

Una Hunt

Pádraig knew where it was; he had been to visit it often with his grand-father. So I decided to go and take a look. Apparently, the plant grew for many years just inside the main gate of the gardens but was moved a few years ago to just outside the director's residence where it is surrounded by railings bearing the sheet music of the famous ballad.

'Just up the hill to the right of those tall trees,' said the caretaker at the entrance to the Botanic Gardens. It was a nice day, rather cold, but bright and almost sunny and there were a number of people out and about. When I turned to the right, I saw it immediately – three plants enclosed with railings. I hardly noticed the pretty house opposite, with the quirky tower and two rabbits in the window, for my attention was fixed on Thomas Moore's Rose. It was perhaps not the most wonderful plant I had ever seen, and it was not yet in full bloom, but still it held extraordinary fascination, for me at least. The mid-pink roses were described in the caption close by as 'Rosaceae, Rosa odorata Pallida'.

Denis, the Grounds Foreman, went on to explain, 'Botanically it is a form originating in China where it has been growing for over a thou-sand years. There is confusion as to who introduced it into Europe but it is generally accepted it came into commercial production from a garden near London in 1793 and it's from this source that it received its cultivar name of Parson's Pink China. Over the years, slightly different forms have been given the names Old Blush, Common China, Old China and Monthly Rose.'

The plant at the National Botanic Gardens was presented by the Thomas Moore Society in 1950, a propagation from the original plant growing in Jenkinstown House, County Kilkenny. Legend has it that Moore was inspired to write his famous song while strolling in the Kilkenny gardens and, right beside the rosebush, stands a reminder of the sheet music:

> Tis the last rose of summer
> Left blooming alone
> All its lovely companions
> Are faded and gone ...

What a sad romantic picture those few lines conjure up; I just couldn't help contemplating that even Thomas Moore himself could hardly have guessed how this rose, that inspired his immortal verses, would touch the lives of millions of people around the world.

There is a line of portraits inside the visitor's centre, commemorating past directors of the Botanic Gardens — among whom, appropriately enough, I spotted Moore's contemporary namesakes David Moore along with his son, Sir Frederick Moore — needless to say, neither was related to the poet. As curator of the gardens back in the nineteenth century, David Moore did research on growing orchids from seed and, indeed, came very close to discovering how the potato blight was spread. And yet another coincidence, David was born in 1808, the year that Thomas Moore first published his *Irish Melodies*.

Despite the other works he wrote — biographies, novels, the oriental epic poem *Lalla Rookh* and several other musical collections — Thomas Moore's lasting reputation still rests on his ten immensely popular books of drawing-room songs known as the *Irish Melodies*, published between 1808 and 1834. Even today, when Moore's star has fallen almost from view, 'The Last Rose of Summer' continues to remain famous around the world. It elicited a standing ovation when I played it in a little arts centre in midwest America, and that from a non-Irish-American audience. Little wonder then that, in Moore's lifetime, the sheet music of the song sold no fewer than 1.5 million copies in America alone and became, quite simply, one of the most popular songs of the century.

It is also symbolic that Moore was able to promote Irish music around the world, by using mostly the ancient harp airs as the basis for his songs. And, he did this at a time when the nation was in one of its darkest hours.

Many of the great sopranos of Moore's time sang it, among them Marie Louise Albani, Adelina Patti and the Limerick soprano, Catherine Hayes. The song crossed over from merely popular repertoire and was quite likely to turn up in the middle of an unrelated opera. This is how it worked: if, during the opera, the soprano received rapturous applause, the whole proceedings were halted to allow her to sing a song of her own choice. Invariably, that would be 'The Last Rose of Summer' … Then, Friedrich von Flotow used the air in his opera *Martha*. As transcriptions frequently highlighted the most popular vocal music of the day, countless pianist-composers and other instrumentalists used the air in their music. The list includes a bewildering array of composers long since forgotten, yet it hardly seems right that such a great song could suddenly have been deleted from the instrumental repertoire! As a song it endured, just like the rose itself, up into the twentieth century, the choice of endless great sopranos and popular songsters; the list itself reads like a hall of fame. Even Edison's earliest cylinder rolls contain recordings of Moore's 'Rose'.

The last verse is a particularly poignant reminder that, despite his success and fame, Moore's life was essentially very sad. All his children died one by one, the resonances of which are immortalised in 'The Last Rose of Summer'.

So soon may I follow, when friendships decay
And from Love's shining circle – the gems drop away!
When true hearts lie wither'd, And fond ones are flown
Oh! Who would inhabit this bleak world alone?

SEPTEMBER

MARKED PRESENT

Seamus Heaney

The photograph shows two little boys with two guitars slung round their necks, their left hands on the frets, their right hands flung high in the air, as if the photographer had snapped them in the final triumphant moment of a performance. They are up on a pretend stage, a picnic table in a woodland picnic area, and they look as if they might be the children of hippies living in some nearby commune: their hair is just that bit longer than you'd expect and there's something about the amount of denim they're wearing that suggests an alternative lifestyle, late 1960s Calfornia, perhaps.

But the photograph was taken in County Wicklow in the early 1970s, although the young brothers had, in fact, spent the academic year 1970–71 in the San Francisco Bay area. One of their most memorable experiences was attending an open-air concert given by the folksinger and storyteller Pete Seeger. 'If I had a hammer …', 'Where have all the flowers gone …', 'Casey Jones', 'Abbey Yo Yo', 'John Henry': they listened that sunlit morning to the thrilling, beguiling songs of those glamorous radical times and, during the coming months, they would listen to them over and over again on a big long-playing record until Seeger's voice and music began to represent the music of what happened in the course of that liberating year.

But now the year of liberty was at an end. I took the photograph of those boys in the Devil's Glen Wood, the evening before they started school in Ashford and I remember well the sadness I felt as their father, the bittersweetness of that moment which is both the end of a child's brief freedom as a creature of family and the beginning of his or her life as a citizen, the exit from Eden, as it were, before the entry into the roll book.

And yet it may be that the photograph affects me because it marks an unforgettable moment of beginning and ending in my own life. The next morning, which would introduce the children to their first taste of the discipline of the classroom, would give me my first morning of escape from it. A few months before, I had given notice to the English Department at Queen's University that I would resign in the summer, and now it was early September, and my wife and I had made the move from the semi-detached security of a house and a job in Belfast to the chancier life of a full-time writer in the adventure playground of Wicklow. So the toy guitars held aloft, the dramatic gesture on the picnic table, the call of the wild green woods in the background have come to represent that moment of change.

I remember very clearly coming back from enrolling the boys with Master Whelan and going upstairs to inaugurate my own new freelance life in front of the blank page. Sitting there, under the low tongue and groove ceiling of the gate lodge we had rented, I was very conscious of the silence in the house and the absence of the children. But I was also conscious that, for the foreseeable future, our livelihood would depend not on the monthly salary cheque but on the muse's favour, on my pen and ink, and my own writerly confidence and stamina. So it was a happy coincidence that the work I started on that morning was my first go at translating the story of Suibhne Gealt, the legendary king who deserted his former responsibilities to become a man of the woods. Just as there had been something marvellously fortifying about a thing that happened earlier down at the school, when Master Whelan was filling in the children's particulars on the roll book. When he came to the column where the father's occupation had to be registered, he asked me no question but wrote down in his firm clear hand, *as Gaeilge*, '*file*'. And I knew that, from then on, I was going to be a poet in earnest.

THE MAN ON THE STAMP

Mae Leonard

Everything in Dublin was new and exciting to me back then – having moved from the confining walls of Limerick to, as we called it, 'the big smoke'. It was 1968 and I was looking at the world through the rose-tinted spectacles of a newlywed.

Dublin that September was a comfortable city at night. There were girls in daring mini skirts, there were street photographers – and there was Cabaret at The Chariot Inn in Ranelagh with *Buachaill ón Eirne* himself, Breandán Ó Dúill and the ballad group We 4 with Suzanne Murphy. I loved the thrill of a late-night horror film at the cinema on Saturday nights and buying Sunday newspapers on the way back to the flat.

Another treat was a pint in Dawson's Pub in Rathmines – a place to relax and, as a couple, we would sit and plan or meet friends. There were others of like mind there also and the two men who sat at the counter on tall stools were there for the same purpose. The difference was, they conversed in Irish with the *blas* of native speakers. I was fascinated listening to them. Fascinated by one of them in particular. The man with the spectacles and the tightly cut iron-grey hair. This man had a peculiar way of enunciating words and delivering them rapidly like the pik-pik-pik of a startled blackbird. I never knew his name but his fluency and command of Irish was spectacular.

My schoolbook Irish hadn't brought me to this level of expertise. My ear was attuned to the soft, rounded tones of Munster Irish but this was something else – this was harsh – as harsh as the landscape of Connemara.

I leaned forward to catch snatches of the conversation – it was difficult – but I managed to understand a few bits and pieces. One evening the two were discussing the recent invasion of Prague by the Russians and what might happen to Alexander Dubèek. Another time, it was about the American presidential election and Nixon came in for a roasting. Soon, I found that I could follow the conversation a little better and heard them discuss the dangers of the Fosbury flop – the head-first jump introduced at the Mexico Olympics that year. And the discussion became quite heated on the protest by the clenched fist salutes of the American Black Power athletes.

Our own discussion was a lot more mundane – mostly about the house we were about to buy and our move out of Dublin to the country. I never knew who that glorious Irish speaker was. I doubt if anyone in Dawson's Pub, Rathmines, in 1968 knew either. He was just part of the scene.

I bought some postage stamps the other day and *there he was* – the gaelgóir – looking at me just as I remember him. But I didn't know him. I didn't know of his political activities or of his internment in the Curragh military prison during the Second World War. Neither did I know that he is universally acknowledged as a pioneer of Irish language modernism. There are books – in particular *Cré na Cille* – a tale of the dead in a graveyard talking to each other, which was translated into several languages – and he wrote short stories too.

We bade goodbye to Rathmines in September 1969 ignorant of the fact that he was a Professor of Irish at Trinity College. Neither did we know that he had passed away the following year. I look at his face on my postage stamp and I tell the man in the post office – I remember him – I remember that man – Máirtín Ó Cadhain.

THE DIVINITY OF RIVERS

Malachy McKenna

Some years ago, while working on a Canadian tobacco farm, I was disappointed to discover that Niagara Falls, one of the Seven Wonders of the World, was not, as I had childishly imagined, a hidden waterfall beyond some unassailable fence in the wilderness, but, rather, a defiant force pounding its aged reminders against a commercialised village that has become the honeymoon capital of the world.

Recently, I stood again, within feet of the horseshoe falls. And while its environs continue to develop, the timeless force of the falls remains. Nothing but a low railing separated me from the churning torrent as it plunged two hundred feet into the gorge below at one and a half million gallons a second. Some people have gone over these falls in barrels and survived. Some haven't survived. In the nearby Niagara Museum, there's a picture of a seven-year-old boy who, having fallen from a boat up river in 1967, was swept over the falls wearing only a flimsy life jacket. He survived. I wonder where he is today? What's his story?

I was in Niagara as part of an annual charity cycle.

We cycled five hundred kilometres in five days. Physically hardened and mentally toughened, we were left to our own devices for a day or so.

I took this opportunity to visit the old tobacco farm, where, for many summer harvests in my youth, I found a home from home in a claustrophobic bunkhouse, built to house seasonal labour on the farm.

On a sunny September morning, my dear old farmer friend, Marius Van Besien and his eternally youthful wife, Mary Anne, picked me up at the Americana Hotel, Niagara, and drove me to the farm. His parents had emigrated from Belgium in the 1940s with nothing but a suitcase and worked so hard subsequently, they left separate farms to three sons. As Marius gripped the wheel on our journey south, I saw, in the clay hardened cracks of his hands, clear evidence that his parents' work ethic is still alive. As we neared the tobacco belt near Tillsonburg, I readied myself for the hum and bustle of a thriving harvest; picking gangs, harvesting machines, smoke rising from curing kilns, coffee breaks outside barns and the urgency of tractors eager to get their loads to the farmyards.

And so, it was a shock to discover that the fields, which once nurtured such industry have given way to less profitable soya beans and cowcorn and, in some cases, weeds.

The farms that once proudly boasted their success with gleaming paint were now crumbling and in need of repair. As field after fallow field presented itself in gloomy silence, Marius turned to me and said, 'It's almost all gone.'

It seems the tobacco industry has moved to areas of the world where costs are lower. There are still a few die-hard growers clinging to the only routine they know, but soon, they too will succumb.

There's an irony in bemoaning the disappearance of such an industry, but, for generations who have known nothing else, the alternative looks bleak.

Later, after we had visited and drank with farmers I'd grown to know over the years, Marius and Mary Anne took me out on their boat, *The Moonlighter*, on Lake Erie.

We dropped anchor off-shore of an American peninsula, a forbidden no-go tract of land known begrudgingly as 'Millionaires'. And, as the sun went down on an evening's reminiscing, I realised I had come full circle on this lake. Years ago, I had sat in this spot on this very same boat, an adventurous young buck, brimming with green enthusiasm.

Now, on this quiet lake, as the conversation lulls, I find I'm missing my wife and two young children. I sit at the back of the boat, my legs floating in the water. This very same water that tomorrow will make its way to the Niagara river and over the falls en route to Lake Ontario. Against all the changes I've known, here and elsewhere, the only constant has been the river.

And yet, geologists tell us, that some day, millions of years from now, the thunderous roar of Niagara will retreat to a mere trickle. Maybe, on that day, a young farmer will help his new wife over some freshly-painted fence in the wilderness.

They'll lay out a picnic and drink Molson Canadian beer, while he worries about the price per pound of whatever cash crop is cracking his hands and breaking his back. And they'll never know that the little brook, gently gurgling beside them, was once one of the Seven Wonders of the World.

IN NOMAD'S LAND:
LOUIS MacNIECE (1907–1963)

Liam Harte

'Speaking as an Irishman of Southern blood and Northern upbringing, whose father was a Protestant bishop and also a fervent Home Ruler … ' – Louis MacNeice's circuitous self-introduction in a 1953 review article is that of a writer whose identity was an amalgam of diverse and competing influences, which rendered him continually uncertain about where he belonged.

Displacement, indeed, was MacNeice's birthright, since home, for him, was always elsewhere. Born in Belfast on 12 September 1907, he grew up in the Church of Ireland rectory in Carrickfergus, where his father ministered. But birthplace and home were not coeval, not least because the claustrophobic rectory and its environs were full of Gothic terrors. Wherever young Louis turned within this 'cramped acre', as he called it, he felt besieged by sinister, static forces: a daunting cemetery on one side; a dour granite obelisk on another; a forbidding Norman castle behind; and everywhere the sound of church bells, factory klaxons and shipyard hammers reverberating in a cacophonic tumult.

Within the rectory walls, MacNeice's kindly but austere father was given to nocturnal praying that sounded to his son like a frightening 'conspiracy with God', as he described it in his posthumously-published autobiography, *The Strings are False* (1965). Add to this a pious children's nurse who indulged in sadistic threats and warnings, and a gentle but

infirm mother who died when Louis was just seven, and one begins to
see why the poet would always associate the North with tyranny.

MacNeice's sense of inner exile was deepened by his discovery that
his parents were themselves displaced people from the west of Ireland.
His mother's homesickness for Connemara bred in him such a profound
yearning for an imaginary homeland of windswept mountains and
welcoming cottagers that the pastoral west became, in the words of his
sister Elizabeth, 'a kind of lost Atlantis where we thought that by rights
we should be living ... We were in our minds a West of Ireland family
exiled from our homeland.' And so Connemara became a 'dream world'
for MacNeice, a mystical, unseen realm where a fresh identity might be
forged. 'Born here, I should have proved a different self,' he conjectures
in 'The Once-in-Passing', and in 'Day of Renewal' he reflects:

> Where I was born,
> Heckled by hooters and trams, lay black to the west
> And I disowned it, played a ticklish game
> Claiming a different birthplace, a wild nest
> Further, more truly, west, on a bare height
> Where nothing need be useful and the breakers
> Came and came but never made any progress
> And children were reborn each night.

Such hankering after an illusory elsewhere is one of the hallmarks
of MacNeice's life and work. Elsewheres play a vital role in his imaginative geography since they hold open the possibility of defying the
deterministic imperatives of history and subjectivity. In 'Valediction', a
love-hate letter to Ireland written in 1934, he acknowledges:

> I cannot be
> Anyone else than what this land engendered me ...
> I can say Ireland is hooey, Ireland is
> A gallery of fake tapestries,
> But I cannot deny my past to which my self is wed,
> The woven figure cannot undo its thread.

Yet the desire for self-unravelment remained, being the corollary of
a physical and metaphysical restiveness. MacNeice is a poet caught in a

perpetual vagrancy, forever poised at some threshold of travel, chasing an illusive authenticity here, courting self-dispersal there. His description of himself in his autobiography as 'a mere nomad who has lost his tent' suggests that homelessness was, for him, a mode of being in the world. Repeatedly, we find him in transit in his poems, from the early 'Ode', in which he resolves to become a 'migrating bird following felt routes', to the late 'Solitary Travel', where he admits 'the futility of moving on/To what, though not a conclusion, stays foregone'. All of which makes MacNeice the supreme poet of unsettled exile, whose 'glad sad poetry of departure' speaks to the unrooted Irish everywhere.

And so if, having read his verse, we feel we still don't fully know him, then perhaps that is as it should be, for part of MacNeice remains permanently unhoused, tantalisingly eluding full and final definition. His epitaph for his friend and fellow poet Dylan Thomas could also be his own: 'What we remember is not a literary figure to be classified in the text-book but something quite unclassifiable, a wind that bloweth where it listeth, a wind with a chuckle in its voice and news from the end of the world.'

OUT-HALVES: IRELAND V. FRANCE, SEPTEMBER 2007

Brendan Graham

My father would have loved Ronan O'Gara; his fluency of foot; the tantalising touch kicking; the grace under pressure. My father, too, was an out-half and on Friday, in Stade de France, I will remember him.

But I will remember him, not as I last knew him, beaten down by infirmity, fumbling for life in the Mater Hospital. I will remember him in *his* time of grace; *his* time of fluency.

On the cover of Donal A. Murphy's book, *Nenagh Ormonds Century 1884–1984*, is a smiling young man being shouldered by a jubilant crowd through the streets of Nenagh. In his hands the Munster Junior Cup to which, in 1935, he captained the Ormonds. The young man, my father, was twenty-one years old.

On the way to victory, Nenagh had beaten Munster's finest: Garryowen, Young Munster and Ronan O'Gara's club, Cork Constitution, against whom my father had scored the winning drop goal.

For the final against Killorglin, the match report records that 'the Nenagh out-half played a very brilliant game and his defence by way of touch kicking drew rounds of applause whenever he was forced to do so.'

He played a key role in Nenagh's 1938 Mansergh Cup victory, too.

Describing a game in which he scored a try, a conversion, a penalty and a drop goal, the match report declared the Ormond captain worthy of 'Field Marshal rank, a judicious distributor or kicker as the moment demanded ... a scoring virtuoso'.

And in the final, the papers commented that his 'left-footed drop goal from near halfway was the highlight of the match and won the cup for Nenagh'.

His association with Ormonds ended in 1943, when he married my mother and the National Bank transferred him away from Nenagh, but his passion for rugby was rekindled in 1956 when the family moved to Castleisland: home to the Doyles, Mick and Tom ... and later Moss Keane and Mick Galwey.

There, with Mick Doyle Senior, he became heavily involved with the local club, which boasted among the forwards one Con Houlihan, a scribe and a mighty man – a Chabal of his day, when boots for mighty men were not that easy to come by in those thin times of the 1950s.

In those years, too, my father would bring me to Lansdowne Road. A reflective observer, he noted moves that hadn't yet happened, understanding things about the line lying flat in defence, deep in attack – stuff to make a young boy feel important, knowledgeable, all grown up.

Those were the times of great Welsh teams but it was the male voice choirs who came with them that my father most marvelled at – raising the roof with their songs of pride and passion ... and of longing.

Hiraeth, the Welsh called it. *'Longing'* – longing for victory ... for homeland, for the indefinable heartland, where love or beauty or music – or the joy of the singing drop goal, can sometimes take us. For that, my father knew, is what Welsh rugby is.

He admired the French ... to a point – their flair, their panache, their lack of predictability. How, when we played them, we should turn the latter to our advantage, exploit their volatility of temperament – go at them ... rattle them.

When we moved to Mullingar, the disease came, rotted his legs. 'Kicks from playing that old rugby,' my mother always said.

Finally, he was transferred to the bank in Ballinasloe. He would be manager there – the prize at last achieved, my mother so proud of him. Then, in one of those savage ironies of life – the very night we arrived, he was rushed to Portiuncula Hospital in the town. The following morning we moved in to the Bank House – *his* house ... without him.

'Pericarditis' they said. You wouldn't think a word like that could kill a scoring virtuoso like him. But it did.

The night before he died, on my way to a basketball match, I dropped in to see him. He told me not to be delaying and wished me a good game. Not always easy with affection, that night he took my hand — held it a little while. 'You've always been loyal,' he said, close in to my eyes. I never felt less so than when I left him there, rushed to my game.

If *I* didn't know it was to be our last goodbye ... he did.

But on Friday next in Paris you will live again: be there guiding those long defensive kicks to touch; there behind the singing drop goal; or when, from afar out field, our out-half will sail the impossible ball high above the world and into the dizzy Parisian blue.

In my head, then, a story told of a young man who had, in the Mardyke once, kicked a penalty from inside his own half; how even his opponents had stood and cheered.

You will be there, I know, when wonder comes; that flickering moment between worlds, when the unseen gap opens — and the young out-half from Munster shape-shifts and shimmers through it like a god, untouched ... and untouchable.

And then, both you and he — out-halves together — will glide beyond time and space, seem to disappear, materialising only when boundaries are broken and that mercurial white line between Heaven and Earth is crossed. Then, will I see you in your time of beauty and youth, your virtuosity, your glorious, smiling moment.

And, as all of Ireland rises, as the Stade de France bursts its banks in a sea of green, I will turn to the young woman beside me ... and see in your granddaughter's eyes ... that *you* are smiling still.

WHERE BAGGOT STREET MEETS PEMBROKE STREET

Phil Herbert

Mapping time and place comes easily to me now. Mapping a person's life is not so easy. I'm walking down Lower Baggot Street, past Doheny & Nesbitt's along the road from O'Donoghues's pub then Toner's and I stop at 132 Baggot Street where Gaj's restaurant used to be. I allow myself to walk back a few decades. I stop at the early 1970s and I walk up the stairs, open the door into a Georgian dining room, where I first encounter the smiling face of the owner, Margaret Gaj. She is talking with her friend Lady Longford. It is a cold day and the red coal fire offers a warm welcome. It is lunchtime and all the solid mahogany tables are occupied. Mairead, the friendly waitress from Donegal, calls me over to a table by the window. There is one empty chair. Goulash is the special of the day. My first ever introduction to beef goulash. The menu is the cheapest in town; the customers the most exotic.

I sit beside a well-known poet from Northern Ireland, he is talking to a theatre critic. I am included in the chat. I listen to the music of different accents from the four corners of Ireland. There are freshly cut flowers on each table. I light my cigarette after my first course and order freshly-ground coffee. I listen to the debate at the table and watch the smoke curlicue towards the high ceiling along with the high-minded words. The aftertaste of the meal and the conversation revive and exhilarate me. On my way out, I notice posters announcing more than one protest meeting in the area.

I come down the stairs and face Dublin of 2007. I turn into Pembroke Street, where time has stood still, and walk by an unbroken line of Georgian houses and up to the Focus Theatre in Pembroke Place. This tiny theatre is forty years old. The small cottages that surrounded it forty years ago have been knocked and have now become fancy apartments. Again, I allow myself to travel back to the late 1960s, early 1970s. I enter the theatre and meet Deirdre O'Connell, her blue eyes sparkling beneath a crown of reddish-blonde hair draped on her head in a chignon.

The play is *Huis Clos* by Jean Paul Sarte and I remember Mary Wilson and Sabina Coyne's brilliant performances. The audience is transported, the atmosphere electric. At the interval, the little coffee room back stage is decked with flowers and the walls are covered with black and white photos of scenes from plays by Ibsen, Strindberg, Chekhov, Tennesse Williams, Doris Lessing. Photos of actors like Mary Elizabeth Burke-Kennedy, Tom Hickey, Joan Bergin and, of course, Deirdre herself. The big portrait of Deirdre by Brian Bourke takes pride of place.

I'm back to reality again. Deirdre is no more. She is sadly missed. In June 2001, she made her final exit. But her Focus lives on. It was Deirdre's vision and dedication in the early years that made it possible for the Focus to survive. The building itself was bought with Deirdre's personal savings and the help of her husband, the late Luke Kelly. She introduced the Stanislavski method of acting to Ireland and taught aspiring and experienced actors on Saturdays and Sundays for a ridiculously low fee. There were many years when she struggled to survive but always put the theatre first. When the theatre was in danger of closing its doors, she would go to work in New York. The money she earned was sunk back into the Focus. Deirdre provided a rare theatre experience in Dublin back then. She not only acted, but directed and taught and mapped the route to the skills needed to provide good theatre.

I make contact with Margaret Gaj, now eighty-eight years of age and as passionate as ever. She had just heard news on RTÉ Radio I's *Liveline* about the condemning of the six most dangerous species of dogs. She showed me photos of her two sons when they were around four and six years of age playing with the family pet, a Doberman Pincher. She said they are very affectionate animals and the fault always lies with the owner and the environment.

She showed me a book called *Monday's at Gaj's: The Story of the Irish Women's Liberation Movement* by Anne Stopper, published in 2006. In it,

I learned for the first time that Margaret Gaj was one of the founder members of the movement. The group met in the room over her restaurant from 1970. The first chapter in the book entitled 'Not Just a Restaurant' covers the story of her life during those days. It pays tribute to the enormous generosity and compassion of the woman in whose restaurant customers were invited to eat without payment, the waitresses knowing not to give them a bill. Her most defining characteristic was her sense of equality and social justice. She had many political affiliations. She was a great friend of Dr Noël Browne. She was instrumental in the creation of the Prisoners' Rights Organisation in 1973 along with Joe Costello. Deirdre O'Connell was a regular visitor to Gaj's restaurant, after all, she had only to walk up Pembroke Street from her beloved theatre in Pembroke Place.

These two women had a lot in common. Both had Irish ancestry. They came to Ireland as young women where they embraced a vision of excellence, established a setting and opened their doors to those seeking the best food and art for mind and body.

THUNDER AND LIGHTNING FINALS

Leo Cullen

'The Thunder and Lightning final of 1939,' my father would say. 'Cork versus Kilkenny, it rained and it rained.' He would shake imaginary rain off his shoulders for emphasis as he described that game to me. And I would picture him on the open expanses of the old Cusack Stand. 'Thunder and lightning,' he would say, 'but not a soul left the ground until the final whistle, so gripping was that game that Kilkenny in the end won by a single point.' And he would continue his reverie, falling into a sadder note, 'I remember walking up Grafton Street after that match. There were people standing in shop doorways, white-faced with fear, cowering from the sound of that thunder. And do you know who they were?'

'Who were they, daddy?' I would ask.

'They were Poles. Polish people. Airlifted to Dublin from Warsaw, escaping from the Nazi bombings. First casualties of war: the children looking up into the parents' faces for comfort, but all they saw was fear.

Oh, my father told important All-Ireland stories; he was important on atmosphere.

'You were born in the early hours of a Sunday in 1948,' he would tell me, 'in which Waterford, led by John Keane, brought home the McCarthy Cup across the Siur for the very first time.'

Now, wasn't that a great thing for any young lad to know … on what day of the week he had been born! In that way, my father unwittingly filled in a lot of my early curriculum vitae for me.

And I don't know if it was that revelation which started my own fascination with All-Irelands and the teams that played them. But what I do know is I can name the winners of every All-Ireland final going back to the year of my birth: Waterford, 1948, Tipperary, 1949 and so on … phalanx after phalanx of heroic fifteens.

Some dates shine out above others: 1957 – a great new Waterford team had emerged on the scene. They were back in an All-Ireland final again, facing the craft of Kilkenny. That date shone out because, on that year, I had got something new. My mother had died a few years previously and, that year, I got a new mother. My Tipperary father had remarried. She came from County Kilkenny, rural Kilkenny, a Rose of Mooncoin. And she had a sister living in Waterford, married to a townie and that sister was loyal to her adopted town and to townie life. Waterford and Kilkenny: I had married into one of the great rivalries of hurling. Unmercifully, those two chided and teased one another over the fortunes of their favourites. The victorious one would crow and tease, the vanquished would be close to tears.

In 1957, they travelled to Dublin, those sisters, and it was the turn of my step-mother to tease. Unemotional woman as I had estimated her, she brought home to our house that night something of the atmosphere of Croke Park. Her hair stood wild, there was colour in her cheeks; her eyes danced. She filled our house with an afterglow, just as my father had done with talk of his Thunder and Lightning All-Ireland.

Nineteen fifty-nine came, a hot summer in which the country's wells went dry and my family went to the sea at Clonea into October days on which we came home to milk the cows in the dark. The blue and white flags fluttered in the Deise that year. The team of Tom Cheastey, God rest him, carried home the cup that Waterford had first carried home on the day of my birth. That year, it was the turn of my step-mother to show her tears.

Came 1963, the third and last All-Ireland encounter between those two. The sisters travelled again. Waterford scored six goals. And from where I listened at our kitchen radio in neutral Tipperary, I heard the clash of each goal in Croke Park. I heard my Auntie Mary scream six times. Kilkenny did not score as many goals but Eddie Keher scored the points and I heard my mother's more muted exhortations high in the Hogan Stand. Her team prevailed that day. What a game.

And here we go again … well not quite. And it is to my father I must return, to introduce the team who stand against Kilkenny in 2007 – his most heroic phalanx of them all. He never tired talking of them, and of the man from Aghane. Mick Mackey, his own personal hero. He described him to me, 'Barrel-chested and fearless, he would go through anything. He would put his head where another man wouldn't put his hurley.' I wondered how a barrel could go through anything, but my father's enthusiasm carried my imagination. 'Munster hurling,' he said, 'close, tight, pull on the ground and in the air – is best typified by Limerick. They were the team of the 1940s.'

Yes, and now Limerick are back again, with that blend of city grit and Golden Vale extravagance. They too have had their many clashes with lissom Kilkenny. Today begins a new era.

So let there be once again on the stands rivals shouting support: the heart-in-the-mouth roars of Auntie Marys and the quieter exhortations of Mothers. I can hear them. It is happening again. And I can see them: the stories of my father – the Polish immigrants and their children who were with us then and now are again. The Thunder and Lightning finals. Let this one begin!

A LIMERICK HERO

Mae Leonard

I didn't know him back then when the Limerick Minor Team won the All-Ireland Hurling Championship in 1958 – in fact, I had never seen a hurling match in my life. Coming from The Parish – The Isle – in Limerick city, I was heavily into swimming and rugby and rowing. Hurling didn't even enter the equation.

I didn't know him throughout the early years, when his hurling skills were developed to the point where he was one of the chosen few to wear the green and white of his county. But, thanks to my mother-in-law, I have been afforded the privilege of sharing her pride, excitement and devotion to his, and Limerick's, sporting career of some fifty years ago. I have inherited her scrapbook. A scrapbook of everything to do with the hurling career I really know very little about.

But it is not just the scrapbook itself. It is the way it is lovingly put together – or I should say – not put together – nothing is in proper sequence – there are no dates on the yellowed newspaper clippings and there are reports of matches between teams from clubs that have long since faded away. There are action pictures that any press photographer would be proud to claim. There are home-made badges and paper hats all stuck between the pages of the huge old diary of 1958. Now, leafing through it, some of the pasted items become dislodged and in my mind's eye I can see her, his mother, mixing a bowl of flour-and-water paste. It is probably late at night when she has the eight of them asleep. Then she takes the most recent newspaper match reports and pictures, carefully cuts around them, applies the paste and smoothes them onto the pages with her son's face scowling up at her. He never seemed to smile in those pictures.

The one I like best is a mid-air clash with a Waterford forward when he clears the sliotar away from the goalmouth. I've heard Limerick followers describe him as talented, strong, reliable, always first to the ball, solid and skilful in holding his half-back position. But I think the best description of him is in an article by An Mangaire Súgach – Manachin Seoighe – in the *Limerick Leader* sometime in the early 1960s. Manachin reports of attending a Limerick hurling match when he overheard a supporter remark, 'Boy that Leonard is a quare hawk', and, depending on the way you look at it, that's admiration indeed.

By the time I met him and we started to see each other regularly, he was playing on the Limerick Senior Team. And then came the time he had to meet my parents. My mother suggested that I bring him to tea one Sunday evening and, horror of horrors, he was late. When he finally arrived, he had a black eye, three stitches over his right eyebrow and his knuckles were raw and bloodied. However, he was welcomed and, over mother's high tea, my father – a rugby follower – pulled out all the stops to discuss the greats of current-day hurling – Tom McGarry and Dermot Kelly of Limerick; Jimmy Smyth of Clare; Donie Nealon and Tony Wall of Tipperary; Pat Fitzgerald and Jimmy Brohan of Cork. Things went just fine and my father would joke about it afterwards in his father-of-the-bride speech, 'When this fellow came across the bridge into the Parish famed for rugby carrying a hurley, everyone stared at it and asked, 'What's that?'

FROM MORTAL TO MYTH: GARY McMAHON

Cyril Kelly

Did I realise, I wonder, on that September Sunday of 1962 that my last Listowel summer had just elapsed, that the final summer of my youth had just passed by? As I strolled around the streets of the town that morning, did I realise that life was about to change irrevocably? Within a year, I would have done my Leaving Cert. I would be departing for Dublin, taking the first tentative steps towards adult life. Was it this twilight zone between Blake's *Songs of Innocence* and *Songs of Experience* which enabled me to turn a local mortal into myth in the space of forty seconds that very afternoon?

On that All-Ireland Sunday, when Kerry took the field against Roscommon, a local lad, a lad who lived a few doors down from myself made history. Within forty seconds of the throw-in, Gary McMahon had scored a goal, the fastest ever in the All-Ireland annals.

For months, the town had been preparing for the races. They took place on the week immediately after the All-Ireland. Known as The Harvest Festival, the very name was redolent of a bountiful countryside; of bog and meadowlands around north Kerry. Rails of turf trailed scents of darkness through the August town; stately domes of hay blessed the streets with the scent of light. For months, Jackeen Godfrey, reeking of turps, gasping with painter's colic, had pumped his blowlamp throughout the town. It was a dragon spitting lilac fire. But then, with oily linseed smells, he magicked in his wake a pristine town.

Night, noon and morning, Mosheen Carmody, ensconced on a cushion of straw at the front of his dray, bobbed from the railway yard. Half-tierces of porter sloshed around him to the silvery tune of the chuckling harness. At the back gate of every pub, Mosheen toppled casks from the cart on to his cushion of straw. With a well-aimed boot he sent them barrelling in along the flagstoned yards, rumbling like thunder, disappearing one by one into the cockroach sheds.

Tadhg Brennan, long tongs in hand, is standing beside the fire at the back of the forge. On a plinth of blocks, the fire is level with his hip. Crunching another shoe into the black bed of slack, Tadhg reaches for the hickory bellows handle. In the darkness, his face reflects gushes of firelight. His chomped lips are pink against his soot-grained skin.

Roger True Blue totes another sack of sawdust from the mill. He's bound for John B. Keane's decent pub. And none better than J. B. himself – me oul segotia – to proffer a reward; one more creamy pint, Roger True Blue's elixir of life. And down by the river, a wagon train of Tinkers is circling in primary colours. Canvas covers baskets of trinkets, holy pictures, miraculous medals and sheafs of ballads to sell and sing during race week.

And into our expectant town, a town stacked with crubeens and mutton pies, stroll the troupe of autumn players. The strong man gnawing six inch nails; nifty chancers complete with butter box and three-card tricks, tic-tac men and the Pecker Dunne, serenading the bebuntinged streets with 'The Moon Behind the Hill'.

Finally, McElligots of Castleisland come to erect loudspeakers on telegraph poles throughout the town. Great grey foghorns of speakers that will broadcast Radio Listowel for the week. But before 'Bridie Gallagher' or 'The Gypsy Rover' or 'She Wore Red Feathers on her Hooley Hooley Skirt' can come through those speakers, the All-Ireland Final of 1962 is relayed thoughout the town. Micheál O'Hehir's heroic tableaux pitched the length and breadth of each deserted street.

Standing that Sunday in wonder and awe outside my own hall door, lace curtains ballooning softly through nearby windows, I saw Croke Park more clearly than if I were there. Echoes and reverberations had three or four simultaneous versions of the National Anthem pulsing in the air. And O'Hehir was welcoming Radio Brazzaville and immigrants from Boston to our town. Then, almost catching me off guard, the ball was thrown in. I could see it, could see it clearly, a dark orb rising in the sky. The blaring commentary bounced off John R's shop, ricocheted across the road to resonate from Farrell's wall, suspending the ball aloft interminably. At last, it dropped into a thicket of grasping hands. Some giant in blue and gold emerged, clutching it to his chest, booted it towards the Kerry goal. But a quick clearance landed it back outside John R's, where Kerry got a free.

From O'Connell's unerring boot, Micheál O'Hehir described the magnificent trajectory of the ball. It sailed over bunting and strings of coloured lights to land amid a cluster of players on the edge of the Roscommon square. And there, it hobbled and it bounced and, at last, broke free, right into the path of a stalwart in green and gold. And he, delirium of deliriums, punched it straight into the net. Forty seconds since the game began, the fastest goal in history, by Gary McMahon.

As O'Hehir's voice was still ringing from the rooftops, I looked at McMahon's house. A few doors down from my own. Brothers in school with me. Taught by his father Bryan, The Master. But in that forty seconds, in that moment caught between a time of innocence and experience, Gary McMahon, a young man not much older than myself, a man I'd seen playing for our street, The Ashes, could with one flick of the wrist, launch himself from ordinary mortal status to take on the mantle of myth.

HENRIK IBSEN (1828–1906)

Mary O'Donnell

I saw the former Abbey actress Kate Flynn play a luminous Hedda Gabler back in the late 1970s, and, since then, have never ceased to be interested in Henrik Ibsen, who died one hundred years ago in May of this year, 2006.

Born in 1828, this Norwegian playwright was to change the shape of European drama forever, introducing audiences to natural-sounding dialogue and realistic-looking situations. Although he adhered to the classical unities of time and place, he avoided the stiffness of the soliloquy and happy endings when such outcomes could only be illogical. This was, at the time, dangerous material, the like of which had not been seen before inside Norway or, indeed, outside of it. Ibsen did not achieve the recognition he deserved until he went into exile in 1864, spending time in Italy and Germany, producing *Brand* and *Peer Gynt*, two dramatic poems which eventually astonished his compatriots and made him famous.

But before all that, young Henrik Ibsen had grown up in poverty, after his father's fortunes failed. He knew all about living in humble quarters, about thinking small and eating humble pie, and suffered many privations. Keen to be a painter, he was discouraged and forced to take on an apprenticeship at an apothecary shop. Naturally, this didn't suit him and, influenced by the revolutionary wave spreading across Europe in the 1840s, he turned to writing poetry. Tired of small-town living, frustrated, ambitious, Ibsen finally went to Christiania in 1850 where he eked out an existence in journalism. But he had friends and, in the end, they got him an appointment as 'stage-poet' in Bergen. Five years later, Ibsen returned to Christiania as artistic director of the new Norwegian theatre which had set itself up in direct rivalry with the town's old theatre. It was a disaster. Rebuff after rebuff, bankruptcy for the theatre, Ibsen was frequently driven to fall back on his painting to earn the price of a meal.

Around this time, he made repeated efforts to get a civil-list pension, but this, too, was refused him, most likely on the grounds that he had unstintingly satirised officialdom in his writings and now they were going to get even with the young dramatist.

And so Ibsen followed that great tradition of artists who go into exile and, with the success of *Peer Gynt* outside Norway, people at home eventually sat up and paid attention. The long-applied for civil pension could no longer be denied and Ibsen's time of penury was over. He began to write the series of prose plays on which his wider reputation rests, the last of them published in 1900, when their author was seventy-two.

After 1866, his work mainly took the form of political or social satire, for which he found no shortage of themes in the narrow provincialism of Norwegian town life. *A Doll's House* was written when Ibsen was fifty-one. Shortly afterwards, it was performed in Copenhagen. It was first staged in London in 1889 and in Paris in 1894; subsequently, it has been widely translated and the part of Nora, its heroine, has been included in the repertory of many a famous actress.

In Dublin, I remember Ingrid Craigie performing Nora, as clearly as I recall Kate Flynn's Hedda Gabler. Both plays seemed strikingly modern in tone and theme, and in the late 1970s and early 1980s, they struck an obvious chord of recognition for young women like me. They displayed the ills and inequalities that so many Irish women were at that time conscious of. Nora was a gem of a part for any actress to play. Her character is at once glorious and bored. She is intelligent but fragmented, revealing a life without focus that in the end is totally destructive.

A Doll's House and *Hedda Gabler* were successes *before* feminism and they remain so today, with brilliant female character roles, where you feel that these are real people and not just appendages in a mostly male cast. The playwright was greatly concerned that in his contemporary dramas the audience, and readers, should witness trains of events that could just as easily have happened to *them*.

This required that his characters spoke and behaved naturally and that the situations had the stamp of everyday life about them. Monologues, asides and stiltedness were ruled out. This carried on through Ibsen's later work, such as *An Enemy of the People* in which Dr Stockmann, Chief Medical Officer of a tourist town, opposes the opening of the municipal baths because he has discovered pollutants in the water. Steven Spielberg's film *Jaws*, was based in part on this play. Instead of polluting the water with a toxic acent, Spielberg polluted it with a gigantic shark. In *Jaws* the residents ignore all evidence of danger in their midst, aided and abetted by a corrupt mayor, just as in *An Enemy of the People*, the advice of the idealistic and educated doctor is thwarted at every turn. The Hollywood version of *An Enemy of the People*, directed by George Schaefer and filmed in 1978, was never released. It starred Steve McQueen.

Ibsen returned to Christiania in 1891 with a European reputation. He somewhat cynically enjoyed the hero-worship showered on him by those who had formerly dismissed him – but enjoy it he did. In 1889, his seventieth birthday was enthusiastically celebrated and the following year a statue of him was erected outside the Christiania theatre. And the final accolade, when he died after a long illness in May 1906? He was given a public funeral.

STANDING ON MY HEAD

Chuck Kruger

Hoping that what woke me up would wake my students too, and believing that you don't teach only a subject but who you are yourself, I had no hesitation as a secondary school literature teacher to be passionate about the novels and poems and plays I assigned my students. And I tell stories. Pose riddles. Have anybody late to class tell the biggest lie as to why, the bigger the better. Kids weren't late often and, when they were, we had fun.

All the paper grading, however, required much of my evening and weekend time, until I discovered a way to shorten my written comments. For each paper, instead of my usual paragraph, I finally learned how to concentrate my evaluations. No matter how weak a paper was, I'd comment on its best quality in one sentence – and, in my only other sentence, I'd constructively comment on the paper's weakest characteristic. And no matter how good a paper was, I'd do the same thing. Two sentences, strength and weakness. At home, I began to have more time to play with my own children.

Realising that I learned more when I had to teach a class than when I simply sat in a class, I'd have each student become responsible for two classes a year. I also encouraged my students to ask questions – and reassured them that sometimes the more silly or even stupid the question might seem to them, that those were the very questions that most often got to the heart of the matter.

One day, having just finished reading aloud a poem by T. S. Eliot or Allen Ginsberg — I can't remember which — a student raised his hand and asked, 'But, Sir, how does your archetypal poet *see* this world?'

I felt stumped, didn't know what to say, and remained quiet for several minutes, suspense building. Then I did something I'd never done before — and never since. I removed my shoes and crawled onto the large sturdy oval wooden seminar table, right to its middle. Surrounded by twelve utterly quiet students (in that international day school in Switzerland we never allowed more than twenty in any one class), I lowered my head to the table, raised my knees to rest on my elbows, and then slowly, tentatively, lifted my legs toward the ceiling. While standing on my head, and wondering if I would ever more be seen as an utter idiot, forgotten pens, pencils, car keys and loose change falling out of my pockets, I waited for the silence to return, and then, from some up-side-down somewhere else, said, 'A poet sees exactly the same world you see, but from a different perspective.'

I kept standing on my head for a few more scarily silent minutes, then lowered myself to the table, collected my belongings and crawled back to my chair.

THE BAKING OF BREAD

Patricia Clarke

I grew up within an austere Calvinist sect in the North of Ireland where contact with the world at large was pared to a minimum and all celebration strictly taboo. We marked neither birthdays nor anniversaries, observed neither Christmas nor Easter and all forms of entertainment were shunned as 'instruments of the Devil' which, as we well knew, were 'an abomination to the Lord'. Eating or drinking in public places was strictly forbidden, as was any form of contact with people who were not members of our sect. 'In this world though not of it', was the abiding admonition to anyone intrepid enough to show curiosity about – never mind make any connection with – the world in which we lived. We endured a relentless round of daily Scripture readings and prayer meetings while Sunday – or the Lord's Day as we called it – brought a marathon scrutiny of our sinful, worthless, wicked ways. And so we dwelt in dreary isolation as we sojourned in our Vale of Tears, within the Valley of the Shadow of Death.

But there was one event in this round of unrelieved drabness that brought the merest glimmer of drama to our lives. This was the early Sunday morning service known as the Breaking of Bread which formed the individual's weekly covenant of faith with the Divine. By 6 a.m. on the Lord's Day, flitting like moths through the darkness before dawn, a handful of men clad in sober suits and women whose hair had never felt the snip of scissors gathered in a plain clapboard meeting house. We sat in two concentric circles; women seated in the outer, men in the inner row around a linen-draped table set with a silver chalice and a willow basket containing a loaf of bread. Heads bowed, we waited in silence until at some unspoken signal a senior member would rise to his feet and pray sonorously over the bread.

With his bare hands, he would then tear the loaf asunder and pass the basket from hand to hand so that all present could pluck a morsel from the soft crumb of the loaf. A further impassioned prayer was spoken over the chalice of wine which then passed from mouth to mouth.

Years later, after I had severed my links with the sect and made my escape to Spain, I found myself living near a baker's shop in an old quarter of Madrid. It was on languid mornings when sunlight streamed over the rooftops and the chirping of sparrows mingled with the murmur of voices in the sunlit square, intoxicated with the rich scent of fresh bread rising on the air, that I learned to forge my own point of connection with the people in this world around me. Here, I learned the rhythm of friendship, experienced the sheer pleasure of people gathered to share conversation, laughter, life.

This is a country where bread forms part of every meal. You break off a crust and dip it into a glass of wine as you wait, with a rising sense of anticipation for the food to arrive. You linger at table long after the food has been eaten, having mopped up the juices on your plate with a morsel of bread. And all the time relishing the lazy buzz of conversation and outbursts of laughter – that easy, uplifting contact with people that was spurned so strenuously in my childhood.

Now that I live on the edge of the Burren, with a daughter of fitful appetite, I have taken to baking my own bread. I have grown to savour the heady aroma of yeast gently dissolving in water as I sift flour in great powdery drifts and add a glug of olive oil, its fruity green scent recalling warmer lands to the south. I knead and steadily work the mixture to a smooth, elastic dough as soft and sensuous as flesh. Then, silently, the dough swells to a glorious frothy puffball – by the same mysterious process that was discovered in ancient Egypt and still works its simple magic today. Until, at last, the warm, delectable, celebratory scent of newly-baked bread fills the heart of my home.

These days, friends drop in for a coffee, a chat and leave with a warm, crusty loaf. In a sort of informal barter, I sometimes swap a newly-baked loaf with my neighbour for half a dozen freshly-laid eggs. A loaf becomes a thank you for minding the dog or feeding the cats. The simplest of meals is transformed into a feast when you add freshly-baked bread. And any gathering at which fresh bread is produced becomes a banquet, a feast of conversation, laughter and life.

And that very moment at which the crisp golden crust emerges from the oven in all its glory forms, for me, a private ecstasy of passion, my own personal expression of covenant with this world. Through this magical rite, I can now freely connect with my fellow beings. I am in this world and very much of it. And that for me is the stuff of life itself.

BÉ SEÁN Ó RÍORDÁIN
AN FEAR

Liam Ó Muirthile

Bé Seán Ó Ríordáin an fear. Pé bóithre, pé ceantar samhlaíochta a bhí siúlta aige ina chuid dánta, b'sheo féna hata anois é anuas ceann de shráideanna na cathrach. Feairín fáiscthe, tochraiste. An file ar an dtairseach againn féin ag triall ar lón sa Five Star Supermarket. Cé chuimhneodh ar an Five Star don lón ach file ag déanamh ceap magaidh den saol, nó máithreacha? Cuma an cheardaí amuigh don lá air, na súile bíogtha úd ina cheann, bheifeá ag tnúth le caint éigin uaidh, léargas a bhainfeadh barrthuisle as an saol. Fonn rógaireachta air, agus ráfla á scaipeadh aige, go bhfuair a leithéid seo de phearsa phoiblí bás obann. Bheadh an ráfla cogainte, slogtha i gcaitheamh an lóin ag daoine agus chloisfeadh sé féin an leagan díleáite de thar n-ais ag cúinne sráide éigin fé mar gur scéala tur te é. Léargas ab ea an rógaireacht leis, is dócha.

Baineann oiread tábhachta le pearsa an fhile, le linn ár n-óige, agus a bhaineann le saothar an fhile. Níos mó go minic. Focal mór sna Seascaidí ab ea *saoirse*. Bhí sé i mbéal gach éinne. Bhí sé le clos amach as siopa ceirníní Hennessy's sa tsráid chéanna a bhí siúlta ag an Ríordánach. Sheol sé isteach ar na tonnta aeir. Pé tiúineáil a bhí déanta ag an Ríordánach ar na haintéiní aige, bhí sé ar an minicíocht chéanna leis an ré agus a chasadh féin bainte aige as. Ringeáil *scillingsmaointe* agus *snabsmaointe* le rithim na *blues* i Me and Bobby McGee. Chaithfí a seanchulaith a bhaint anuas den Ghaeilge, agus *denim* a chur uirthi. Seán

Ó Ríordáin athstruchtúraithe ag caitheamh Levis. Bhainfí casadh as línte eile dá chuid … *Ní ar bheith ann, Ár n-aire ár mbeann, Ach ar gan bheith ann a bhrath.* Nach aige a bhí an fhírinne nuair a dúirt nach raibh istigh i gceart ach Suibhne Geilt? Gealtachas an freagra. Tír na nÓg. An saol anchruthach a chur trína chéile féachaint cén cruth a dhéanfaí de. Dul ar an ól, ar an ngal agus an domhan a fheiscint soiléir, nite ina nádúr féin. Triail a bhaint as an mé seo, an mé úd, féachaint cén mise a dhéanfaí den iomlán dá ndéanfaí go deo. Saol fé chló agus athchló síoraí a bhí sé a thairiscint, daoine ag malartú a gcló féin le hainmhithe, solas á shlogadh, an oíche ag léimt sna scamhóga, cait ag crú gréine nó ag titim ina gceathanna de réir na haimsire, fear á fheistiú amach i dtreabhsar focal, conas go ndeirimid an rud ná rabhamair chun a rá?, leamhain ag síneadh a sciathán le fairsingeacht ainglí aníos as an aigne chomhfhiosach, fóthoinn. Cén treoir a thugann sé dúinn? Cén bóthar atá le leanúint isteach sa tír aineoil? Ligeann sé a rún linn:

Téir faobhar na faille siar tráthnóna gréine go Corca
Dhuibhne…
Sin é do dhoras,
Dún Chaoin fé sholas an tráthnóna,
Buail is osclófar
D'intinn féin is do chló ceart.

Ní raibh ann, ar deireadh, ach leathdoras. D'oscail an leath eile amach i gCalifornia – portach Chalifornia mar a dúirt an bhean i gConamara ag féachaint uaithi ar an gceo brothaill anuas ar an bportach agus an baile i bhfad ó bhaile.

Saghas fiabhrais ab ea an rud ar fad. Fiabhras aigne agus choirp in éineacht. Ceann de na rudaí nár thuigeamar agus sinn óg, chomh breoite agus a bhí an fear. Níl le déanamh ach an bheathaisnéis liteartha le Seán Ó Coileáin a léamh. An dialann. An eitinn. An mhíthrócaire. An beannú uafáis ag freastalaí le tráidire mugaí do na seilí, ceann de na maidineacha in óispidéal: *Good morning, my tubercular friends.*

Gnéithe aiceanta an fhiabhrais atá againn sa dán *Fiabhras.* Réigiún sainiúil Ríordánach lena aeráid ardbhrú. Na línte mar a bheadh líníocht déanta le pionsal agus iad ag titim ina mbuillí rithimiúla leathstadúla agus lánstadúla. An pheirspictíocht, an greim ar an saol á chailliúint, agus an fócas á fháil thar n-ais lena mhéar a chrochadh in aghaidh na

spéire. É gafa trí aoitheó an fhiabhrais áirithe seo. Na nótaí a bhreac sé
lá sa dialann i dtaobh ba a fheiscint go neafaiseach, á bhfeistiú anois ina
n-íomhánna a ardaíonn an dán amach as gnéithe aiceanta an fhiabhrais
go dtí diminsean eile ar fad. Filíocht ar deireadh, is ea dul sa bhfiabhras,
sa tír aineoil, é a mhapáil go sainiúil as an nua, agus a rá leo siúd nár
chuaigh fós ann conas 'tá. B'fhéidir go n-aithneoidís féin na comharthaí,
lá. Á rá, bhíos anso cheana le Seán Ó Ríordáin.

FIABHRAS

Tá sléibhte na leapan mós ard,
Tá breoiteacht 'na brothall ina lár,
Is fada an t-aistear urlár,
Is na mílte is na mílte i gcéin
Tá suí agus seasamh sa saol.

Atáimid i gceantar braillín,
Ar éigean más cuimhin linn cathaoir,
Ach bhí tráth sar ba mhachaire sinn,
In aimsir choisíochta fadó,
Go mbímis chomh hard le fuinneog.

Tá pictiúir ar an bhfalla ag at,
Tá an fráma imithe ina lacht,
Ceal creidimh ní feidir é bhac,
Tá nithe ag druidim fém dhéin,
Is braithim ag titim an saol.

Tá ceantar ag taisteal ón spéir,
Tá comharsanacht suite ar mo mhéar,
Dob fhuirist dom breith ar shéipéal,
Tá ba ar an mbóthar ó thuaidh,
Is níl ba na síoraíochta chomh ciúin.
(Seán Ó Ríordáin: *Brosna*)

LOOKING WEST

Bláithín Ní Liatháin

Room 202 in Kylemore College in Ballyfermot, on the second floor, west-facing, has been my classroom for the past ten years. Originally, Coláiste Lorcáin and a product of the 1960s, its only architectural merit is its four over-large windows.

Directly outside these windows is a row of poplar trees; forty years on and their branches reach higher than the roof of the school building.

These trees have swayed in winds, have greened, have coloured, lain bare and in March and April when morale is low, have budded, have leaved, have heralded the arrival of summer, of June, of July, of August.

Together, the students and I have been distracted from our lesson by the nest-building of magpies; each day for some days we watched their bringing of little bits and pieces and watched the intricacies of their weaving these bits and pieces into their little home high up off the ground just outside the window.

Beyond the trees spread out in an indecernable pattern are the grey-green roves of Lally, of Decies, of Inagh, of Spiddel, of 'me gaff', 'me nanna's', 'the Gala'. Once upon a time a picture house, now snooker hall, the Gala is the centre of the universe that is Ballyfermot. Everything, every direction is 'just up from the Gala', 'd'ja know the Gala?', 'when ja come to the Gala, well go on straight past the Gala...'

And why these Galway names in an Eastern place? A Galway builder planted Claddagh where there is no Cladach; Kylemore where there is no Coill Mhór. Dublin Corporation imposed a people on these lands, a people who know not the names before the Galway names who know not Ballyfermot. Is it Baile Formaid or Baile Dhiarmada or Baile Thormaid?

And why California Hills and why the Ranch? Was it because of the Westerns watched or because of the alien, rural setting of the houses built when slums were cleared and suburbs created by country men for city people? Is the Killeen Road now no more than a factory-lined mess? The road that once led to the *Cillín* in which were buried, in the sanctuary of walls of the ancient church, those born to another life who died before being baptised. Men walked this road by night, this road of the dead, with their lifeless bundles hidden, wrapped and ready for burial in the days when every second child born in Dublin died.

Go straight on past the Gala leaving Ballyfermot, Grange Cross, Cherry Orchard, Balgaddy behind and look west; west into the mountains that rise up to encircle Dublin – thus far and no farther shall the city go. The mountains that are different every day, some days blue, some days so green that fields can be seen, some days a purple-coloured mystery, some days snow-capped, some days a white wonderous winterland, fully snow-covered.

Many an evening, I have remained behind after the last bell of the day has rung and sat and watched a September sun setting in an orange splendour on these westerly Wicklow hills, as she has set long ages before the Corpo houses, long before the Gala, long, long before all of them.

OCTOBER

GATHERING CHESTNUTS

Paddy Murray

It's nice to finish a career as you started it. In my case, my rugby career ended some thirty-three years after it began. And, in a scene worthy of the *Twilight Zone*, it ended exactly as it began – with the referee pointing to the dressing room and telling me to get myself there forthwith. I dispute both decisions.

Let me start with the first one. It was in Willow Park school. I had proudly lined out in my blue and white hoops for the first time. Willow Under 9s were taking on their arch rivals from St Mary's.

It was a fresh autumn day, I remember. We were winning. They scored a consolation try. We retreated behind the posts for the conversion which was duly missed. And then fourteen of our team ran to the halfway line for the kick off. I, alone, remained behind the posts.

It was, as I said, autumn. The leaves were brown. And the ground behind the goal was covered in fallen chestnuts. It was too good a moment to miss.

I mean, we'd won the game. There were only minutes left. And I felt it would not have any influence on the result if I were to take the opportunity to stuff my pockets with conkers. I was sure I was doing nothing wrong.

Brother Luke, however, took a divergent view. He believed, mistakenly I was certain, that collecting conkers during a game was against the laws of rugby. He duly sent me off in disgrace.

In the intervening years, I happily played rugby having studied the laws to ensure that no such fate would befall me again.

I was, of course, correct about the laws in relation to collecting conkers and Brother Luke was wrong. Nowhere is it written that collecting conkers, during a game is an offence. In fact, it is perfectly legal to collect conkers during a line out, scrum or maul, though I must admit, it is not something I have seen happen since at any level.

If they wanted it to be an offence, it would be. The laws of rugby run to some 30,000 words when you include myriad subclauses, additional regulations and referee instructions. Law 19, subsection 13, for example, states:

> A player not carrying the ball is offside if, after the ball has touched a player or the ground, that player steps in front of the ball, unless tackling (or trying to tackle) an opponent. Any attempt to tackle must start from that player's side of the ball.

I hope that's clear.

Having digested at least the important laws, I began a memorable career. The first try – in the snow – on the front pitch at St. Mary's in Rathmines. The match-winning try against Pres Bray on the pitch near the tennis courts in Willow. The fumble on the line against St Michael's that resulted in their last minute try and our only defeat of the year at Under 13s. The moment Fr Nudie Boyle told me I was dropped by the junior cup team. The heady heights of the thirds at senior level. The third Es in the club. And the World Golden Oldies in Dublin in 1993.

And that's where it all ended. On a muddy field in Belfield. In ignominy.

The first two matches were grand. The CYM Olden Golden Stars, as we were called, walked them. When it came to the third and final match, I was asked if I would like the honour of being captain against the Australian side. Brilliant, I thought, though I did wonder why some team-mates were sniggering.

The Aussies emerged, brick outhouses to a man, with two former internationals in their side. It didn't augur well. And it only got worse when the referee arrived and bid us all 'G'day', in a broad antipodean accent.

He gave us nothing. Not a scrum, not a penalty, nothing. It was all too much. I cracked.

I can't remember what I called him. I think one of the words was 'biased'. The other was something along the lines of 'cad' or 'bounder'. Maybe a bit stronger. He wasn't impressed.

And for the second time in my long career, I was asked to leave the pitch. I walked the long walk to the sideline, my head hung low.

In shame? Not one bit of it. It was autumn again. And I was looking for chestnuts.

THE DEVIL WALKS

Fachtna Ó Drisceoil

> Now over Polegate vastly sets the sun;
> Dark rise the Downs from darker looking elms,
> And out of Southern railway trains to tea
> Run happy boys down various Station Roads,
> Satchels of homework jogging on their backs,
> So trivial and so healthy in the shade
> Of these enormous Downs

For me, John Betjeman's poem, 'Original Sin on the Sussex Coast', always brings to mind the seemingly innocent scene of two boys playing football on the lawn behind a large Victorian-era house. One of them, tall, handsome and fair-haired, about ten years old. The other, a bit older, dark-haired, large and overweight, but strong. But there is another boy here, hunched glumly on a garden seat at the back of the house, fair-haired also but smaller than the others, watching them warily and making no move to join them. It is my ten-year-old self.

While the other boys are bathed in sunshine, I am in the shadow of the house, its redbrick walls looming high behind me. The tall fair-haired boy we will call Edward, not his real name, the son of friends of my parents. My mother works outside the home, so I am often collected from school by Edward's mother and spend much time in his house. My parents are very grateful to Edward's mother for this. The other boy is Robert, a neighbour of Edward's. I can tell from the recurrent whispered conferences on the lawn that they are plotting against me, so I ignore their pleas for me to join them. They put on an obviously staged display of laughter and enjoyment in an attempt to entice me, but still I hold out. They even appeal to Edward's mother in the kitchen, but she doesn't intervene.

Finally, they abandon their pretence and make their way over to me. 'Come with us or else,' they command, their fists threatening, their voices menacing. I could have shouted out to get the mother's attention, but I didn't. Meekly and fearfully, I surrendered myself to their custody, allowing them to escort me down to the back of the garden. Perhaps Edward's mother saw us and smiled at the seemingly benign scene of childhood friendship. They forced me to climb a wall with them into the back garden of Robert's house. There was an old shed here, one door allowing access from the garden, the other opening out into a laneway behind it. I was taken in and Edward locked the door behind me. It was a dark and dirty place, the single window covered in grime, rusty paint tins on the shelves and a bunch of yellowed newspapers on the ground. My captors began ridiculing me, hurling abuse at me. I stood mutely in front of them, humiliated, scared.

Eventually, they tired of this sport and looked for a new way to use me for their entertainment. In one corner was a large blackened and oily wooden box turned upside down. There was something alive inside it, for the sound of scraping claws and growling could be heard from within. Edward went over to the box and lifted it up. A pair of frenzied eyes leapt forward out of the darkness but fell back again in a whine of pain as Edward kicked at them. I could just about make out the dirtied white and shaggy fur of some type of mongrel, a dog bred in terror, stench and darkness. Edward turned his attention towards me. 'Get in there quick,' he shouted. My first reaction – shock, for even I was surprised at how far they meant to go this time. I had known fear before but, now, my stomach was sick, my body tense with a new and unfamiliar terror.

What happened next took all of us by surprise.

I heard myself shouting at them that I wouldn't do it, I wouldn't get in the dog's box and, as the older and bigger boy came at me, his arms reaching out to grab hold, I found myself striking him as hard as I could on the side of his face. He reeled back in pain and shock, calling on Edward to stop me escaping. But not only did Edward step aside, he actually opened the door to let me out, suddenly afraid of my new-found willingess to fight back. Suddenly, I was in a blaze of evening sunshine, running up the back laneway, out of harm's way, running home.

> And when they're home,
> When the post-Toasties mixed with Golden Shred
> Make for the kiddies such a scrumptious feast
> Does Mum, the Persil-user, still believe
> That there's no Devil and that youth is bliss?
> As certain as the sun behind the Downs
> And quite as plain to see, the Devil walks.

PAYPHONES

Conor O'Callaghan

First time I got to America was the spring of 2000. I had no idea that Americans called mobile phones 'cell phones'. So when a friend told me a pal of hers out there would like me to meet and suggested that she would pass on his cell number, I had some understandable reservations. A fortnight, I figured, would go in no time. I really didn't want to blow a whole day of LA sunshine visiting an inmate of some local prison.

I don't carry a mobile. There have been odd moments, sure, when the handiness of such a possession has become abundantly obvious. But, mostly, I figure it would be a waste of good pocket space. I get no calls on the landline at home. I possess no life-saving skills. Who could possibly be so desperate as to need me in that much of a hurry?

One of the more regrettable results of Ireland's mobile mania over the past decade has been the demise of the traditional Irish common-or-garden payphone. They have become almost obsolete. When was the last time you used one? It occurs to me that, very soon, there will be a generation who won't know what they are: a new wave of fans of the latest *Dr Who* who don't understand that the external dimensions of the TARDIS are those of an old-fashioned police phone box; a fresh posse of awestruck kids watching the new *Superman* with no idea that that minute fitting room Clark Kent enters is actually a payphone kiosk.

Recently, in the nation's capital, your correspondent asked a newsagent's assistant if and where they kept a payphone. There was a moment's silent hesitation, during which I assumed that she was not native to the English language. I therefore repeated the question slowly, making an elaborate phone gesture with my right thumb and pinkie. I may even have mimed popping coins into the slot and pressing the old A-button, for heaven's sake. After the assistant's face had passed through several phases of horror, she asked in a thick Dublin accent, 'You want a top-up?'

All of which, as you've probably deduced, is a source of great sadness. Some of the happiest memories of my teens and twenties involve payphones. My mother didn't get a phone into the family home until the early 1990s. I wooed my wife by ringing the payphone in her flat in Ranelagh from a coin box outside the Harp brewery in Dundalk. The first flat I ever had in college had one payphone on the landing upstairs. Since we were in the basement, tenants in the flats upstairs had to answer and trundle down the steps to say it was for one of us. It took the guts of twenty minutes and a small fortune before the caller got us on the line. Often, there was nobody home upstairs. To this day, I think of that sound – a payphone ringing itself into silence in the fusty hall of a south Dublin Victorian house owned by a midland's farmer who surfaced once in a blue moon – as the sound of all youth.

I was informed that my first book had been accepted for publication down a payphone. The editor described his selection process at length while I banged a torrent of fifty pences to counteract the insistent pips. I had no money left to celebrate, but it was worth it. A double bedsit that I shared with my brother on Grosvenor Square in Rathmines had a payphone with a faulty lock. Whatever money you put in was easily retrieved at the other end. Our landlady, who had a fondness for bottles of stout, several times said she thought we must be the quietest boys in Ireland since we never made any phone calls. And who among us will ever forget the controversy of 1999 when that year's pound coin had to be reminted because no payphone would accept it?

All things of the past's foreign country. Recently, in a pub on the Cooley peninsula, I spied an old A/B payphone in the corner and went over to call my wife for old times' sake. I had just got the dead receiver to my ear when I heard giggling behind me. The staff were laughing at this last man on the planet to realise that it was just another part of the

scenery. Now, it seems, payphones and coin boxes adorn those traditional tourist pubs that punctuate the roads of Ireland, much as kettles
and bicycles hang inexplicably from their ceilings and black-and-white
road signs tell you that Killarney is a mile and three quarters away. What
they didn't know was that I had already inserted €2 – €2 that I will
never see again. Someday in the future, it will be found, probably by lads
redecorating the same pub and replacing the A/B payphone with
another Irish fetish fallen into obsolescence in the interim, such as Ye
Olde Mobile.

FROM BONDI TO BALI

Cyril Kelly

Bondi beach, byword for carefree days, zest for life. The concrete wall at the back of the beach is a kilometre long. Covered in graffiti, it is one extended mural, one ardent memorial to youth lost in the Bali bombing. Slowly, I walked the wall from end to end. A kaleidoscope of aerosols, blue and gold, bronze and blonde. The colours of sea and sand, sun-bleached hair, torsos tanned. Clichés, admittedly, of Shangri-la, yet, for all that, disturbing. Every youth sprayed to posthumous psychedelic stardom, carved biceps, sculpted abs, as they lounge against surfboards with a self-absorbed Adonis air. The girls, all caricatures of post-pubescent beach babes, sultry eyes, pouting lips, voluptuous breasts slung in skimpy bikini tops. One is called Chloe. Bubble writing below supplies stark birth and death statistics – '8th of May '84, 12th October '02'. Just eighteen years old. Above her, like an epitaph: 'Chloe, the girl with frangipani in her hair.' 'Frangipani'; I looked it up. Tropical red jasmine, with perfumed flowers. Far from cliché that; beautiful, poignant elegy more like.

Bali, 12 October 2002. At twenty-three hundred hours, local time, one incognito backpacker, rucksack bulky, entered Paddy's Bar. An accomplice was pulling up outside in a white van. Having learned to drive the previous week, the accomplice still did not know how to reverse. In any case, lest he had second thoughts, the device in the back of the white van was rigged with a remote control.

In surfers' lingo, a 'sleeper set' is the biggest wave of the day, the one that catches them off guard. On October 12th in Paddy's Bar, at twenty-three zero five local time, a backpacker's bulky incognito bomb exploded. A transfiguring 'sleeper set' of flame and shrieks flashed through and past the revelries. The inferno lasted but a millisecond. Followed by a deafening aftershock of silence before the vacuum imploded. Revellers, lungs cauterised by scorching air, eyes frantic for a future, began groping their way from the rubble where Paddy's Bar used to be. Just outside, waiting in the balmy night, primed to greet them, a white van. An unremarkable white van waiting to blast a crater in the roadway, one metre deep.

In surfers' lingo a 'bomb' means an enormous wave. On the wall at the back of Bondi beach, there they all are, waiting nonchalantly for just such a bomb. All the vivid graffiti figures, waiting with the indolence and insouciance of youth. Watching the sea. Watching avalanche after avalanche of Pacific water curling towards the shore. Dreaming of the 'feathering', that first filigree of foam on the rising crest of a wave, the ecstasy of carving a manoeuvre in the ensuing barrel of blue, the fan of water, a translucent blade in their wake.

They never needed, after all, to ring that huge 1800-number sprayed on the poster beside the Jimmy Hendrix figure: 'Satellite Sexual Health,' the poster proclaims. 'Free check-ups for STDs. No medical card required.' Never needed to heed that warning about rip currents, those rip currents which the gallows humour of the beach nicknamed 'back-packers' express'. So there they all are, brudda with waiting brudda, sista with sista, watching for that one 'big bomb' whose explosive power could propel them to the ultimate thrill. Then again, it could plunge them playfully beneath the briny ocean. A debacle which they themselves call 'wipeout'.

HEARING THINGS

Gerald Dawe

I had taken a turn for the worse,
when the chambers of the heart
mysteriously close, or oxygen
to the brain falters suddenly,
and there's a disconnect,
the light hesitates for a split –
second, the room closes
and the drumming begins,
anyway, that day I thought
of falling down a steep chasm,
the rift between here and now,
shifting on the earth's axis
of you and I, as waves parted –
to an exodus in search of home,
the prelude to new beginnings,
scaling different heights! –
then, as all came to rights,
I heard amid the pounding seas,
the most unlikely phrases, such as,
'The world and its mother',
'Music of the Spheres', 'Safe havens'.

SPIES

Peter Jankowsky

Strolling around the very outskirts of a little town in Cyprus – a town simply called '*Polis*', 'Town' – my wife and I found ourselves in a very promising locality, for a painter and a bird-watcher, that is: there were neglected gardens, shrubs ran wild and abandoned houses and, if there's anything my wife can't resist, it's abandoned houses. So she disappeared into one of them while I ambled on, listening, watching.

It was high noon and very hot. Soon, I came across a charming sight: a morning glory plant had climbed up the side of one of the derelict houses, had covered the roof and now fell down the other side like a sparkling blue waterfall. My wife would be thrilled. Also, on the horizon, in the middle distance, there were two old women standing on an earthen mound, in deep conversation, so deep, indeed, that they seemed to be motionless, like sculptures. I looked through my binoculars and saw that they were two strangely-shaped ventilation pipes sticking out of that mound. What to make of that? An answer of sorts came with the cocking of a gun at my back. Turning around, I saw that I was just twenty or so yards away from a high fence, with a watch-tower behind it and, farther back, a number of well-camouflaged army trucks. From the box of the watch-tower, a young soldier was levelling his machine-pistol at me and shouted something. He was very young, and good-looking, wore only a vest on his splendid torso and was glistening with sweat – up there in this box, being on guard duty must be boring as hell. I called up to him, gesticulating, 'Come?'

'No!' he shouted back. 'Go!'

OK, so I turned around and trotted back. It still hadn't clicked with me that we had blundered into a military No-Go area, and I still wanted my wife to see those morning glories. So I brought her back to them, in the fullness of our innocence, and she, of course, was so excited that she had to take a photograph of them. But with that we had crossed the line – again the cocking of the gun, and this time the barrel indicated that we were to proceed to the fence. There the young soldier, in very poor English, demanded the camera from us. When we refused, he called his officer on duty on his mobile phone, all the while keeping his gun at the ready.

While we were waiting, he stood there in his archaic beauty, as we, two elderly tourists, didn't know whether to worry or laugh. Had we been caught – spying? Gradually, the suspiciousness of our actions dawned on us.

When the officer appeared on the scene he was still chewing on his lunch, and his shirt was out over his trousers. In much better English, he also demanded first the camera, then, as we refused again, the film. There were family pictures on it, valuable to us, so we launched a counter-attack: there had not been the slightest indication that this was forbidden terrain, no signs, no barriers. Whereupon he threatened to call the police!

'Excellent!' we replied, and he made the call. By now, the situation had become a bit absurd: our inquisitor was confined behind a wire fence and, although with armed assistance, was forced to call the police for help, while we, the suspects, made ourselves comfortable in the sparse shade of a whispy tree. Actually, I hoped this would go on for a while and develop into a story...

While we were waiting, we thought it might be wise to try a friendly conversation. Reluctantly at first, but more and more readily, the officer opened up. We told him we were Germans living in Ireland and that, therefore, he and ourselves had something in common: divided home-lands! As soon as we mentioned that, we noticed, as we had before with other Cypriots, that his brow darkened, the tone of his voice became bitter. The partition of the island was obviously the sorest point one could touch here. But having spent the first half of our lives in a divided Germany, the second in Ireland, we felt entitled to make a few optimistic noises: surely, after German reunification and Ireland's Good Friday

Agreement, there was hope for Cyprus too, in the context of the EU? We saw him consider for a moment, and then he answered calmly, sadly, 'Perhaps, but I don't think so.' And we felt ignorant and rash, and kept our mouths shut for a while.

There we stood and sat, united in silence and the midday heat, and by experiences the citizens of most other countries are spared. The partition of a country affects, if not everybody's heart, certainly everyone's mind and consciousness – the distraction, that come with it from everyday life, difficult enough for most of us, the endless blame game, the corruption of ideas and ideals, the ever-present web of suspicion that had momentarily entangled us here, with our spy-glass and our camera.

We didn't think such burdened thoughts while we were waiting, we swatted flies, wiped sweat and tried to be as reasonable and civilised as we really were. The police arrived, with speed and bravado, and the rigmarole started all over again: demands, refusals, explanations, reproaches, warnings – and the situation had exhausted itself. A call to our hotel proved that we were who we claimed to be, and everybody was satisfied. The police departed, we shook hands with our friend through the wire fence, congratulated the young god with the thunderbolt for his watchfulness and resumed our perambulations. No story then, unfortunately. But I wish you could have seen those morning glories, the way the blue waterfall spread on the ground, shading it, refreshing it, before trickling away in the parches soil!

The photograph captured it perfectly.

MY FAVOURITE
STUFFED BEAR

Sherra Murphy

My favourite stuffed bear is showing his age. His once-white coat has
yellowed and his stuffing has shifted, spoiling his shape a little. His glass
eyes bulge and his nose is cracked. A colony of insects has taken up residence somewhere inside. Lately, I've noticed that the bullet holes he's
had for years seem to be getting bigger.

He stands in place, my bear, at the Natural History Museum in
Dublin, silent ambassador for his polar kin. He's been there so long that
his presence seems a given, one of the things about Dublin that will never
change. So long that the account of his arrival has been forgotten,
unknown to the visitors who exclaim over his great big teeth and the hole
in his head. I'm partial to this bear because he embodies the idea that
knowledge renders the familiar new again, that history enriches understanding. The clues to his past are in the display case for all to see, but the
story, once widely known, has been largely erased from popular memory.

The label at his feet says he was a gift to the Museum from Captain
Francis Leopold McClintock and that he comes from Baffin Bay.
McClintock, a Dundalk man, was a skilful and veteran polar explorer
who participated in four separate attempts to locate the lost expedition
of John Franklin, which had disappeared while searching for the
Northwest Passage. On the fourth try, requested as captain by Lady

Franklin, McClintock succeeded in finding records and artefacts demonstrating that Franklin's entire crew had perished. Though the bearer of sad news, McClintock was celebrated as a hero for finally having solved the enigma, and his memoir of the expeditions was a nineteenth-century bestseller.

McClintock encountered this bear when his team struck out from the main ship by sled to search in small groups, travelling light, carrying minimal provisions. In his memoirs, he describes how the bear wandered into their newly-pitched camp, sniffing his way while the crew paused, silent.

After a short chase and six bullets, the bear became much-needed food; along with blubber and bear steaks, the men even made use of the seal the bear had eaten previously, still undigested in its stomach. Though coping with an extreme environment where space and energy were precious, McClintock, a keen naturalist, dedicated some of that limited space on the sleds to storing the bear's skin so that he could be shipped home for the museum's collection.

The bear and his bullet holes are not what they seem — what at first appears to celebrate the machismo of a big-game hunt in fact recalls that, for the Arctic explorers, the struggle for survival and the quest for knowledge were the same thing. For McClintock, the bear was both a means of seeing the next day and a way to show the world something of his experiences in that harsh, beautiful terrain. The bear creates a link to a time when explorers tackled unknown and demanding environments with equipment, technology and nutrition we would now consider laughably inadequate.

Therein lies my fascination with this bear; he embodies the idea that it's possible to connect with people long gone, using the objects they've left to us as stepping stones. Material culture, as it's known in anthropology, is nothing more, or nothing less, than the idea that things are meaningful, and that why and how we save or use things says something about us, about our time and our priorities. At first glance, the holes in his pelt suggest bloody-minded sport, reckless arrogance. On reflection, they describe the conditions of science and exploration in the nineteenth century, speak of the sacrifices involved in gathering new information. Victorian viewers of the collection would have instantly understood that this bear was not simply a type specimen representing his kind, but that he was also a remnant from a dangerous and melancholy journey to find a dead hero. Public obsession with Franklin's fate meant the label describing the bear would read as a short synopsis, a snippet from a well-known story. Today, the references are a mystery to the average visitor to the museum.

Investigating this bear has deepened my understanding of a time I assumed I knew fairly well; he has spurred me into a new way of thinking, a renewed passion for searching beyond the obvious to uncover the hidden story. Only at the Natural History Museum can one's intellectual process be influenced by a deceased bear. Long live the Dead Zoo.

THE GADFLY AND LILY BOOLE

Betty Nunan

We first heard of *The Gadfly* when Enda Rohan of Galway played an excerpt of the Shostakovich film music on a piano at Tirana University in 1991. Enda had brought *The Gadfly* score for the music professor, a man who had also read and enjoyed *The Gadfly* novel, published almost 100 years earlier by Heinemann in New York, for safety because of its theme, but written by a young woman who was born in Cork.

The Gadfly, a riveting novel of intrigue and betrayal by E.L. Voynich, was published in 1897. It's still an exciting tale of revolution! After the Second World War, possibly because of the release of *The Gadfly* film on the life of the master international spy, Sidney Riley, sales of Voynich's novel zoomed behind the Iron Curtain until Russian readers classed her with Dickens, as one of Britain's greatest novelists. Yet in Cork she was called plain Lily Boole.

Lily's story must begin with her amazing parents. Her father, George, was the brilliant mathematician after whom the Boole Library at Cork University is named. Her mother, Mary Everest, another genius, was born in 1832 in England. At five, Mary and her brother moved with their parents to live at Poissy in France because her father's health had become fragile. He had been a Church of England minister. In Catholic France, the children might have felt isolated, but Mary was soon introduced to mathematics by a brilliant tutor, Monsieur Deplace, who taught her to love learning as a game for her own pleasure. 'Monsieur Deplace,' she wrote, 'was the hero of my idyll. I wish I could convey an adequate impression of the way in which he enveloped my life with a protecting influence, without the slightest interference with either my thoughts, or feelings.'

The family moved back to England and, at eleven, Mary was taken out of school in order to help her father. Soon, in his library, she was learning calculus from his mathematical books. Then, on a visit to her uncle and aunt in Cork, she was introduced to George Boole, who taught mathematics at the university. Socially and intellectually, George and Mary were ideally suited. He was seventeen years older, but soon they fell in love, married and had five young daughters when tragedy struck. Lily, the youngest, was only six months old when George died suddenly of pneumonia, caught after he walked through driving rain one day to deliver a lecture to students.

Mary was forced to provide for her children. She worked as a librarian and as a teacher and educator. She had many works published into her old age. Her youngest daughter chose to become a novelist.

Lily Boole was the first woman to recognise Sidney Reiley's genius. She was beginning to gain recognition as a writer in the London of 1895 when she fell in love and had a torrid affair with Georgie Rosenblum, later known as arch spy Sidney Reiley.

Together, they moved to Catholic Italy where the charmed lover bared his soul to his young mistress, telling her of his southern Russian birth into a minor aristocratic family, that his father had been an army general with direct links to the Czarist court. At home, Georgie and his sister, Anna, were taught by private tutors, Georgie showing insatiable curiosity and genius at mastering languages. He had also become an excellent swordsman and a crack shot with the pistol.

Georgie had respected his father but loved and trusted his mother as honest, always despising Jews. But when she had been young she had become ill and almost died until a Jewish doctor, Rosenblum, had restored her to health. While at university in Vienna, Georgie had grown to love this doctor, only to discover, on his mother's death, that he was Rosenblum's illegitimate son with her. Devastated, Georgie feigned suicide and stowed away on a ship to Brazil where he worked as a labourer, circus clown and doorman to a brothel. He now mastered Portuguese and was employed as a cook by British explorers travelling to the Amazon jungle. When the convoy was attacked, grabbing a pistol, Georgie defended them single-handedly, finally leading them back to safety. One of the explorers, Mary Fothergill, gave him a large cheque, (most of which he spent on Lily Boole) and introduced him to life as a spy in Britain's secret service.

The affair with Lily lasted only a few months but, charmed by his intelligent mistress, Georgie forgot his grudges and – for the only time in his life – bared his soul to her. Soon, he ended the affair, abandoning her in Italy.

The following year she wrote *The Gadfly*, basing the early part on Rosenblum's actual life. That year, Lily married a revolutionary named Voynich, a man who had fought for Poland's freedom from Russia. After his death, she lived on quietly for many years, a widow in New York, always dressing elegantly in black until she died peacefully in her ninety-sixth year in 1960. Of all Lily Boole's novels, only *The Gadfly* survives.

TINY TIM

Steve MacDonogh

At her home high up in Beverley Hills, Zsa Zsa Gabor held a birthday party in 1968 for the unconventional crooner Tiny Tim. As we approached the house, lights came on and water flowed over concrete cliffs into an artificial rock pool; the view over Hollywood and LA was spectacular.

I arrived on the arm of a Hollywood starlet named Lara, and in the company of actors Dennis Hopper and Severn Darden, and poet Michael McClure and his wife, the two of them sporting unusually identical haircuts.

On our arrival, Zsa Zsa was all effusiveness, hospitably offering her breasts for the males amongst us to fondle. Dennis and I briefly fell into conversation with Peter Fonda, whom Dennis was trying to get involved in the film that would become *Easy Rider*. The problem for Dennis was that people who mattered in Hollywood thought of him only as Jimmy Dean's sidekick and it was difficult for him to get his project taken seriously. Peter was interested, and he and his father had real clout in the industry, but Dennis was concerned about what the Fonda money might do to the integrity of his idea for the movie.

Dennis introduced me to Mama Cass Elliott of the Mamas and Papas and both Lara and I took to her immediately. She had just bought a Harley Davidson, which she was delighted with, but she was worried about her eight-year-old daughter's reaction: she was seemingly becoming sensitive to her mother's large size, which was all the more evident when she rode the bike. The Mamas and Papas had been high in the charts for several years and we chatted, too, about a relative newcomer I'd met in San Francisco, Janis Joplin.

Dennis Hopper, Severn Darden and I had been meeting up most nights of the last week at Barney's Beanery and, one night, Tiny Tim had joined us and invited us to this birthday party. Tiny Tim had shot to stardom not from nowhere, but from the relative obscurity of a novelty act in which he dubbed himself 'The Singing Canary'. Another of his pseudonyms was Larry Love, though his real name was Herbert Kauhry. He was the son of a Jewish mother and an Armenian father. Six foot three tall, with a beak nose and prominent teeth, he had real, if unusual, vocal talent and was no mean player of the ukulele. He was best known for his falsetto-voiced rendition of Rudy Vallee songs, but he also had a tremendous vocal range. At a time of youth culture, he was incongruously middle-aged, and he wore clothes that seemed to date to the 1940s, but, more incongruously still, this large man had the character of a giggling young teenager. 'If I could only stay sixteen forever,' he sang in one of his songs, yet he more often seemed to inhabit a sense of himself as a twelve- or thirteen-year-old.

An extraordinary number of great rock albums came out in 1968, but his first album was not one of them, though it made quite an impact. Despite his new management, his record deal and high-profile promotion, he remained essentially a novelty act, singing songs like 'Tiptoe Through the Tulips'. He possessed an enormous enthusiasm for old songs, which he would sing at the drop of a hat, but it was the high range of his voice which was exploited in most of the songs he recorded.

Now, when he arrived rather late at the party, he was in great spirits, and Zsa Zsa Gabor gleefully presented him with a new ukulele case as he blushed to the roots of his long hair.

'Oh, Steve,' he warbled to me, 'I am so thrilled, just *so* happy!' Then he confided with a guilty giggle and a toothy smile that he was too attached to his old ukulele case to use the new one.

That night, after the party, Dennis Hopper, Tiny Tim, the McClures and I all stayed over at Severn's house, talking into the early hours, Tiny Tim relentlessly punctuating his conversation with snatches of songs.

ISLAND SURRENDER

Elaine Sisson

There is an island in my mind's eye. It is a real island although I have
never been there. It is rocky and inhospitable, pyramid-shaped; certainly
not conventionally idyllic but when I think of it, it fills me with a yearning and a longing that I cannot put into words. I first glimpsed my
island when I lived in Dingle last year. It belongs to the crop of the
Blaskets sprinkled off the coastline but is the farthest away. An Tearacht:
the far island.

I came across my island almost by accident. Driving along the peninsula intent on some banal errand, my eye was caught by the October
light slipping over the water. Looking out to sea, the triangular shape of
a distant island came into sharp relief. I pulled over and got out of the
car. Despite the clarity of the day, the distant imprint of the island's
shape was like a mirage coming in and out of focus. It was there and
then not there. Captivated, I walked along the cliff for a time realising
that there were only certain places from where the island could be seen.

In the following weeks, I discovered that there were days when the
island was invisible and not necessarily on those misty days as would
be expected. Sometimes, the low autumnal light masked it from view,
but it was always there – is there still. I made detours during my day
seeking it out – going out of my way to look for it and yearning for it
in its absence. I realised that getting closer did not necessarily give me a
better view – like an ageing beauty, distance was kinder. Now, back in

the city, it is my computer's screensaver — a poor but necessary approximation. The sight of it centres me, stills me.

After a certain age, life is a series of small subtractions. They are miniscule at first and then a little bigger until, one day, you realise that you have reached a tipping point: not exactly old but no longer young. And you have to readjust your thinking about your life — maybe in little ways, maybe in full-blown crisis mode. Perhaps you have more days behind you than in front of you; although each of us, regardless of years, lives with a degree of uncertainty. Is it possible that you have already had your best memories? It is with a degree of resignation that I recognise I am unlikely to usurp the intensity of the experiences of late adolescence: staying out dancing all night and walking home barefoot in a May dawn; freewheeling down a mountainside in the dark with a potential boyfriend; discovering poetry and literature and music as if I was the first one to stumble blinking onto new land. I can still do all of these things, of course, although these days I'd probably wear more sensible dancing shoes and make sure I had a cycling helmet. It is the joy and the newness and the possibility of those experiences — when we ourselves are fresh and new — which keeps them vivid for us.

It is an obvious truth that we must each discover what it means to be mortal. And while each must learn for themselves, there are plenty of pointers and signs which have been left behind for us. We age day by day, slowly, imperceptibly but inevitably. We are constantly in transition, shedding and becoming, shedding and becoming.

In chemistry, there are substances which can pass from one state to another without going through an interim state: a process called sublimation. Iodine, for example, passes from a solid to a gas without first becoming liquid. There are times when what we are feeling and how to express it are disconnected: we cannot find the words. We are unable to move from feeling to articulating to understanding. Yet, sometimes, we can short-circuit language and connect emotion directly to understanding by hearing music or looking at a painting or a landscape. This is sublimation of the soul; it is what art offers us.

My island is teaching me about mortality and how to be alive. It is timeless, immutable, immortal — was there before me and will be there after me. It holds the promise of boundlessness, of wordlessness, of eternity, not of annihilation, but of surrender. My isle of the blessed; my sublime.

THE FORM OF INHERITANCE

Anne Hartigan Le Marquand

'Dear little Angie,' was the way my mother always referred to one of her sisters.

I never met Angie, but I know her. She rests there light and delicate in a sepia photograph of the whole family formally posed in their childhood. From this photograph, I can see how her fine bone structure has been inherited by my third son. How a few words and stories told to you as child can paint bright pictures of people you will never know.

This Aunt Angie lives with me, her short and young life lies with me in my cupboard where the delicate china she sent home from Shanghai is now kept. I use it with great pleasure always remembering her life and the poignancy of the fact that things have longer lives than those who owned them.

Angela Josephine Halligan was born on 22 October 1885; my grandfather recorded her birth, in his elegant copperplate writing, in his farm day book, which he started in 1856. All his daughters and one son were well educated and, very talented musically; Angie played the cello, my mother and all her sisters played at least one instrument. Angela must have trained as a nurse, probably with her sister Frances Clare who trained at the Meath Hospital in Dublin, and who worked there, in the operating theatre with Oliver St John Gogarty, the writer and man who was surgeon during the 1916 Rising.

Angie, however, took the adventurous trail to go nursing in China, to Shanghai, where she worked in a large hospital. I feel she was probably inspired by nuns and her own warm Catholic faith to do this, a form of missionary spirit, the desire to help those in need, the desire to do good. And good, she did. She worked there during the First World War, and my mother told me made good friends with one of the doctors of the hospital and with his wife and family. The population of Shanghai and, of course, the patients in the hospital fell prey to the dreadful flu that ravaged the world after the First World War and that killed more than all those who died from the fighting in the war itself. Angie's doctor friend and his family were struck down by the flu and Angie left her work in the hospital and went to nurse the family in their own home. She nursed the whole family back to health, but she herself caught the disease and was not so lucky. She did not recover. Angie, only a young woman herself, far away from all her loving family in Ireland, died.

I have a photo of her tombstone, taken by a sailor from their village at home. He sailed to Shanghai years later and found her grave and took the photo for the family brought it home to my mother and her sisters. Many years later, in the 1980s, my youngest daughter was travelling the world with her husband. They went to India and Thailand, cycled down Malaysia and on to Australia and New Zealand. They then travelled back to Hong Kong and, from there, took a slow boat to China and came to Shanghai. I was very moved when she told me later that they tried to find Angie's grave. She could not, because no trace of it remains.

She was told that during the Communist Revolution, all the western graves were ploughed up and destroyed. So even the memory of her brief life, of giving help to the sick in a foreign country, is destroyed and forgotten.

But I still have the delicate china tea set with its green dragons with blue faces that curl and writhe on the yellow background, china so thin you can see through it; this china itself reflects Angie's own delicate nature that I see in that photo of her as a child. I enjoy this tea set with its cups and plates, the jugs and teapot, that she sent home to her sister, my mother. I use it with delight and celebrate her, sharing tea at family parties, christenings, birthdays, Christmases and the thin china tea cups carry her delicate life story to us, her family, on and on.

HIDDEN HISTORIES

Viktor Posudnevsky

It happened in Brussels, just a block away from the European Commission. The building is in the shape of a star. Four wings radiate from the central tower. It's made of grey steel and glass.

Not more than 200 metres from there, in a traditional Belgian bar, there was a short roundish man in the corner, standing by the counter and drinking beer. He had a fixed stare with a kind of glee, even triumph, in his eyes, no matter where he looked. He seemed very pleased about something and when he raised his glass, it was as if to toast everyone around. Apart from him, there was just a group of us, students – and an elderly barmaid.

The man in the corner radiated excitement which seemed a bit out of place and it looked like he'd love to share it. Finally, I went over and talked to him.

His name was Giles. He was working for the post office, and every day his white pick-up van would bring correspondence to the European Commission. He blurted out straightaway that he called in sick this day and would do so again in the morning. He made a dramatic pause, as if inviting me to appreciate the great form he was in.

Outside, you could see the dark silhouette of the Commission building. He was drinking beer literally under his bosses' noses and they were paying him thinking he was out sick. He laughed and gave me a schoolboy accomplice look full of joy.

Giles told me he lived some twenty kilometres away from the centre of Brussels. He was going to stay in the bar all night and catch the first train home in the morning. What did he do on his sick leave? He'd spent the whole day in the library.

It was an unexpected answer and it didn't really tie in with the triumph in his eyes. What did he do in the library? He was researching his ancestors and got some extraordinary results. He patted the file that was lying on the counter next to him. He patted it as if it contained a treasure map.

He took a sheet of paper from the file. It was a printout. A portrait of a man was on it. The man was in eighteenth-century military uniform and wearing a cocked hat. Some medals were pinned to his chest. The man's face was proud and romantic, like a war hero from an old novel.

'That was my great-great-great-great-great-great-grandfather. Yep, that's it, six greats,' Giles said and gave me a triumphant smile.

His grandfather was British and he was an officer in Admiral Nelson's fleet. That day, Giles finally found his name in the library archives. When he Googled the name, he got a picture.

Genealogy was the man's passion. He spent most of his free time researching his ancestry. It's a very long and painstaking process, Giles explained. You have to stay in the library for days, looking up various records. You start with the oldest family member you know, and slowly make your way down the genealogical tree. Down to the roots. Most of the time, all you get is a name and bits of circumstantial evidence, pointing to where your ancestors lived and what their occupation was. But if you get lucky – like he got that day – if your ancestors made it in life and their name left a trace in history – you'd get so much more. A complete biography, and a picture.

Quickly, he produced another sheet of paper from the file. This one was a photocopy of an old newspaper cutting, with a photograph of a group of people. One of the faces in the background was circled in red. Giles pointed his finger at the circle, almost spilling his beer.

'The nose! Look at the nose! Is it not very much like mine?'

I couldn't see. The photo was very old, you could barely make out the people's features. And the light was too low.

He went on with the story. The naval officer was his mother's ancestor. Two centuries ago, he had commanded a ship in Nelson's fleet and had fought against Napoleon. But the most exciting thing was, his six-times-great grandmother, on the father's side, worked on a French wharf. She had built the very same ships that his mother's ancestor – the British navy officer – had fought.

Giles raised his glass and toasted me. He looked like his team had just won the World Cup. I looked at him amazed, and could only congratulate him and the discovery.

So his ancestors were involved on two different sides of a conflict two centuries ago. And their eventual offspring was a quiet man living in the suburbs of Brussels and delivering post for the European Commission, the body that implements decisions across the twenty-seven countries of the union. And Britain and France are no longer sworn enemies – they are parts of this formation. That's hardly something Giles' ancestors would have imagined.

What do we really know about ourselves? If anyone of us was to look at our past, what strange connections and interrelations would we find? And what, if we could look into the future? What strange shapes will our genealogical trees take?

We glide on the surface most of the time. We live in the here and now and take things as they appear before us. It's only seldom that we see them in their changing nature.

Take Europe for example. It's a structure whose half a billion subjects are controlled from several buildings in Belgium and France. One of them – a grey star of steel and glass – was before me that day. Somehow, it didn't seem so massive now. The bar where I'd met Giles seemed more real. It had been there for much longer than the Commission building. And whatever happens in Europe as we know it, it would stay and welcome new generations, just as it had before.

MARATHON MAN

Paul Cullen

I have a woman waiting for me in Kimmage tomorrow morning. She'll be there from early morning, with a bottle of holy water in one hand and a hard-boiled sweet in the other. I don't know her personally but that won't stop her shouting at me in public. That's all right, though, because she'll be shouting at all the runners in tomorrow's Dublin city marathon.

I normally go for the sweet. The glucose gives me a small sugar high, sustenance for another stretch of road as the last miles approach. The benefit is more psychological than real, I'm sure, but any distraction from the hardship of running twenty-six miles has to be welcome.

The start will be fun, 10,000 of us setting off in giddy spirits, cheering at the cameras and our loved ones. Those early miles will glide along, plenty to see as we travel the city's empty thoroughfares. Familiar faces from previous years are sure to pop up – the tartan-clad Scotsman with the orange wig or members of that small and dwindling band of men (and one woman) who have run all twenty-six previous Dublin marathons.

Then, there's the middle stretch, when the race meanders through outer suburbs and the going gets tougher. A strange silence will descend, broken only by the footfall of expensive trainers. This being Dublin at the end of October, a sudden squall will blow up to buffet us and prick our earlier confidence, and there'll be few spectators.

This is payback time for all those hours of training. The endless circuits of the park, the sweat-racked runs on now-distant summer days, the nightly trudges through mounds of fallen leaves as autumn and the day of the race draw near. Reservoirs of stamina built up for sudden dissipation on this bank holiday marathon.

Now, as the strength drains from my legs, my body starts listing and I slow to a crawl, I'll be asking that same question I asked last time I ran a marathon, and the time before that, and before that again – why? This can't be good for us – after all, didn't the first marathon-runner, Pheidippides in ancient Greece, drop dead at the end of his exertions? Why inflict such pain on myself? Why subject my body to such shocks? And what was it I said the last time? – 'Never again.'

Pounding the streets of suburban Dublin while the rest of the city rests, I'll have plenty of time to come up with an answer of sorts.

Because? Because I can. Because I'm here and I'm healthy. Because this discomfort, being self-inflicted, has an end. Because I have a short memory. Because the guy in the white T-shirt who I passed a few miles back has just caught up with me. And, finally, now that I've twenty miles of running behind me, because stopping is arguably more painful – physically and psychologically – than continuing.

And so I'll go on, on to the finish, now looming, with the cheering of the crowds a fuzzy din, as though I'm hearing it from under water. I'll be struggling, now, listing like a sunken trawler, my face contorted in pain and my brain telling me to pack it in. Tightening muscles will force a shortening of my stride, the lightness in my head, the only counterpoint to the dead weight of tired limbs. I might hear a friend call my name from the crowd, but I'll be too weary to look.

Most of the city centre shops will be closed, but their appearance will be comforting nonetheless, for it means the end is nigh.

Suddenly, I'm rounding the corner onto Merrion Square, striding with new-found energy to the succour of the finishing line. Hands aloft, I'll pass under the bright clock and crumple once I'm on the other side. It's over now, once again. I've done it. That's that.

But as the pain subsides, optimism will grow. Within minutes, I'll start thinking about next year. Just one more go. For my woman cheering in Kimmage. Only this time I might ask her for the holy water.

NOVEMBER

THE FACTORY OF DREAMS

Katrina Goldstone

My mother and her sisters were film-star crazy and movie mad, their imaginations fired up on an endless diet of black-and-white American films. The effortlessly glamorous lives of the stars influenced their fashion sense, even though as young Catholics in 1940s Belfast, their budgets couldn't match up to their idols in a month of Sundays. Whenever they got a chance, they'd be down at the Princess Picture Palace. Otherwise they'd while away the hours poring over the pages of *Picture Goer* magazine, searching out tips on style, deportment and the right way to smoke a cigarette. Given this family history, it's hardly surprising that I have a passionate devotion to old movies too.

I was watching *The Maltese Falcon* again the other night, crashed out on the sofa. Old black-and-white classics nearly all improve on second or even third viewing – the sets, exquisite costumes, quick-fire repartee – things I didn't appreciate first time round on grey Sunday afternoons in my callow youth. Even the bit players in these films exude class. Peter Lorre, with his *Mitteleuropa* drawl and opium-addict eyes; Sydney Greenstreet, a rotund malevolent figure with cut-glass diction who landed his first film part at the grand old age of sixty-two and Elisha J. Cook Junior, who in *Falcon* plays a baby-faced psychopath sinister enough to rival any Mafia mobster.

Lying on the couch, the words of writer Raymond Carver, a kind of literary Bogart, drifted into my mind. There's that iconic photograph of him, cigarette slouching out of his mouth, an image that could just as well be a promo shot for a Bogie flick. Carver and his poet partner Tess Gallagher liked old black-and-white movies too and Carver immortalised their companionable relationship in 'Proposal', from the poetry collection he wrote and compiled in the final year of his life. Carver's preoccupation with luck, chance and that last click of the gun chamber in Russian roulette – it's all there in 'Proposal'. For him, the last chamber did indeed hold a bullet – inoperable lung cancer diagnosed at the age of forty-nine.

The decidedly unromantic setting for 'Proposal' has Carver and Gallagher half-dozing on the sofa whilst a Bette Davis film noir plays out on the small screen – Davis edging her way, shoulder pads first, down an elegant staircase. The poem describes their subsequent wedding in Reno, divorce capital of the world, with a honeymoon at the gaming tables – all of it, a kind of defiant two fingers to mortality and dreary romantic convention.

Carver claimed that he'd always squandered – a strange confession from someone who wrote a slew of prize-winning short-story collections and even before his death was compared to Chekhov. Still, his troubled first marriage and a battle with alcoholism seemed to leave him with the sneaking suspicion that he'd thrown away more than he'd stored up for himself in life.

When his hopeless prognosis was confirmed, Carver set about finishing one last cherished project. Together with Gallagher, he struggled in the last year of his life, eking out the small bits of energy left to him to fashion something new, a literary form between poetry and prose, and inspired by the precision and emotional honesty of his literary hero, Anton Chekhov. Gallagher describes how, painstakingly, the two worked on this last book. The hours spent literally piecing the texts together like patchwork on the living room floor. So, it unfolds the parallel track of luck and misfortune that informs a poem like 'Gravy'. After all, Carver himself had gotten a reprieve from death once already – and eleven extra years of hard work and happiness with Gallagher by his side. Gravy indeed. And then there's the surreal honeymoon with a final gamble, one last throw of the dice. It's all there in the pages of *A New Path to the Waterfall*, a moving epitaph to a great writer whose life with its grand themes of tragedy and redemption had all the ingredients of some gritty black-and-white movie you might see by chance on a chill winter's afternoon.

UNSPOKEN TRUTHS

Enda Wyley

for Rozika Parker

To kick the empty pram
way down the street
over the Ha'penny Bridge
and far into the west,
from Burren limestone
to the Hudson river,
there to drown
over New York City –

to kindle the bonfire
with wooden jigsaws
startle-eyed dolls,
nursery rhyme noise,
lego dinosaurs and
Barbie balls,
the Green Party
yelling, indignant –

to burn all bibs and teats,
beakers and soothers,
late night fevers
and to only have
you and me as it was before,
alone again in November stillness,
the clock ticking and the sky
a pumpkin orange –

the future flaring fluorescent
with each firework bang,
our life vast, exploding
with light.

But the monitor flashes,
a strange language
gurgles from above.
Cot bars rattle –

then each thump,
each stir, tugs back the pram
and those dribbled-on,
well-loved playthings,
pulls me again
to the little warmth,
wraps my arms
forever around her.

THE BOY NAMED IGNATIUS

Iggy McGovern

I was the only one in the class, the only one in the school, and, by virtue of Northern religious labelling, the only one in the town. I was an Irish version of the boy named Sue; the boy named Ignatius. And although he might live, however uncomfortably, among the Patricks, the Eoins and the Seamuses, there could be little understanding from the Victors, the Trevors and the Douglases. The only solution was the diminutive Iggy, accepted by all except my mother, who would revert to full-on title in the presence of the Holy Trinity of teacher, doctor and priest.

And so the name and its possible origins became a vague memory, but a memory that surfaced recently, prompted by seemingly unconnected events. I was in Rome on a tour that included the room where Ignatius of Loyola died. Responding to some gentle teasing from the others, I protested that I was most certainly not named after that intense Iberian, and left it at that. The same evening, however, I saw on the internet that the writer John McGahern had died, but only made the connection some weeks later when I read his splendid *Memoir*. There, McGahern reports that when his mother's health was threatened by another pregnancy, his father pressed her to see a healing priest, a Fr Ignatius.

I once heard my own father's name read out in a local history lecture; it was a dramatic epiphany for me. I felt something similar now, reading of this Fr Ignatius, suddenly aware that here was the man I was named for. I could now picture my own mother making her long journey to see this priest and, in gratitude, as the phrasing has it, for favours received, naming her first son after him.

The priest was born Thomas Francis Gibney in Dublin in 1889. His early education was with the Christian Brothers and he was a regular mass-server for the Jesuits in Gardiner Street. Eventually, he was attracted to the Order of the Passionists, the self-styled 'black-robed army of the crucified', badged with the characteristic wooden heart, the mission cross tucked into the sturdy belt. He joined the novitiate in Worcestershire in 1907 and, acknowledging perhaps the Gardiner Street influence, took the name Ignatius.

Ordained in Dublin in 1913, he ministered in Belfast and Sutton before being appointed to The Graan, the newly founded Passionist monastery in Enniskillen. His reputation as a preacher was well established by then; dramatic and versatile, according to one obituary, he could equally 'entrall a church of tiniest children' and 'enrapture a congregation of Cistercian monks'. But the same writer notes that his preaching was 'but a shadow of his greater quality, his appeal as a confessor'. And, although for Sargeant McGahern and many others, The Graan was the acute hospital of its time, this would suggest that Fr Ignatius' true gift was the healing of the mind, the counselling of the worrisome, the scrupulous, the mildly depressed and the plain worn-out.

And, yet, there is much anecdotal evidence of physical cures, of maladies that range from hair loss to alcoholism. He himself had a stammer but, in a case of 'physician heal thyself', when he rose to preach he was word perfect. It was also said that the local doctor would invite the priest to accompany him on his rounds. What is certain is that in many homes throughout the border counties, his name is still remembered with deep affection, long after his death in 1952. And it was in one such household in Belcoo earlier this year, that I came face to face with him, so to speak, coming away grateful for the sepia photograph of my namesake.

A final connection occured in a pub in County Mayo. A local writer introduced me to a man considerably younger than myself, saying, 'Iggy, meet Iggy.'

'Do you mind me asking you—' I began.

He interrupted with, 'Father Ignatius of The Graan.' But, in his case, it was his maternal grandmother who attended, and who, with no sons of her own, deferred the gratitude to the next generation.

2007 is the centenary of the entry of Fr Ignatius into the Passionist Order. I have marked it by visiting his grave in Mount Argus. I have recalled his ministry and his generosity to my mother, but I have also thought about his eponymous family of sons and grandsons, the boys named Ignatius.

SEÁN Ó TUAMA (1926–2006)

Eoghan Ó hAnluain

It is natural, I suppose, how, on hearing of the death of an admired and cherished writer, we turn to the written word — partly out of nostalgia, partly out of homage but partly also out of the need for reassurance in the face of loss.

I have in front of me, a copy of an old journal, somewhat tattered now from much handling over the years by myself and by students. It was an instinctive response to reach for it when word came from Cork of the recent death of Seán Ó Tuama. It is an edition of *An Síol*, a journal published by An Chuallacht Ghaelach, the Irish Langauge Society of University College Cork. Its date is 1950, over half a hundred years ago. It has been a treasured possession for many years and all the more so now since Seán Ó Tuama's death.

In this edition of the journal are included two remarkable essays in literary criticism: one by Seán Ó Tuama and one by his former Professor of English, Daniel Corkery, whom Ó Tuama regarded as the finest teacher of literature he had ever met. Corkery's essay is an incisive analysis of a sixteenth-century poem by the poet Tadhg Dall Ó hUiginn, while Seán Ó Tuama writes a remarkable seminal introduction to the little-known but emerging poet from West Cork, Seán Ó Ríordáin.

What is remarkable about these two essays is that one can trace the influence of Corkery on Ó Tuama quite clearly. Corkery's essay is a close and intimate reading of the poem and concerns itself not, as was the accepted approach, with examining the external forms of syllable count and correct rhyming, but rather that inner dynamic which gives a worthwhile poem its distinctive artistic quality and human appeal.

This same approach to literature was to be the hallmark of Seán Ó Tuama's own criticism, whether of a traditional folk love song or a mediaeval literary love lyric, or of contemporary writing in prose or poetry.

Born in 1926 in Cork City, Seán Ó Tuama attended the North Monastery Christian Brother's School and University College Cork, where he later became Professor of Modern Irish Literature. He was a visiting professor at Harvard and at Oxford. His anthology *Nuabhearsaíocht*, poetry in Irish from 1939-1949, first focused critical attention on the achievement of contemporary poets of that period. Since then Seán Ó Tuama's influence as a writer, dramatist, critic, teacher and mentor has been pervasive. He also played hurling with the famous Cork Hurling club Glen Rovers. How right that a camán should be central to his funeral rites.

An early recollection of mine of Ó Tuama was his challenging lecture, Fáistine na Litríochta, on the prophetic nature of literature, delivered at the Oireachtas, the Irish language festival in 1961. The lecture was attended by President Éamon de Valera and Sinéad de Valera in the Old Hibernian Hotel in Dawson Street, Dublin.

Apart from the superb lecture, which can be read in his collected essays, *Tuath agus Bruachbhaile*, what remains most vividly in my memory of that night in the Hibernian is the haunting image of the late John Jordan, critic and lecturer in English at University College Dublin and an esteemed poet and regular contributor to *Sunday Miscellany*, along with the distinguished portraitist Seán Ó Súilleabháin RHA, as they made their unsteady way to the front of the crowded room and sat themselves in close proximity to His Excellency, *Uachtarán na hÉireann*. They were both well on.

But their presence that night was an indication of the high regard in which they both held Seán Ó Tuama as a critic and literary commentator. Throughout the brilliant lecture from highlight to highlight, and at the appropriate time, they unobtrusively growled their inebriated approval. A fitting contribution indeed. It was a memorable night. For Ó Tuama and for his audience it was, as so often with him, 'something to perfection brought'.

Those of us who were trying to find an appropriate form of language in which to discuss literature in Irish were offered a critical voice by him, and not only in concise and adequate vocabulary but in articulation. Some time ago, I saw and heard on television the self-same voice and rhythms and precisely shaped sounds in the remarkable tones of the late Bab Feiritéar, the renowned West Kerry storyteller.

I had never heard or seen her in person before that but I could hear and see then the precision of language and articulation which Ó Tuama had made his own and then transformed to an imaginatively intellectual medium for his own original readings of life and literature and for his distinctive voice in poetry and plays.

That remarkable individual, yet rooted voice is to be heard in all his great scholarly works — *An Grá in Amhráin na nUaisle* and probably most memorably in his masterly introduction to his edition of *Caoineadh Airt Uí Laoghaire*. His voice lies gently but insistently on the ear and asks persuasively to be heard. That same voice had a particularly vital realisation in his many plays which must now await new and re-imagined productions.

It was a phrase of Mícheál Ó Guithín, *an file*, son of Peig Sayers, which inspired one of Seán Ó Tuama's most moving short poems. It evokes with great tenderness the vulnerable world of an adolescent girl who has been chastised by her elders. He called it, so very appropriately, 'Rousseau na Gaeltachta':

> Lig di a dúirt an file
> Is ná smachtaigh í,
> Níl inti seo ach gearrchaile
> Is is breoiteacht é an t-eagla
> A chrapann an nádúr.
>
> Lig di a dúirt an file,
> Is ná smachtaigh í,
> Lig di fás gan bac ar bith
> Go dtína hairde cheapaithe,
> Tá an t-aer fós bog os a cionn.

IN FLANDERS FIELDS

Val Mulkerns

When I was in Belgium recently I remembered something I thought I'd forgotten. It happened on a dark November evening when my brother Jim and I were taken to Dorset Street for the first fitting of new winter coats. My mother always preferred to walk, if there was time, instead of taking a bus or a tram, so when we emerged from the tailor's into some sort of confusion on the street, we were surprised when she told us to be quick and we might catch the approaching tram. She could run faster than either of us, and so we were dragged on board and in a position to look down from a safe height at the angry crowds who were jostling and shouting at two or three women shaking collection boxes.

'Stupid, stupid people,' my mother muttered. 'They can't see that other people have a perfect right to buy and wear poppies in memory of those poor slaughtered young men – many of them Irish anyway.'

It was grown-up talk, and it didn't particularly interest me then, but the words came back vividly as we stood on that bleak cold day in Flanders Fields. In the grey gloom, the thousands of small white crosses seemed to stretch for miles in every direction. On the horizon, just beyond the cemetery, a tall trio of soldiers stood among the trees as though on guard. They turned out not to be real, but a very fine and moving piece of sculpture.

When we drove on to Ypres we found under the Menin Gate, and covering every inch of the town walls beyond it, many thousands of names similar to those under the entrance to St Stephen's Green at home, names like Murphy and Fitzgerald and Kelly and Mangan and O'Neill and O'Connell. They mingled with the thousands of Welsh and English and French and Belgian names of men who had fought and fallen too and it was extraordinary to learn, by looking at the archive photographs in the Cloth Hall, Market Square, that this small town which we were exploring had been completely gutted by shells and canon fire, and meticulously rebuilt exactly as it had been before the First World War. Nobody looking at the tall fourteenth-century cathedral could believe that it too had been gutted. But the people of Ypres have done more than just rebuild. Every morning and every evening to this day they sound the 'Reveille', in memory of those innocent dead, and townspeople gather in the square to stand in silence for the duration of the ceremony in winter and summer alike.

It seemed fitting, somehow, to be exploring, in sleety cold, places like the awful Death Trenches, and the grave of Francis Ledwidge who was blown away by a shell not far from there. That grave, unlike those of Wilfred Owen and Siegfried Sassoon, was not actually part of our itinerary, but when we mentioned Ledwidge to the knowledgeable gentleman from Bruges who was our guide, he at once decided to include it. And so we discovered, eighty years after his death, that somebody had left fresh spring flowers on the grave of the young Irishman, and nearby was his memorial sculpture. When he died, he was only twenty-nine years old, so maybe Seamus Heaney is right in the closing paragraph of his introduction to Ledwidge's *Collected Poems*:

> Ledwidge solved nothing. As a poet his sense of purpose and his own gifts were only beginning to come into mature focus. As a political phenomenon he represents conflicting elements in the Irish inheritance which continue to be repressed or unresolved.

Indeed, since that disgraceful scene on Drumcondra Road, all those years ago, not much has changed. One sees a tiny minority of people in Ireland wearing a poppy on Remembrance Day, as I do myself, despite an acknowledged republican background. But it takes a long search to find a poppy seller.

For all that, the First World War and its Irish connections have continued to provide inspiration to writers as far apart as Neil Jordan and Sebastian Barry, or Frank McGuinness and James Plunkett. It's there still as a tantalising contradiction, and it seems it won't go away.

> In you, our dead enigma, all the strains
> Crisscross in useless equilibrium
> And as the wind turns through this vigilant bronze
> I hear again the sure confusing drum
>
> You followed from Boyne water to the Balkans
> But miss the twilit note your flute should sound.
> You were not keyed or pitched like these true blue ones
> Through all of you consort now underground.
>
> from 'In Memoriam Francis Ledwidge', by Seamus Heaney

CUIMHNE AN UISCE

Nuala Ní Dhomhnaill

Uaireannta nuair a bhíonn a hiníon
sa seomra folctha ag glanadh a fiacla le slaod tiubh
is le sód bácála,
tuigtear di go líonann an seomra suas
le huisce

Tosnaíonn sé ag a cosa is a rúitíní
is bíonn sé ag slibearáil suas is suas arís
thar a másaí is a cromáin is a básta.
Ní fada
go mbíonn sé suas go dtí na hioscaidí uirthi.
Cromann sí síos ann go minic ag piocadh suas
rudaí mar thuáillí láimhe nó ceirteacha
atá ar maos ann.
Tá cuma na feamaní orthu –
na scothóga fada ceilpe úd a dtugaidís
'gruaig mhaighdean mhara' nó eireabaill mhadraí rua' orthu.
Ansan go hobann téann an t-uisce i ndísc
is ní fada
go mbíonn an seomra iomlán tirim arís

Tá strus uafásach
ag roinnt leis na mothúcháin seo go léir.

Tar éis an tsaoil, níl rud ar bith aici
chun comparáid a dhéanamh leis.

Is níl na focail chearta ar eolas aici ar chor ar bith.
Ag a seisiún síciteiripeach seachtainiúil
bíonn a dóthain dua aici
ag iarraidh an scéal aisteach seo a mhíniú
is é a chur in iúl i gceart don mheabhairdhochtúir.

Níl aon téarmaíocht aici,
ná téarmaí tagartha
ná focal ar bith a thabharfadh an tuairim is lú do cad é 'uisce'.
'Lacht trédhearcach, 'a deir sí, ag déanamh a cruinndíchill.
'Sea,' a deireann an teiripí, 'coinnibh ort!'
Bíonn sé á moladh is á gríosadh chun gnímh teangan.
Deineann sí iarracht eile.
'Slaod tanaí, a thugann sí air,
í ag tóraíocht go cúramach i measc na bhfocal.
'Brat gléineach, ábhar silteach, rud fliuch.'

A RECOVERED MEMORY
OF WATER

Paul Muldoon

from the Irish of Nuala Ní Dhomhnaill

Sometimes when the mermaid's daughter
is in the bathroom
cleaning her teeth with a thick brush
and baking soda
she has the sense the room is filling
with water.

It starts at her feet and ankles
and slides further and further up
over her thighs and hips and waist.
In no time
it's up to her oxters.
She bends down to pick up
Hand towels and washcloths and all such things
as are sodden with it.
They all look like seaweed —
like those long strands of kelp that used to be called
'mermaid-hair' or 'foxtail'.
Just as suddenly the water recedes
and in no time

the room's completely dry again.
A terrible sense of stress
is part and parcel of these emotions.
At the end of the day she has nothing else
to compare it to.
She doesn't have the vocabulary for any of it.
At her weekly therapy session
she has more than enough to be going on with
just to describe this strange phenomenon
and to express it properly
to the psychiatrist.

She doesn't have the terminology
or any of the points of reference
or any word at all that would give the slightest suggestion
as to what water might be.
'A transparent liquid,' she says, doing as best she can.
'Right,' says the therapist, 'keep going.'
He coaxes and cajoles her towards word-making.
She has another run at it.
'A thin flow,' she calls it,
casting about gingerly in the midst of words.
'A shiny film. Dripping stuff. Something wet.'

CREGGAN GRAVEYARD

Éamonn Ó hUallacháin

Nestling in the hills of south Armagh, on the road to Crossmaglen, you come on Creggan churchyard, and I know of no more enchanting grave-yard anywhere in Ireland. An Creagán, named after the rocky outcrop on which it stands, is an open page from which the story of this area, and indeed of the whole island, may be read. This has been a sacred spot for 1,000 years or more, and it is now in the attentive care of the local Church of Ireland community, who minds it well.

As you wander in through the old iron gates, you soon notice that Catholic, Protestant and Dissenter are all buried together in the clay of Creggan. Pat Loye, a small farmer who died in 1685, and whose grave has the oldest dated stone, lies between a Jackson and an Eastwood. Creggan is no respecter of status either:

> Sceptre and crown must tumble down, and in the dust be
>   equal made
> with the poor crooked scythe and spade.

A few steps past the peasant's grave is where the chieftains of the area, the O'Neills of the Fews, were laid to rest for hundreds of years. Their tomb was lost until quite recently, when three local men came on it by chance while tidying up the graveyard for a poet's commemoration. When they descended into the vault, they found the remains of sixty people. Amongst them was Turlach Mac Enrí Ó Neill, half-brother to the Great Hugh of Tír Eoghain, and it was Turlach's ability to keep a foot in both camps in the late sixteenth century that ensured south Armagh was not planted.

It was in this same tomb, 200 years ago, that the poet Art Mac Cumhaigh took shelter on a bitter winter's evening shortly before his death:

> *Ag Uirchill an Chreagáin sea chodail mé aréir faoi bhrón.*
> (In the graveyard of Creggan, I slept last night, in gloom.)

A vision came to him in the form of a lovely young woman inviting him to leave his pathetic, miserable existence and to go with her to a honeyed land where the foreigner's sway did not hold. He thought of going with her but was reluctant to leave those he loved, and asked, if he did go, if it would be possible for him to be buried, in the end, in the fragrant soil of Creggan, which is indeed where he does lie today, though his escape to Utopia never did occur.

As you pass the tomb of the O'Neills, and before the ground falls rapidly down the Creggan river, we come on the burial place of Séamas Mór Mac Murfaidh, rapparee and poet from the eighteenth century. Betrayed by his lover to the Chief Constable of the area, he was tried in Dundalk and executed in Armagh Jail at the age of thirty. While awaiting his death, he foresaw, in poetry, his remains making their way home, finally, to south Armagh:

> '*Triailfidh mo thórramh tráthnóna Dé hAoine* ...
> (My funeral will make its way on Friday evening
> And on Sunday morning, in silence, through the little roads;
> Caití Óg Ní Dhónaill will be there and all the young women
>   around
> And I'll be listening to their voices though lying under the
>   ground.)

Close by is the enclosure of the Donaldsons, Gaelic-speaking Presbyterians who came from Scotland and became the leaders of the United Irishmen in this area in the years preceding 1798. One of them, known to all as Peigí Bán Donaldson because of 'the shock of white ringlets that fell around her shoulders', was the founder of the United Irishmen in south Armagh and her brother was the first chairman. Not too far from the Donaldson plot lie some members of the Creggan Yeomanry, whose sworn aim in those years was to destroy the United Men.

On the way out of the graveyard, under the yew trees, there are two gravestones which stand quite close to one another; one to Fr John Campbell, a Catholic priest, and the other to the Rev. Daniel Gunn-Browne, a Presbyterian minister. They both stood courageously with the people of Creggan during the Great Famine and went to London together to plead with the Committee on Outrages in Ireland on behalf of the starving population. When the opposing lawyer put it to them that a 'landlord had a right to do whatever he liked with his own' Gunn-Browne's reply was, 'No man has a right to do what is wrong.'

As I wander out of Creggan, out through the old iron gates, I find it most striking how those of other generations, friends and foes, noble and lowly, Planter and Gael, now lie side by side in this one small acre of land: O'Neill and Loye (Great chieftain and small farmer); O'Callaghan and Ball (Catholic landlord and Protestant landlord); Mac Murfaidh and Johnston (Rapparee and Chief Constable); Donaldson and Crawley (United Irishman and Yoeman) all together now under the sod, in the fragrant soil of Creggan. '*Faoi fhód le chéile i gCill chumhra an Chreagáin.*'

A TIN OF PUMPKIN

Mary Mullen

A tin of pumpkin. That's what I want when asked if I need anything
from the States. Always on the outlook, I've never found a tin of
pumpkin for sale in the west of Ireland.

The low light of November makes me long for the smell of
pumpkin mixed with eggs, milk, sugar, cinnamon and nutmeg warming
the kitchen and my memories.

There was one Thanksgiving, though, when I was so sick with the flu
that the combined smells of pumpkin pie and the all-morning aroma of
the turkey roasting made me get sick into a blue plastic basin. I was ten
years old. My family, busy preparing the traditional feast for twenty
people, moved me from our couch to the neighbour's house, so I could
be sick in privacy. I lay on the unfamiliar plaid couch and listened to
Alaska's famous Kenai river, twenty feet down a steep embankment,
tinkle, then rumble as it froze solid. I dozed in the dark, thankful for
the sound of my mother's boots on the crunchy snow when she came to
touch my forehead.

The next most memorable Thanksgiving took place in Astoria,
Oregon. I was nineteen. A few of us Alaskan girls were working in a
tuna cannery. We stood on the tort-line for eight hours a day scraping
the maroon blood line from the cooked tuna. We had rented an unfur-
nished Victorian house up the hill with a view of the Columbia river.
We purchased a used refrigerator which smelled and looked clean, but,
unbeknownst to us, had cockroaches living in the back of it. Undaunted,

we invited a dozen other Alaskans who were attending universities in Oregon to join us for giving thanks. Joni Mitchell's album *Blue* blasted out of the record player as we filled the waterbeds and baked as though we were Francie's mother in *The Butcher Boy*. We passed a chalice of wine around and toasted Alaska; loving the idea that you can't ever take Alaska out of us, even though we were 1,000 miles from home.

Nearly thirty, I found myself teaching Inupiat Eskimo children in a small village west of Point Barrow. A whaling captain had landed a bowhead whale, and a feast for Thanksgiving took place in the school gym. Two hundred people packed the gym. They danced and laughed while waiting for the revered captain to share the whale meat and muktuk. Holding a huge butcher knife, he and his assistants made their way slowly around to each family.

'How many?'

'Eight,' replied a mother next to me. He whacked off a massive roast of chocolate brown meat, and an equally colossal hunk of black and pink muktuk. While plopping it into their black rubbish bag, he looked at me and said, 'OK, teacher-girl, muktuk for one!'

Years later, I cook a Thanksgiving dinner for my eight-year-old, dual-citizen daughter in our south Galway home. Joni Mitchell sings of drinking a case of her lover and remaining on her feet.

'What does that mean, Mammy?' she asks while gingerly ironing eight cloth napkins.

'It's a love song, Lily. It means you are as delicious as hot chocolate, as sweet as pumpkin pie. What are you thankful for today?' I ask as I baste the turkey one more time.

She says, 'I'm thankful that Pádraig the Postman gave us that tin of pumpkin, that all the children of the world are safe.'

My soul cringes as I offer her prayer to the universe and stir the gravy.

DECEMBER

JOHN MILTON: CROMWELL'S SPIN DOCTOR

Mary Russell

When the King of England, Charles I, was beheaded way back in 1649, it sent a shiver of fear throughout all the other crowned heads of Europe. What if the same thing happened to them? What if they were called upon to be accountable to the people? What if their soldiers were allowed to question their officers? In England, this is exactly what happened, for the world was turned upside down by the trial and execution of Charles I.

Then, in order to counteract the anti-republican propaganda that followed, Cromwell, the leader of the Parliamentarians, decided it was important to put forward the pro-republican point of view to explain to the rest of Europe what had been done and why. But who would be the best person to take on this important task? Whoever it was would have to have a good working knowledge of Latin, which was the lingua franca of the day. He – it goes without saying it would be a man – would have to have a commitment to the ideals of republicanism, to accountability and to the rights of the common man.

Thus it was that John Milton was chosen, charged with the task of writing about the evils of the monarchical system and of the benefits of a republican one, which he did persuasively, eloquently and in Latin, of course, leaving no stone unturned in his effort to make sure that the Parliamentarian point of view was understood.

He was, therefore — to use present day parlance — Cromwell's spin doctor, appointed to the Council of State with the title of Secretary for Foreign Tongues.

As a schoolchild, I had been forced to learn off by heart large tracts of *Paradise Lost* and *Samson Agonistes*. The poem 'Lycidas' I could relate to because it was Milton's lament for a young friend who had drowned but, by and large, I found him a difficult poet whose writings were dense and hard to understand. He was also a bit puritanical and we all knew that puritans were never any fun. But beyond that, I knew nothing about the man.

And then, one day, I visited the house he retreated to in Buckinghamshire during the Great Plague. He came to this house a couple of years before the monarchy was restored, bringing with him his third wife and his daughter Deborah who helped him once his blindness made it impossible for him to read.

It's a lovely old timbered house with an inglenook fireplace and a ladder leading to an upstairs bedroom which Milton, then seventy-three, was unable to climb. Instead, he used a room to the right of the front door which served both as a bedroom and as a study.

Here in the pre-dawn stillness — he got up regularly at 4 a.m. — he completed *Paradise Lost*, which deals with the restitution of the monarchy, and then he started and finished *Paradise Regained*. In fact, on the wall is a framed receipt for £5 — a lot in those days — which was the first half of the payment for *Paradise Lost*.

Milton had always been a political animal who would have made common cause with many political activists of today. In the run up to the Civil War, he had published numerous pamphlets dealing with issues such as divorce, which he favoured. This last was written when his first wife, Mary Powell, left the family home and returned to live with her mother. They had married when she was seventeen and he was thirty-four. The Powell family didn't at all like his views on divorce but, far worse for Milton, was that the Powells came down on the Royalist side so that, politically, husband and wife were seriously divided. This treatise on divorce caused mayhem and was finally banned. This led to further trouble when Milton wrote *Areopagitica* which denounced any attempt by the powers that be to silence a writer or to ban a book and which showed him to be a passionate champion of freedom of the press. 'As good Almost to kill a man as kill a good book,' he wrote.

Two weeks after the execution of Charles I, he published a pamphlet called *The Tenure of Kings and Magistrates* which sets republican principles against those of an arbitrary, and therefore undemocratic, government and which has led him to be called England's greatest republican.

A NOBEL BANQUET

Gerry Moran

Last month, I came as near as I'm ever going to come to the Nobel Prize for Literature. I was in Stockholm in Sweden, the birthplace of Alfred Nobel, the inventor of dynamite and whose vast fortune funds the Nobel prizes. I was also in Stockholm's City Hall, where the prize winners will assemble for a banquet tomorrow night, the 10 December, after the prize-giving ceremony in the Concert Hall.

Both ceremonies always take place on the 10 December, the anniversary of Alfred Nobel's death in 1896 at the age of sixty-three. What I was doing in Stockholm's City Hall, however, had less to do with Nobel prizes and more to do with hunger.

It's our last night in Stockholm and my wife and I decide to go somewhere different for our last supper, so to speak. Browsing through an 'Eating Out' guide we come upon the following:

> Stadshus Kallaren – found in the basement of City Hall, come here to savour a Nobel Banquet. Your dinner will consist of the menu and wines served to the Nobel Prize winners the previous 10 December.

I book a table.

The Stadshus Kallaren, in the basement of City Hall, is long and narrow, the walls and ceiling elegantly decorated with frescoes, and it resembles a small, ornate church.

We are handed our menus by Crister, a silvery, long-haired, elderly gentleman, who is a dead-ringer for the actor Michael Gambon. Crister would slot easily into any Agatha Christie novel.

As I study the 2006 Nobel Menu, my wife points to the small print: 'This menu must be booked twenty-four hours in advance.'

Oh, oh. I explain to Crister that we are leaving Stockholm tomorrow. Crister, a man of few words, consults with the manager who hastens to the kitchen to see what he can do. We're in luck – the Nobel Banquet can be served, but, first, Crister prepares a special table for us, a table that replicates in detail, including the candelabra and gold-plated plates, cutlery and glasses, the exact table set-up for the Nobel Banquet that will take place upstairs in the Blue Room of Stockholm's City Hall tomorrow night.

The preparation of the tables for tomorrow night for the 1,318 guests, including the King and Queen of Sweden, will occupy twenty-eight people for eight hours. Thirty-eight cooks will be on duty, two hundred and twenty eight waiters will serve the food and five people will work flat out, uncorking bottles of champagne and wine.

No such fuss tonight, however, as Crister uncorks a bottle of Montaudon Brüt Reserve champagne which is served with our starter: mosaic of salted salmon and scallops, served with cucumber and apple salad. It is delightful, as is the champagne and Crister, God bless him, is not slow to refill.

The main course is lamb. On 10 December last year, the Nobel Prize winners tucked into: herb-baked back of lamb with olive-glazed vegetables, potato and Jerusalem artichoke puree, served with Port wine sauce and accompanied by a red Shiraz from South Africa.

There was no lamb on the menu in 2005 when Literature winner, Harold Pinter, in his Nobel lecture, referred to his native England, as 'a bleating lamb'. Instead, Harold had mountain grouse breast, baked in black trumpet mushroom.

Three different menus are prepared each year and are tasted by members of the Nobel Foundation at a trial dinner. The selected menu takes into account the different cultural backgrounds of the guests while incorporating a Scandinavian flavour.

Back in 1995, Seamus Heaney, our Nobel Laureate, enjoyed west coast special salt cod for starters, herb-fried fillet of red deer for main course and Nobel ice-cream parfait with spun sugar for dessert.

Our desert tonight is pineapple parfait on an almond and cinnamon biscuit accompanied by a glass of Sauternes dessert wine. We finish with coffee and a chocolate replica of the gold medal the prize winners will receive tomorrow from the King of Sweden along with their diplomas and substantial cheques.

What Doris Lessing, the 2007 Nobel prize winner for literature, and her fellow prize winners will tuck into tomorrow night is anyone's guess, but from the 11 December on, and for one year only, the Nobel Banquet can be savoured in the unique atmosphere of Stadshus Kallaren in Stockholm's City Hall.

HAPPY CHRISTMAS '78

Tommy Sands

Eileen Paisley opened the door and assured me with a wide smile that I was welcome. 'You're welcome,' she said. 'Wait in here.' It was near to the Christmas of 1978 and, outside, the snowflakes were bouncing off the Free Presbyterian windows, like drunken seagulls in search of the seven seas. It was getting dark.

'He'll be here soon,' she said.

It had been a bad year. Eighty-one people had been killed and there were no talks going on between the Northern leaders. There was not even talks about talks. Some people thought I must be either mad or naïve to invite them all to this kind of Christmas get-together. I asked for no talk of politics or religion, just a yarn or a story, maybe a song to inspire the humanity and the neighbourliness within us.

They wouldn't come to the same studio, I knew that, but I could bring the studio to them and bring them together later. I fingered the microphone of my brand-new black Marantz tape machine as nervous as a Catholic in a Paisley Manse and waited, wondering what manner of man this reverend man was.

My first visit had been to a socialist sinner called Paddy Devlin, the most socialist of the Social Democratic and Labour Party. He threw back his head and sang a song, then threw back a vodka and sang another. Hardline Unionist leader of the day, Harry West, spoke softly of his Christmas childhood and the two primates in Armagh, archbishops Simms and O'Fiach, rose to the occasion with relish in recitation and song.

Soon, I was walking into the house that Gerry Fitt would soon be burned out of. 'Some people call this a tin sandwich,' he said, putting the harmonica to his lips.

He was like a stand-up comedian, firing out one-liners like spits of tobacco, aimed at myself and a journalist who had arrived to take photographs. Some of Fitt's jokes were black, others blue, but few would not have raised a chuckle on that cold night in the bleak Ulster winter of 1978, when a bit of laughter was a rare and sacred thing.

Paisley would be most difficult, I was told. His pulpit-pounding fundamentalism didn't make him an obvious candidate for merriment and frivolity, particularly in the company of political papists and social-ist sinners. But he was a 'must'. He would have to be there and I would have to wait a little longer.

Suddenly, it seemed the house began to shake.

'He's coming,' said Eileen, putting her head around the door.

I heard footsteps getting closer and I shivered slightly, hoping it wouldn't show. The footsteps grew louder and the house seemed to shake more. Then, standing at the door was one of the biggest men I have ever seen. He had a large head, large ears, large teeth, large eyes, large everything. He seemed to fill the whole doorway. As a child, I had nervously watched the television screen as he controlled thousands with a single roar. Now, he was standing right in front of me, like a giant.

'How do you prefer to be addressed, by the way?' I asked, trying to break the ice lightly. 'Do you want me to call you Reverend, or Doctor, or Ian?'

'You can call me anything you like, providing you don't call me early in the morning,' he boomed, with a loud laugh. 'I hear you have Fitt playing the mouth organ?' he said. 'I don't know how good he is, but the more he plays in my constituency, the more the people vote for me.'

'What about a song or a story from yourself?' I said.

He put his head in his hands and began to think.

'As you know,' he said, at last, 'I'm an unreformed jailbird and the first time I went to prison, the prison doctor examined me from head to toe and said, "You're fit," and I said, "No! I'm Paisley."'

This was a Paisley I had never envisaged, relaxed and radiant with boyish devilment and humour. He regaled me with joke after joke, gradually drawing me into a web of companionship. The man was powerful. I was mindful of this Redemptorist who could kick you verbally heavenwards by scaring the very hell out of you. He portrayed a rare mixture of charisma and awfulness and you were inclined to laugh at the joke before you got to the punchline.

I walked away from the door with a well-filled tape and a well-shook hand, and the longing for a future Christmas when this man's power might be used to make the world a brighter place to be.

THE WORD

John F. Deane

I stood in the chill of deep winter dusk. I was with my father, down along the grit-track that was made for donkey and cart out into the heart of bogland where turf was saved. Now, there was only that chill wind coming from the north, shushing the rushes and heathers into a heartless sound. From the distance came a sound that lifted my breathing into excitement; it was as if a flock of lambs called out from the high reaches of a mountain slope, a high-pitched, insistent baaing call. But I knew what it was, and father knew. For we were standing, skulking rather, behind a ragged thorn bush, there near the rim of bogland lake, the drooping reeds just visible through the dusk-light. This was the antici-pated arrival of the greylag geese, those plump and lovely wild creatures that had mated and bred among the distant marshes, the watery waste-lands of Siberia, of Iceland, flying now towards us to winter on our less-frozen soil, our more gentle waterways and wet-heaths.

Then I saw them, making their way through the evening in a strag-gling chevron shape, like that wavering chalk line I had drawn on the school slate-board to shape an inverted V. They were coming down out of some great height of sky, down to splash-land, gratefully, on our small and intimate bogland lake. Unaware of a human presence that was awed but threatening, the lead bird fell back from that wedge-shaped working across the air, to give place to another bird that might lead the flock down to where we waited. Father had the rifle; I held his hand.

I was excited, part of it, a shadow among shadows, a wedge out of the darkness of the earth, a piece of the land. Dangerous. And cold.

Later, I touched the ashen-grey, still-warm breast of the grey lag, flung down across the scrubbed-deal scullery table, and, when I took my hand away, the fingers were tipped with blood. I put my fingertips to my lips and tasted something of the awful labouring of the earth, the salt suffering of distant frozen lands, the warm fluidity of blood that had pumped through a body urging its way across thousands of miles towards unexpected death, and the raw and unhappy violence offered to the world by my own father. But I, too, was raw then, and unlearned and knew no sorrow, nor any grief for the lovely creature beaten too soon into death.

Later still, that very evening, I stepped out again, holding once more my father's hand, out into the chill and urgency that was Christmas Eve. It was a ritual, this walk up to the top of a low hill to see how the night looked, this special night. I watched, intrigued, our breathing shape angel-ghosts about us on the air; frost was hailing across the fields and hedgerows a chill and feather-delicate scattering of white. It was very cold and we moved quickly together. There was not a cloud to be seen in that wonderful sky and when, soon, we were standing high on the old quarry hill, we could see the village laid out breathless in expectation below us. There was a candle lit in every window throughout the town-land and the sky above us, too, was rife with its own special and winking candlelights. It was all wonder, breathtaking, the chill and the stillness and the heart pounding with a scarcely understood excitement.

I was clinging to my father's hand and even he was quieted, a silence growing between us that was, somehow, much more companionable than when earlier we had headed out together, that rifle held cautiously in father's hand. I stood in awe and I know that he, too, big and experienced and eternally wise as he was, was held by that same simple awe that held me. I know that what was happening within me was a level-ling of all my senses to a notion of peace that was almost physical, that made me and my father part of that sacred universe, this time offering no danger to it but a kind of love, a sharing in the mystery, a pulsing small part of the pulsing of all of creation. Something to do with tenderness, and with hope.

It was Christmas Eve. Again, in time and in space, there was that happening which cannot be spoken in words, but what was happening was everything whereby the Word itself was spoken. And it happens again, and again, in time and in space, the flight of flocks of wild geese crying through the stillness of twilight towards their resting places, the opening out above their flight of a sky so magnificent in extent and beauty that it silences all language, and the Word itself is spoken through that silence, in the faithful candlelight that is prayer and welcome and hope in every innocent window. And when, at last, we set off homewards, father and I, I was big with love and I danced on stars that were singing their hosannas in each frosted-over bog-pool.

BEANNACHTAÍ NA NOLLAG

Liam Ó Muirthile

Aer caol na maidine os cionn na cathrach
oiread is a líonfadh bairille
ag bolgadh na matán.

Na héin ag canadh aria Montenotte
is mé ag gabháil de choiscéim éalaitheach
lem mhálaí thar an ardán.

Tugann mo chroí léim ag an mbácús
is guíonn sí beannachtaí na Nollag orm
lem mhála aráin.

Oíche Nollag ag fágaint an bhaile
sínim mo lámh i mbrothall na mbuilíní
taobh liom ar an suíochán.

Téann arraing trín traein ag tarraingt
go géar ar bhéal an tolláin;
ar a laghad, beidh an bolg lán.

CHRISTMAS GREETINGS

Ciaran Carson

from the Irish of Liam Ó Muirthile

The clean dawn air above the city
is inhaled in barrelfuls
to swell the muscles.

Birds sing the Montenotte aria
as I sneak with my bags
past the high terraced houses.

My heart leaps as I reach the bakery
and she offers me her Christmas greetings
with my bag of bread.

Leaving home on Christmas Eve
my hand steals into the warmth
of the baps beside me on the seat.

A shudder goes through the train
as it leans into the tunnel's mouth;
at least the belly will be full.

THE WELCOMER

Brendan Graham

I am at the gate, looking east along the road from Finny to where it snakes its way past me, out of Mayo and up to Ireland.

Before me is the Mask, behind me the Maamtrasna mountain: water within water, stone within stone.

I glance back at the house. I have left open the half-door. Always I am in trouble ... for leaving open the half-door – 'letting in the cold'. When, all I am doing is letting in the night – and the phantoms of the night which flit by from farther back in the valley ... and Loughnafooey's swan-less shore.

Now, from the outside I see how inviting is the glow of an open half-door.

The night itself could be any night ... but it is not. It is the night of ... The Winterchild.

Within the kitchen window, framed in the condensation, is the figure of a woman, head downwards to the work at hand, 'readying'.

She looks up, casting an eye down the *bóithrín* to the gate, knowing I am there. Like me, she is watching for lights from the east, not at peace until they turn in the gate ... bringing the first of them home.

I strain against the night to see towards the fork in the headlight-flashed sky – so I will know which way the cars turn ... left for Corr na Mona, or right for the Finny road ... and me.

Nearer, in the cradle of the mountain, a light burns. The man who lives there lives modestly, below notice, but he knows of things like silence ... and stillness.

He would be lost in talk-radio Ireland. *He* is a philosopher of stone walls and hilly, hump-backed fields ... and the wisdom of wool.

In the field by the stream, our two donkeys Jack and Juno are restless, ee-awing into the night, ready to be called – to warm a stable, to carry a Christ.

I look back to the kitchen ... the figure still works. I am reminded of a boy of Christmas past; of coming home from boarding school ... a train, laden with scholars, and civil servants out of 'lodgings' in Dublin, and the hod carriers and tunnel-men fresh off the mail boat. From the motorways and building sites of England *they* came, pockets full of pounds with the Queen on them. They bringing home the Christmas from Croydon or Kilburn, with talk full of McAlpine and the craic ... and the Crown in Cricklewood ... and girls from home danced with at the Gresham ballroom on the Holloway Road.

The Kerry train stopped at every crossroad of a station, tumbling them out into the dark of small-town Ireland. Tumbling them into waiting arms ... back into the old, safe life ... for a while.

In the carriages we waited, impatient. On southwards then, our faces pressed to the windows, the train gathered itself for the mountains. As nearer it drew to that far-off kingdom, in its clackety-clack, I could hear the music of homecoming; imagine my mother 'readying' for our return, preparing the midnight feast, dampening Charlie Lenihan's fresh eggs into ravenous sandwiches; and with slabs of her chocolate biscuit cake stacked on the Wedgewood plate she kept for important occasions.

Then, finger to her lips, moistening it to gather the crumbs from the white-Christmassed table. She casting an eye at the mantelpiece clock, head tilted towards the mirror above it, fixing her jet-black hair, telling my father 'they must be in Mallow by now – they'll be famished'.

My father then, too soon there, in the thick overcoat of a fog at Farranfore, watching for smoke in the night, the wait of four months over. Then, the creak to the station, the shuddering halt, wrench open the door, jump the gap, suitcase following ... and my father suited, tall and timeless, appearing out of the mist ... a hand outstretched before him.

I return again to the now of this night. Picture the inside of the house behind me; the room where the fire is lit, where the Christmas cactus my mother once gave, now every year ignites her memory, flaming her presence back to life again.

Across the room from where the cactus sits is the crib – my father's crib. It is beautifully carved of oak and the bark of oak – and thatched with real thatch. In it a small lamp of sanctuary casts its warmth over the figurines of Mary, Joseph, the empty cradle. A gift from a farmer man my father once helped, chiselled out by the man himself ... lovingly thatched with that most precious of all gifts ... time.

Now, as my mother and father once did, these two, a cactus and a crib sit across from each other. When the travellers whom I await arrive, they will admire them, as they always do, touch them and understand for a moment, both the passing of all things and the never-ending presence of all things.

At the turn for Corr na Móna, I see lights flash the sky ... watch them take the lower road to Finny, look to the window of the house, see their mother, my mother, within. The rise in the road at the Ferry Bridge sends the lights skywards again, only to disappear once more. For an instant, I think they have turned into one of the other houses but I know the road along there, how in that place it dips into a hollow. Nevertheless, my heart rises when, at the turn beyond the *sean bhóthar*, the side of the mountain is briefly lit and I know the travellers still travel.

A voice from the side of the house calls, 'Is that them – I saw the lights?' I turn to answer and notice the kitchen window empty. The voice goes in again ... and in the living room the fire is stoked. I see the smoke plume heavenwards – and, through the glow of the window, a head tilted towards the mirror above the mantelpiece.

The lights bounce towards me, ever closer along the road. Now, an amber light ... indicating safe delivery. The car slows on seeing me. Jack and Juno start up again and the winter night is alive with sound and colour.

Filled with light I walk out of the dark, hand outstretched before me ... and, for a moment ... I am my father ...

I see my daughter's face ... joy like a tear the moon let fall.

The inexpressible beyond me, I touch her cheek through the opening window.

Now, many years later, *I* am the welcomer.

LEMONS

Emma Sides

Lemons are things you buy in supermarkets. They're exotic. But in my sister's garden, they grow on trees. Alongside the oranges, they glow warmly in the winter sun and through tall, elegant windows, the painted shutters thrown back, the Mediterranean can also be seen, sparkling bluely in the distance.

On Christmas morning, we slice open the oranges, each half-filled with precious drops of captured blood, and squeeze them into ruby-red juice; and we put a bowlful of lemons on the grand piano. Breakfast is croissants and pastries from the boulangerie, freshly-squeezed juice and strong coffee. The same ingredients, purchased rather more prosaically from Tesco when at home, are magically transformed into a sophisticated *petit déjeuner*.

I have made a washing line between two chairs for the stockings – a row of stripy knee socks held in place with wooden clothes pegs – and inside little memories of childhood for each of us; a stripy candy cane poking out the top, a net bag of golden chocolate coins (pirate's treasure), real, shiny money (the same amount for each so that nobody can fight), a blank tape, a matchbox containing a miniature box of skittles or perhaps a cardboard cut-out house that must be painstakingly put together, an apple, an orange and, because they grow on trees here, a lemon. Stockings may be opened before breakfast but presents must wait till after.

Later, we slice the smoked salmon we have brought from home (wrapped in newspaper in my suitcase), butter the McCambridge's brown bread and cut lemon wedges to adorn the platter. Then we don our Christmas finery and proceed to the Promenade des Anglais for a people-watching constitutional before dinner and collapse. Despite the presence of a grand piano, the rest of the furniture in my sister's elegant rented French villa is distinctly uncomfortable and, therefore, we are forced to slump in rotation on the only decent sofa.

Two years earlier, in Peru, having descended through the clouds, I lay on the floor of the Colca Canyon on Christmas morning and waited for the condors to rise on the morning thermals. Around me in the lemon grove, the trees dripped yellow, dripped with zest and energy, while, elsewhere, branches groaned with the weight of warm ripe avocados and we ate guacamole sandwiches for lunch. Twice as deep as the Grand Canyon, the walls soared above us and we swam in the warm waters of a thermal spring, diverted into a pool for our pleasure. At midnight, when the day had long since cooled, the steam rose gently from the water and we swam again by moonlight.

Many years ago, when I was a child, we would spend the long, dark, cold winter afternoons camped out in our front sitting room. We liked to make houses out of chairs, blankets, old camp beds, and the red and orange geometrically patterned Marimekko curtains that had adorned that same room in the early 1970s. We would pile cushions and pillows and sleeping bags inside and retreat into our own warm, cosy, private world.

I am caught on camera, curled up asleep in my winter palace, worn out from playing. Now that I am grown up and have my own real bricks and mortar house, I like to curl up in my favourite armchair, the fire lighting, a gin and tonic with clinking ice cubes and a slice of lemon to hand and I remember that on those long, distant winter afternoons, my mother would make lemon juice. Plastic beakers, each a different colour – pale pink and blue and green and yellow – and a plate of iced fancy biscuits whose colours matched the beakers. All brought in to us on a battered pink square tin tray. And in the kitchen the whirr of the blender, a pile of empty lemon halves and, sometimes, not quite enough sugar.

Lemons are things you buy in supermarkets.

THE GHOST OF THE CROPPY BOY

Monica Henchy

My first Christmas in Ireland was unusual to say the least. Three days before the feast, we had left London with its bustling crowds and brilliant lights to come and spend Christmas in a large, draughty castle at the foot of Lugnaquilla Mountain in Wicklow. We had travelled from Holyhead in a boat filled with noisy returning emigrants singing, 'Come back to Erin' while clutching their bottles of stout. In a few days' time, they would be ploughing their lonely way back again. But we were lucky. We were coming home to stay. My father had decided that Ireland might provide more inspiration for his writing and would be a better place to bring up his daughter. Hearing that the Oblate Fathers were offering to let Aughavannagh Castle for a modest rent, we were now on our way there.

On the last seven miles of our journey, we were shaken from side to side as the old Armstrong-Siddeley car ploughed its way over the rocky road. Suddenly, the castle loomed into sight and we could glimpse the long, dark avenue ahead. My father got out of the car and opened the rusty gates, overshadowed by a large, stone arch from which rooks were cawing loudly. These strange birds were flying around us protesting that their solitude had been disturbed. The huge house was shrouded in darkness but I could just make out through the snowflakes the outline of a castle at each end. When we pushed in the front door, it groaned on its hinges to let us into a dark hallway, and then into an enormous stone-floor kitchen lit by paraffin lamps where a huge fire glowed warmly in the open black range. A small man stepped forward to greet us.

'I'm Christy, the caretaker of John Redmond's old home. Happy Christmas to ye all! Ye're very welcome.' And turning to a shy girl beside him he announced, 'This is Kate who will be looking after ye.'

After a hurried meal, candles were lit and we retired to the eerie upstairs rooms. Although I was tired, I was curious enough to look into the room next to mine where a long, rusty bar ran the length of the back window. 'No one ever sleeps there,' said Christy ominously. 'Best to keep it locked.'

I awoke the next morning to a vision of delight. Everywhere was covered in a thick blanket of snow. Feeling hungry, I descended in search of breakfast but, when I reached the kitchen, clouds of black smoke greeted me. Mother and Father with perspiration rolling down their cheeks were looking into the jaws of the black range; Kate was beside them, scratching her head in puzzlement. Finally, Father pulled out the damper. 'Don't you realise, Kate, that you must pull this to create a draught to draw the fire?'

'Well, God Almighty,' said Kate, and this was to prove her continual response to all crises.

We all laughed and Father, who loved writing limericks said, 'After that I must find something to rhyme with Aughavannagh.'

'I bet you won't,' said I. But later that evening when Kate was out of earshot he produced the following verse:

> Kate from Knockananna
> Came to Aughavannagh
> She said, 'God Almighty
> I've forgotten my nightie,
> And now I'll have to sleep without any!'

All the next day, we prepared for Christmas. The turkey was cleaned and stuffed and the ham was put to simmer. Christy cut down a small fir tree and I was given the job of decorating with tinsel and candle-holders. I went out on the white lawn and looked up at the ivy-clad house and counted thirty-six windows. While Christy was cutting holly and ivy, I listened in fascination to his stories. The house, he said, was built as a military barracks in 1798 and it was here, he maintained, that the Croppy Boy was hanged. 'And that's why that room beside you is never used. His ghost has been seen betimes.'

After tea, I was tucked into bed. I hoped to stay awake to see my Christmas presents, but I drifted into that twilight zone between sleeping and waking. Suddenly, I could hear the clatter of horses' hooves as the redcoats galloped up the avenue, the grating sound of a key turned in the lock and the groans of a prisoner. I shouted out from my dream, 'It's the Croppy Boy.' Immediately, my parents came rushing down the corridor, bringing my Christmas present, a small collie pup to keep me company. Reassured, I went back to sleep.

On Christmas morning, we travelled slowly over the snow to the chapel in Askinagap where we listened to a lengthy sermon and Christmas carols played on a wheezy harmonium. After dinner, we gathered around the gramophone with its large brass horn to listen to more carols, and Father read pieces from Dickens. When the Christmas cake was cut, I asked for a piece for the Croppy Boy. I had no fear of him. To me, he was a real person. That night, I tiptoed into the room to leave the cake for him. It was still there the following morning. I never heard the Croppy Boy again!

CHRISTMAS KISS

Julia Kelly

The house on Haddington Road is swollen with merriment and extra wine. Underwear uncomfortable, I force a look of pleasant expectation, press the doorbell and brace myself for an onslaught of lipsticky teeth and high-pitched exclamations.

I'm so dazed by the heady rush to the senses – the over-hot house, the shrieks and roars from the drawing room, animated faces reflected in the mantelpiece mirror, the pop and pour of champagne, winter coats balancing on the bannisters, something burning in the perfumed air – that I fail to spot Aunt Maureen lurching towards me, not quite 2 p.m. and already unsteady in heels.

'Rebecca! How *are* you?' she says, a bubble in her throat, addressing me traditionally, by my sister's name. Glass held aloft, a cheroot in the other hand also held back and above heads, so that only her face and chest protrude, like the maidenhead of a ship. She angles her rigid frame at mine, freezes for a millisecond and hovers, very skillfully, close to, but never quite, touching me.

I put my hand on the small of her back and feel beneath velvet the rigid rod of her spine. A startling close-up of her left eye – wild and bloodshot, the equine flare of her nostrils, features seeming to liquefy in the heat. Our heads do that awkward dance thing, moving out of sync and in the same direction. It is in this moment of disorientation that I kiss my aunt, not on the cheek, or in the air, not on the lips but, ridiculously, on her mole-bedecked neck.

In the drawing room, Coked-up children whine around the wide-hipped and perennially helpful who transport trays of mushroom vol-au-vents from the kitchen, a mortified newcomer stands to the side as spilled wine is fussed over at his feet. I am suddenly in the arms of my teenage second cousin, who only last year was happily employing his tongue to clear gluey snot from beneath his nose.

He seems to have expanded width-ways, his new voice, deep and faltering. With a waft of cheap aftershave, he presses his cracked lips on each cheek, tickling them with downy moustache hair. It takes me some time to realise that he's flirting with me, distracted as I am by the cocker spaniel, stretched and flatulent by the fire.

Several hours later, it happens again, the dreaded convention of the Christmas kiss. This time, it's more precarious. Mr Scott Hamilton pins me to the wall on a poorly-timed trip to the toilet. Tightly fitted in his suit and his skin, spittle shoots from a mouth whose green and black filled teeth bring to mind the underbelly of a pier, and lands on my lip, as he wishes my cleavage a very Merry Christmas indeed.

And then into the elders to say goodbye. There are fewer of them every year, shrinking as they are in number and size, their laughter is not so uproarious, their faces sadder in repose. My godfather compliments my 'snazzy new hairdo' as he fumbles for my Christmas present in the inside pocket of his jacket and I respond in shyness by hugging him for far too long, finishing off with a prolonged back rub. When he escapes my clutches, he looks slightly alarmed and flushed.

On the other hand, Mrs Long won't let go of my hand. Her eyes are wet with thoughts of poor little Hillary, who stood mid-meal the year before, dressed in red but hating Christmas, and recited the Hail Mary, Brussels sprouts rolling from her plate to the floor, where she collapsed lightly, a wooden giraffe.

Head bowed like a penitent, I make my way over to my mother. She's been cross-eyed with concentration all afternoon and hasn't noticed me in the confusion of children. Everything about her – voice, softness, scent – is reassuringly familiar and sincere, as is our little ritual. Still seated, she reaches up and puts both her hands over my ears, tilts my head forward and down to her chest. Then she kisses me, very gently, like the Pope might, on the centre of my head.

EPIPHANY

Anne Sharpe

The word 'epiphany' originally had a meaning that stretched far beyond the events of Christmas. It meant the manifestation of a god, a god who suddenly shows himself to us unexpectedly and undeservedly, often in a flash of glory. While, nowadays, the meaning has been extended to include all the possible ways in which our gods may appear to us, no matter what we worship. An evanescent flash of insight and joyous awareness, all for maybe no more that a few brief concentrated moments, may make up our own individual epiphany. Through it we are stirred or deeply moved, with our full significant attention well held. And, traditionally, too, we may crave a relic, a small evocation and reminder of that rich moment, some particular thing to clutch to ourselves and even hold in our hands, as pilgrims used to do with saints' bones or clothing.

   I have a small ritual of my own, a tradition I tend to carry out on New Year's Eve. For several years now, I've been gathering a bunch of willow wands from the roadside trees at dusk, always from the same trees opposite my house. And once the wands have been planted and established themselves, they are gradually turning into their own small wood. The timing is important. I always do it at that time when light hesitates, when it pulls up short in a deliberate pause before committing itself to blanket darkness. Through it all, the traffic hums and wends past in the continuous urgency of its murmuring rush. But still the willows piercing the fading light have collected a lasting stillness of their own around them. Bare shapes etch mesmerisingly upon the eye. For time and stillness have reduced them to their very essence, as if each time I am rediscovering the core of willowness anew.

I can't say logically why I am drawn again and again to repeat the ritual. After all, the willows are available for cutting anytime, long before or after New Year's Eve. Yet, the simple gathering at dusk makes all sorts of unspoken and subtle connections among the felt contradictions of the season.

It's the dead end of the day and year, yet I'm gathering garden rods for planting and renewal. While the parent tree blazons on, surviving sturdily through the dead stasis of winter. And if the warm bronze of each selected wand is a sort of naked defiance in itself, each still glows through the dusk like subdued winter kindling. As the blanket of night begins to drop closer, I remember that those willow wands will continue to smoulder unseen in the dark like endurance itself.

Through it all on this busy public road, the streaming cars are bright, busy, purposeful, all going somewhere particular if unknown to me, all expectantly heading towards New Year's Day. Each beams briefly, if unintentionally, upon me through its rush and hum, each loading with personal and private expectation. I know nothing of the details of each different set of hopes and needs, of course. But I can assume that most people within will have their spirits raised in some revival of optimism, however unfounded or unfocused this optimism may be. While, as I select and prune and fill my basket, wondering how quickly each will shoot and root this year, I, too, feel both led back and urged forward in a loop or set of continuous loops, like the returning seasons themselves. Busy travellers with focused beams somehow mark and punctuate both endings and near beginnings, in some sense of joyous awareness. For a manifestation of some kind has occurred, some sudden knitting together of tacit contradictions. And it is all so basic, so undeniably there, that it cannot be easily overlooked.

SOMETHING MARVELLOUS

John Boland

In another life, Maeve Brennan could have been my mother, and, in a way, I see her as such. Born within two years of each other, they were Dubliners from neighbouring suburbs – my mother from Richmond Hill in Rathmines, Maeve from Cherryfield Avenue, a mile away in Ranelagh. Both of them were thin, petite, pretty and vivacious, both were fond of a drink, and both were essentially lonely souls, a state recorded by each of them in different ways – by my mother in an occasional and poignant diary and by Maeve in her incomparable stories of middle-class Dublin life in the early decades of the twentieth century.

Ten years ago, almost all of Maeve Brennan's Dublin stories were collected in a volume called *The Springs of Affection*. Until then, and despite the fact that she had died as recently as 1993, she was unknown as an Irish writer. The *New Yorker*, where she worked, had been publishing her fiction since the early 1950s. In the late 1960s and early 1970s, two volumes of stories – *In and Out of Never-Never Land* and *Christmas Eve* – had appeared in the United States, as had a marvellous book of Manhattan vignettes called *The Long-Winded Lady*, but they were never published on this side of the Atlantic and you won't find her name in any of the standard guides to Irish literature.

The story of her later life is as heartbreaking as much of her fiction, though her career had begun with great promise. The daughter of Robert Brennan, Ireland's first envoy to Washington, she went with the family to the US in 1933 when she was sixteen, and she remained on when they returned to Ireland in 1949, soon acquiring a job at the *New Yorker*.

In his introduction to *The Springs of Affection*, her great editor and friend William Maxwell recalled the high-spirited, witty, impish Maeve he first encountered at the magazine's offices on West 43rd Street. But life wasn't to remain like that. 'Many men and women,' Maxwell writes, 'found Maeve enchanting, and she was a true friend, but there wasn't much you could do to save her from herself.' She had an unsuccessful marriage with an alcoholic *New Yorker* writer, then lived alone in various apartments and small hotels in the city, constantly getting into debt.

And it got worse. 'She had begun,' Maxwell writes, 'to have psychotic episodes, and she settled down in the ladies' room at the *New Yorker* as if it were her only home. Nobody did anything about it, and the secretaries nervously accommodated themselves to her sometimes hallucinated behaviour, which could turn violent.' Towards the end, after a couple of unhappy trips back to Dublin, she became hospitalised and died with only a few friends to mourn her passing.

All of this would be just very, very sad if it weren't for the fact that, from the early 1950s to the early 1970s, she wrote a score of short stories as great as any that have been written by an Irish writer. Although she was an exile for most of her life, in her imagination, like Joyce, she never left Dublin and it is there – specifically in the Cherryfield Avenue house of her childhood and girlhood – that almost all these stories are set.

They concern two married couples, first the Derdons and then the Bagots, both of them probably modelled on her parents and, in simple but beautifully evocative prose, they capture the small exhilarations and larger disappointments that happen to decent people trying to find fulfilment but instead encountering the emptiness that lies at the heart of so many of our lives.

But though a profound understanding of loneliness pervades these stories, there's a remembrance of happiness too, as in her final journalistic piece for the *New Yorker* in which she recalls a moment from her girlhood.

> One New Year's Eve, something marvellous happened on our little street. It wasn't called a street; it was called an avenue. Cherryfield Avenue. What happened that New Year's Eve was that in the late afternoon word went round

from house to house that a minute or so before midnight we would all step out into our front gardens, or even into the street, leaving the front doors open, so that the light streamed out after us, and there we would wait to hear the bells ringing in the New Year. I nearly went mad with excitement and happiness. I know I jumped for joy. That New Year's Eve was one of the great occasions of our lives.

And in that glimpse of Maeve the young girl, with all her hopes and dreams still before here, I catch a glimpse of my mother too, before adulthood and age took their cruel, betraying toll on both of them.

RELUCTANT TO LEAVE

Val O'Donnell

A chance meeting with an old schoolfriend recently in the National Concert Hall prompted me to reflect on how my lifelong passion for classical music began.

I trace its origin to those short music interludes on Radio Éireann in the 1950s. That's where I first heard the greatest Irish pianist of the day, Charles Lynch, playing Chopin. It was an epiphany. A door was opened on a new world of exquisite melody and delicious harmony, and I wanted more.

I can still remember the shock when I first saw a picture of Charles Lynch in the paper. The balding head, large physical frame and mischievous smile, correlated very poorly with the romantic image I had created in my youthful imagination.

During my teens, I savoured the musical magic conjured by the magnificent Charles Lynch, through his many radio broadcasts. Then, later, at Prom Concerts in the Gaiety Theatre and recitals at other venues, I became familiar with his dignified platform manner. I always marvelled at the ease with which he could execute the most demanding music and communicate its intellectual essence to the listener.

His was a cool, detached style of playing, with no trace of physical engagement with the music.

But I remained content to the consummate artistry of Charles Lynch from a respectful distance, and never expected to meet so great a pianist in person, much less to enjoy a private recital. But that's exactly what happened.

The office Christmas dinner dance in 1963, at the old Jury's Hotel in Dame Street, was ending in predictable high spirits. The conga chain was winding up the stairs of the hotel, when I noticed a familiar figure relaxing in the residents' lounge. Well fortified by the occasion, I peeled off from the swaying conga line and introduced myself to the great Irish pianist. He was a resident at the hotel and was teaching at the Royal Irish Academy of Music at the time.

I was effusive in expressing my admiration for his playing and the revered status his name enjoyed in our home. Would he, possibly, I ventured, have time to visit us over the holiday period and perhaps play the piano

Surprise at my own brazenness was surpassed only by his response. Yes, of course! He would be delighted. Could we fix a date? Could he be collected from his hotel? I emerged, dizzy, from the impromptu encounter. I couldn't believe it. I had just received the best Christmas present I could have imagined.

The 6 January 1964 was a cold day. My mother had assembled an appetising buffet, with a wide selection of desserts and cakes. Her cousin, Breid, had volunteered to brave the icy roads in her Morris Minor to collect Charles from his hotel. The piano had been tuned on the day. The coal fire was well settled. All was set for the arrival of our famous guest.

When he arrived, I could hardly believe that Charles Lynch had walked in through our front door, was now sitting at our table, dining happily and sharing a miscellany of musical experiences and reminiscences with us, as if he had been a family intimate for years.

Then came the final treat. Moving to the open upright piano, Charles Lynch settled himself on the small piano stool and delivered the most memorable piano recital I ever heard – all from memory!

Chopin, Brahms, Debussy, Rachmaninov – they were all there and many others too, drawn effortlessly from his abundant repertoire. I remember that he seemed reluctant to leave and brave the icy streets again in the early hours of the morning.

When Charles Lynch died in 1984, I read about some of his personal difficulties, including problems in coping with many of the practical aspects of life – not least the management of time and money.

Many other music lovers benefited, like our family did that night, from the sad fact that he never owned a piano of his own. And he had a great fondness for cakes. Clearly, we had struck many of the right chords with the doyen of Irish pianists on that festive night.

My mother cherished the golden memory of the night Charles Lynch visited us for the rest of her life. So do I.

PRIDE COMES AFTER

Denise Blake

That first time, on my knees in Vermont snow,
I needed to do two things;
try to stand up, which is so damn difficult
weighted and bound into concrete boots,
wearing unyielding skis, like an Edward scissor-feet –
and they say those are the shortest, made for learners.

The second mission was the most gruelling;
trying to straight-jacket my emotions,
avoid break-down sobbing.
Nearby a child was throwing a stomping fit –
I can't do this. I don't want to do this.
My every last nerve was shouting the same.

Laurence, with his first plummet,
became the laboratory rat, the instructor
coaching him to roll onto his belly,
his never-ending skis flailing as a drowning man,
as the goggled class stood by, learning the lesson,
don't fall on purpose, it should be a surprise.

There is the knowing you are out of control,
the body pulling backwards when it should hunch.

Those seconds when it all flashes before you;
I'm going to fall; who will I take down with me; how
will I land; will anyone see me? The bone-shocking thump —
why does my hat always fly into the deepest slush?

Crawling on frozen earth — packed ice has passed through
all thermal layers to stick to my back, down my trousers.
Deposited there, I want to just sit and wait for Laurence
to white-knight me away, as helmeted four year olds fly past.
Once I am standing, trying to hold a stance, face forward,
my nursery slope has become Mount Snowdon.

On the last day I rode the ski lift; Killington flowing
away from me. I wove down the novice run, slowly,
over, then back, turning right, turning left, in control.
The sun shone. Fresh snowflakes floated down.
If I hadn't had those falling days,
I wouldn't have had the day I didn't fall.

CONTRIBUTOR BIOGRAPHIES

KAREN ARDIFF: An award-winning actress, she regularly appears on the stage and stars in films, including *Evelyn* and *This is My Father*. *The Secret of My Face* is her first novel.

DENISE BLAKE: Born in Ohio, USA, in 1958, her family moved back to Ireland in 1969 where she grew up in Letterkenny, County Donegal. Her first collection of poetry, *Take a Deep Breath*, was published by Summer Palace Press.

JOHN BOLAND: A literary and television critic for the *Irish Independent* and an arts broadcaster. His first collection of poems, *Brow Head*, was published in 1999.

PAT BORAN: Born in Portlaoise in 1963, his *New and Selected Poems* was published by Dedalus Press in 2007. He received the 2008 O'Shaughnessy Poetry Award and is a member of Aosdána.

CONOR BOWMAN: An Elvis Presley and George Harrison fan.

FIONNUALA BRENNAN: Lived on the island of Paros, Greece, with her young family in the late 1970s and has written a book about that experience, *On a Greek Island* (Poolbeg). She teaches creative writing and tutors on an adult education course at University College Dublin.

CATHLEEN BRINDLEY: Born in India and educated in Ireland, where she received a degree in modern languages, she enjoys travel and has written extensively on the subject.

CATHERINE BROPHY: Born, reared and educated in Dublin, she has written novels, short stories and screenplays and facilitates writing workshops.

TIM CAREY: American-born author and historian, he is currently Heritage Officer with Dún Laoghaire-Rathdown County Council.

CIARAN CARSON: Professor of Poetry at Queen's University Belfast, his most recent book of poems is *For All We Know* (Gallery Press, 2008).

PATRICIA CLARKE: Born in Derry, she studied languages and literature at Trinity College, Dublin. She has lived in Madrid and Seville and is the translator of Spanish Nobel laureate Camilo Jose Cela's novels *Mazurka for Two Dead Men* and *Boxwood*. She now lives in Kinvara, County Galway.

GERARD CORRIGAN: A senior manager with a multinational corporation based in Limerick, he is married to Ann and they have three children. His passions are writing and music and, when not writing, he records and performs with his band Hardy Drew and the Nancy Boys.

JAMES COTTER: A film scriptwriter, RTÉ Television producer and director, his writing for adults and children has featured on RTÉ.

LEO CULLEN: Author of *Clocking 90 on the Road to Cloughjordan* and *Let's Twist Again* (Blackstaff Press). A frequent broadcaster on RTÉ I, RTÉ Lyric and the BBC. He hails from County Tipperary and now lives in Monkstown, County Dublin.

PAUL CULLEN: A journalist and sometime runner.

GERALD DAWE: Born in Belfast, he lectures in English at Trinity College, Dublin, where he is director of The Oscar Wilde Centre for Irish Writing and co-director of the Graduate Creative Writing Programme. He has published numerous books of essays and poetry and his most recent poetry collection is *Points West* (Gallery Press 2008). He is a member of Aosdána and lives in Dún Laoghaire.

JOHN F. DEANE: Born on Achill Island, County Mayo, he writes poetry full-time. A founder-member of Poetry Ireland and a member of Aosdána, his latest work of fiction is *The Heather Fields and Other Stories* and his forthcoming poetry collection is *A Little Book of Hours*. In 2007, the French government honoured him by making him Chevalier dans l'Ordre des Arts et des Lettres.

MICHELINE EGAN: Born and still living in Castlebar, she works as a communications trainer and is a published poet.

ANNE ENRIGHT: Her writing includes short-story collections, non-fiction work and four novels: *The Wig My Father Wore*, *What Are You Like?*, *The Pleasure of Eliza Lynch* and *The Gathering*, which won the 2007 Man Booker Prize and Listowel Writers' Week Kerry Award for Literature 2008. She lives with her family in Bray, County Wicklow. She participated in *Sunday Miscellany Live from Listowel* in 2008.

BERNARD FARRELL: An award-winning playwright who, since *I Do Not Like Thee Doctor Fell* in 1979, has had his subsequent twenty-one plays, which have been seen extensively abroad, premiered mainly at the Abbey Theatre and Gate Theatre.

MICHAEL FEWER: Born in County Waterford, he is the author of numerous books relating to nature, landscape and the environment, most recently *The Wicklow Military Road*.

AUBREY FLEGG: Born in Dublin, he spent his early childhood in Sligo. His first book, *Katie's War*, about the Civil War period in Ireland, was awarded the Peter Pan Award for a book translated into Swedish. His book *Wings Over Delft*, the first in his Louise Trilogy, won the Bisto Book of the Year Overall Award in 2004.

KATE E. FOLEY: Lives in Dublin. Her keen interests in travel and culture are a feature of her writing.

PADDY GAVIN: A native of County Galway and a retired Garda Inspector.

HEDY GIBBONS LYNOTT: A writer from County Galway, her journey as a writer is informed by her childhood in Dublin and in Passage West, County Cork; her career a nurse and midwife; her time as a student and lecturer of psychology and counselling psychologist; and as a mother of four. She has been published in many anthologies of Irish writing and contributes spoken-word pieces to Irish and US radio programmes. She is a founding member of Talking Stick Writers Group, an Irish collective of authors and poets.

KATRINA GOLDSTONE: Works for Create, the national development agency for collaborative arts. She is also a freelance reviewer and researcher.

BRENDAN GRAHAM: A novelist and songwriter, his novels are *The Whitest Flower* (HarperCollins, 1998); *The Element of Fire* (HarperCollins, 2001); *The Brightest Day, The Darkest Night* (HarperCollins, 2005) – a trilogy tracing one woman's journey from Ireland's Great Famine to the killing fields of America's Civil War. Among his songs are 'Rock 'n' Roll Kids', 'The Voice', 'Isle of Hope, Isle of Tears', 'Crucán na bPáiste' and 'You Raise Me Up'. He lives in County Mayo

LORRAINE GRIFFIN: A marketing manager, qualified journalist and freelance writer with a BA in International Marketing, she has lived and worked in Barcelona, Chicago, London and her native Dublin. Her writing inspiration draws from life experience and a carefully-nurtured love of people-watching.

VONA GROARKE: Born in Edgeworthstown, County Longford, she is an award-winning poet and a member of Aosadána. Her many poetry collections include *Lament for Art O'Leary* (Gallery Press). She is a member of the creative writing team at the Centre for New Writing at the University of Manchester.

HUGO HAMILTON: Lives in Dublin. He is the author of the bestselling German-Irish memoir *The Speckled People*, his second memoir is entitled *The Sailor in the Wardrobe* and his latest novel, *Disguise*, was published in 2008. He participated in *Sunday Miscellany Live from Listowel* in 2008.

MICHAEL HARDING: Has written two books of fiction and numerous plays for the Abbey Theatre and other Irish theatre companies.

LIAM HARTE: Lectures in Irish and Modern Literature at the University of Manchester and his books include *Modern Irish Autobiography: Self, Nation and Society* (Palgrave Macmillan, 2007) and *The Literature of the Irish in Britain: Autobiography and Memoir* (Palgrave Macmillan, 2009).

ANNE LE MARQUAND HARTIGAN: Born in England and living in Ireland for many years, she is a poet, playwright and painter. Her sixth collection of poetry will be published in 2008. She has a family of six children and likes a bit of crack.

SEAMUS HEANEY: Since his first collection of poetry *Death of a Naturalist*, he has published numerous collections of poetry and prose. He is the recipient of many awards and honours including the Nobel Prize for Literature (1995). His most recent books are the collection of poetry *Electric Light* (2001) and a selection of prose, *Finders Keepers* (2002). He participated in *Sunday Miscellany Live from Listowel* in 2008. Born in County Derry, he now lives in Dublin.

MONICA HENCHY: A retired Assistant Librarian in Trinity College, Dublin, she was president of the Dublin Spanish Society for several years. Her special interests are writing and lecturing about the Irish colleges of Spain.

PHIL HERBERT: She has a background in teaching and theatre and, in 2008, completed an MPhil in Creative Writing in Trinity College, Dublin. She is published in the anthology *Sixteen after Ten*.

SHARON HOGAN: Born in Drogheda and raised in North America, she is a film, television, theatre and radio actor who frequently contributes to RTÉ as a reader of her own and others' writing. She is also a mask-maker and holds an MA in Dance from the University of Limerick.

UNA HUNT: One of Ireland's leading pianists with a particular interest in the music of Ireland, she has made several ground-breaking CDs devoted to the music of Irish composers. She is also a broadcaster and producer, and was Artistic Director of the Thomas Moore Commemorative Festival 2008.

VIVIEN IGOE: A graduate of University College Dublin, she has a deep interest in all aspects of Irish heritage. Worked on archaeological excavations, as a publicity officer for Bord Fáilte and as a researcher in the Department of An Taoiseach.

PETER JANKOWSKY: Born in Berlin in 1939, he worked for ten years as actor in Germany. He has lived in Dublin since 1971, where he has been teaching, acting and writing. His translations, together with Brian Lynch, of Paul Celan's *65 Poems* was published in 1985. More work with Lynch resulted in *Easter Snow/Osterschnee*, a book of photographs, poems and translations. His memoir, *Myself Passing By*, was published in 2000.

JOE KEARNEY: Born in County Kilkenny, he worked in the oil industry before becoming a full-time writer. He has had prize winning short stories and poems published and is currently working on a PhD in creative writing in University College Dublin.

CYRIL KELLY: Born in Listowel, County Kerry, he was a primary school teacher in Dublin for many years and is a regular contributor to RTÉ Radio. He participated in *Sunday Miscellany Live from Listowel* in 2007 and 2008.

JULIA KELLY: Born in Dublin, a middle child of a large Catholic brood, she studied English, Sociology and Journalism. She escaped, like most, to London for the mad, bad years of life, where she worked as a desk editor in various publishing houses and wrote a monthly column for Irish *d'Side* magazine. She contributed to the Rough Guide series for Thailand and Ireland. *With My Lazy Eye*, her first novel, won an Irish Book Award and was shortlisted for the Listowel Writers' Week Kerry Group Award 2008. She now lives in Bray, County Wicklow.

BENEDICT KIELY: Born in 1919, near Dromore, County Tyrone, his short story collections include *A Journey to the Seven Streams, A Ball of Malt and Madame Butterfly, A Cow in the House* and *The Collected Stories of Benedict Kiely*. His novels include *Land Without Stars, The Cards of the Gambler, The Captain with the Whiskers, Proxopera: A Tale of Modern Ireland* and *Nothing Happens in Carmincross*. His non-fiction includes *Counties of Contention: A Study of the Origins and Implications of the Partition of Ireland, Poor Scholar: A Study of the Works and Days of William Carleton 1794-1869, Modern Irish Fiction: A Critique* and *A Raid into Dark Corners and Other Essays*. His autobiography is *Drink to the Bird: An Omagh Boyhood*. A member of Aosdána, he lived for many years in Dublin. He died on 9 February 2007. *The Cards of the Gambler* will be reissued by New Island in 2009.

CHUCK KRUGER: Grew up in New York's Finger Lakes. In protest against the Vietnam War, he moved to Switzerland. He has lived on Cape Clear Island for many years. A regular contributor to RTÉ Radio's *Sunday Miscellany*, *Quiet Quarter* and *Seascapes* and NPR's *Weather Notebook*.

MELOSINA LENOX-CONYNGHAM: Born in Sri Lanka on a tea estate, she spent her youth in County Louth and now lives in a cottage in Kilkenny. She is the editor of an anthology, *Diaries of Ireland*.

MAE LEONARD: Originally from Limerick, she now lives in Kildare. A broadcaster, award-winning writer and poet, her publications include *My Home is There*, *This is Tarzan Clancy* and *Six for Gold*.

CLARE LYNCH: Born in County Cavan, she has worked in the arts sector in County Sligo for many years. She is the author of two short story collections, *Short Steps in Long Grass* (Black Battler Press, 2002) and *Life Through The Long Window* (Original Writing, 2007).

AIFRIC MAC AODHA: Born and living in Dublin, her poems have been published in several magazines, including *Poetry Ireland*, *Innti* and *Bliainiris*. She has won many prizes for her poetry and was recently awarded an Arts Council endowment. She is working on her first collection of poetry.

STEVE MACDONOGH: A writer, publisher and photographer, he set up his first publishing company in 1968 after spending the summer in the US. Since 1982, he has been editorial director of Brandon, based in Dingle.

CATHERINE MARSHALL: An art historian and curator, she has written widely about art. She is the visual arts advisor to the Arts Council on Touring and Collections.

STEPHEN MATTERSON: Head of the School of English at Trinity College, University of Dublin, and has published widely on poetry and aspects of American literature.

NUALA MCCANN: A freelance writer and journalist, she lives with her husband, Roger Patterson, and their son, Ruairí, in Belfast.

IGGY McGOVERN: A poet and a physicist, his collection *The King of Suburbia* received the inaugural Glen Dimplex New Writers Award for Poetry.

MALACHY McKENNA: Trained as an actor at the Focus Theatre, his play *Tillsonburg* won the 2000 Stewart Parker Trust Award. Recently, he has been dividing his time between his young family, his writing commitments and appearing as Obsequious in *I Keano*. His new comedy musical, *Macbecks*, which was co-written with Gary Cooke, opens in the Olympia Theatre, Dublin, in 2009.

JUDITH MOK: Born in The Netherlands, she now lives in Dublin. An internationally-renowned soprano, she has also published many works of poetry and fiction. Her most recent novel, *Gael*, is published by Telegram.

GERRY MORAN: From Kilkenny, he is a former primary school principal whose writing has featured in various publications. He has written *Kilkenny City and County*.

MARY MORRISSY: A journalist and the author of two novels, *Mother of Pearl* and *The Pretender*, as well as a volume of short stories, *A Lazy Eye*. She holds the Jenny McKeane Moore Chair of Writing at George Washington University for 2008–2009.

ANDREW MOTION: The author of eight books of poems, four biographies, including the authorized life of Philip Larkin, and of critical studies of Larkin and Edward Thomas. He has been the recipient of the John Llewellyn Rhys Prize, the Somerset Maugham Award, the Dylan Thomas Award and the Whitbread Prize for Biography. He was appointed Poet Laureate of the UK in May 1999. He participated in *Sunday Miscellany Live from Listowel* in 2007.

PAUL MULDOON: Born in County Armagh, he has, since 1987, lived in the United States, where he is now Howard G.B. Clark '21 Professor at Princeton University and Chair of the Peter B. Lewis Center for the Arts. His main collections of poetry are *New Weather* (1973), *Mules* (1977), *Why Brownlee Left* (1980), *Quoof* (1983), *Meeting the British* (1987), *Madoc: A Mystery* (1990), *The Annals of Chile* (1994), *Hay* (1998), *Poems 1968–1998* (2001) and *Moy Sand and Gravel* (2002), for which he won the 2003 Pulitzer Prize. His tenth collection, *Horse Latitudes*, appeared in 2006.

VAL MULKERNS: Born in Dublin, she moved to London after working in the civil service. She returned to Ireland in 1952 as the associate editor of *The Bell*. Her novels include *A Time Outworn*, *A Peacock Cry*, *The Summerhouse* and *Very Like a Whale*. Her short stories are collected as *Antiquities*, *An Idle Woman* and *A Friend of Don Juan*. She jointly won the AIB Prize for Literature. She is a member of Aosdána.

MARY MULLEN: Was born and raised in Alaska long before it was a tourist destination and now lives in County Galway with her daughter Lily.

DEIRDRE MULROONEY: A writer specialising in dance, a lecturer in drama and a stage director, her radio series *Nice Moves*, out of which her book *Irish Moves* grew, was broadcast on RTÉ Radio I.

ORLA MURPHY: A writer of fiction, poetry and plays, she has been published in Ireland and the UK, and broadcast on RTÉ Radio and BBC Radio Four. Editor of the catalogue raisonné of (her grandfather) *Joseph Higgins: Sculptor and Painter* (Gandon, 2005).

SHERRA MURPHY: A lecturer in Visual Culture at the Dún Laoghaire Institute of Art, Design and Technology, she is currently pursuing a PhD on the Natural History Museum, Dublin, at University College Dublin's School of History and Archives.

DYMPNA MURRAY FENNELL: Hailing from County Westmeath, she lives in Lucan, County Dublin. A retired teacher, she has worked in many teaching posts from Nigeria to Naas.

PADDY MURRAY: A Dublin-born writer and journalist and a columnist and the associate editor of *The Sunday World*. He is a partner, father, rugby fan, music lover and Irishman.

MAIRÉAD NÍ CHONEANAINN: Born in East Galway and a civil servant for many years. Married to an islander and lived for many years on

Inis Mór, The Arann Islands. She is regular actor in An Taibhdhearc with a long interest in literature.

NUALA NÍ DHOMHNAILL: A poet and mother of four children.

BLÁITHÍN NÍ LIATHÁIN: Born and living in Dublin where she works as a teacher.

SUE NORTON: Having grown up in America, she lectures in the Dublin Institute of Technology.

BETTY NUNAN: Born in Cork, she is married and has six children. She moved to Baghdad with her husband in 1982 and has lived in many countries, including Saudi Arabia, Kenya and Zimbabwe. She has a Masters degree in Semetic languages from University College Dublin.

FACHTNA Ó DRISCEOIL: Brought up in an Irish-speaking family in Dún Laoghaire, he works as a television reporter and radio producer for RTÉ.

TADHG Ó DÚSHLÁINE: A senior lecturer in Modern Irish at NUI Maynooth, he is director of the Frank O'Connor Project, is the writer in residence with Cork Corporation and was the writer in residence with the Munster Literature Centre from 1999–2000. He has published poetry collections and books of criticism.

EOGHAN Ó HANLUAIN: A Senior Lecturer Emeritus in Modern Irish at University College Dublin.

ÉAMONN Ó HUALLACHÁIN: Lives on the border between north Louth and south Armagh. He has long had enthusiastic love of the culture, language and history of his native place.

LIAM Ó MUIRTHILE: A poet and writer, his latest collection of poems is *Sanas* (Cois Life, 2007).

CONOR O'CALLAGHAN: Has published three collections of poetry with Gallery Press, including *Fiction* (2005). His comic prose memoir, *Red*

Mist, (Bloomsbury, 2004) has since been adapted into a television documentary. He lives Manchester and teaches in Sheffield.

JOSEPH O'CONNOR: A Dublin-born, award-winning novelist, his most recent books are *Star of The Sea* and *Redemption Falls*, both of which have been translated into many languages. He has written non-fiction articles and books, as well as film scripts. He participated in *Sunday Miscellany Live from Listowel Writers Week* in 2007.

JOHN O'DONNELL: His work has been published and broadcast widely and his awards include the Irish National Poetry Prize, the Ireland Funds Prize and the Hennessy/*Sunday Tribune* Poetry Award. A barrister, he lives in Dublin.

MARY O'DONNELL: Her novels include *The Lightmakers*, *Virgin and the Boy* and *The Elysium Testament*. Her short-story collection, *Storm Over Belfast*, was published in 2008. Her poetry books include *The Place of Miracles: New and Selected Poems*, *Spiderwoman's Third Avenue*, *Rhapsody*, *Unlegendary Heroes* and *September Elegies*. She is a regular broadcaster and a member of Aosdána.

VAL O'DONNELL: Born in Dublin, and a former civil servant, he has a long association with the theatre as an actor and director.

CLODAGH O'DONOGHUE: Having studied at Trinity College, Dublin, she has worked as an actor with many companies including the Abbey, the Project, Pan-Pan, Pigsback and Fishamble. She has written short stories for children for RTÉ and co-edited *Contemporary Irish Monologues* with Jim Culleton.

EMER O'KELLY: A drama and literary critic, principally with the *Sunday Independent*, she also writes a current affairs column for that newspaper. She was a member of the Arts Council/An Comhairle Ealaíon from 1998 to 2005 and is currently serving a second term as a Board Member of the Irish Museum of Modern Art. She lives in Dublin.

MICHAEL O'LOUGHLIN: A poet, screenwriter and translator, he is currently writer in resident with Galway City.

MARY O'MALLEY: Born and reared in Connemara, she now lives in the Moycullen Gaeltacht. She has written six collections of poems, the latest of which is *A Perfect V* (Carcanet Press, 2006). She broadcasts, travels and lectures widely and is a member of Aosdána. She is currently writer in residence at NUI Galway, where she teaches on the MA in Writing and in Arts Administration.

COLM Ó SNODAIGH: A member of the music group, Kila, he has published a novel, *Úrscéilín*, and a novella, *Pat the Pipe – Píobaire*, as well as a solo album entitled *Giving*.

JOE O'TOOLE: Born in Dingle, County Kerry, he qualified as a teacher at St Patrick's College of Education, Dublin. He has been an Independent member of Seanad Éireann since 1987 and is a former General Secretary of the Irish National Teachers Organisation (INTO) and former President of the Irish Congress of Trade Unions (ICTU). He published his autobiography, *Looking Under Stones*, in 2003.

VIKTOR POSUDNEVSKY: Hailing from a Russian family in Latvia, he came to study in Ireland in 2006 and has lived here since. Viktor works as a journalist for *Nasha Gazeta*, Ireland's Russian community newspaper, and the multicultural weekly *Metro Éireann*. He contributes reports and radio essays to RTÉ Radio 1.

TONY QUINN: A barrister, educated by the Christian Brothers and at Trinity College, Dublin and The King's Inns, he was a member of Irish PEN and a Chairman of the Irish Writers' Union. He is the author of *Wigs and Guns: Irish Barristers in the Great War* (2006). He died in April 2008.

MICK RANSFORD: Born in Athy, County Kildare, he has worked at all sorts of things. He has dedicated himself to short stories, short-shorts and prose pieces. He has had stories published in the *Sunday Tribune*, the *Stinging Fly*, *Cúirt*, *West47* and the US magazine *Me Three*. He has won the Galway Now short-short competition in 2004. He is currently looking for a publisher for a collection of stories he has just completed.

ENID REID WHYTE: Lives in Ireland since 1994. She is a professional theatre arts practitioner and is married to actor, Mal Whyte.

MARY RUSSELL: A journalist and writer with a particular interest in travel.

DENIS SAMPSON: Lives between Ireland and Canada. His most recent book is *Brian Moore: The Chameleon Novelist*.

TOMMY SANDS: A singer, songwriter and social activist from County Down. Part of the acclaimed Sands Family, one of the most important traditional groups in the early years of Ireland's folk revival.

ANNE SHARPE: A psychologist and lives in County Wicklow.

EMMA SIDES: Loves the outdoors and gardening and lives in Dublin.

ELAINE SISSON: An IADT Research Fellow at the Graduate School of Creative Arts in Dublin.

GERARD SMYTH: Has been publishing poetry widely since the 1960s and his most recent collections are *Daytime Sleeper*, *A New Tenancy* and *The Mirror Tent*, all published by Dedalus.

GEMMA TIPTON: Lives in Dublin and writes books and articles about art and architecture. Her writing appears regularly in *The Irish Times* and in many art and cultural publications.

COLM TÓIBÍN: Born in Enniscorthy, County Wexford, and educated at University College Dublin, his first novel, *The South* (1990) about an Irish artist in Spain, won the *Irish Times* Literature Prize in 1991. He has since written numerous novels, short stories, essays and non-fiction works, including the novel *The Master*, which won the Dublin IMPAC Literary Award in 2006. He participated in *Sunday Miscellany live from Listowel* in 2007.

ALISON WELLS: Living in Bray, County Wicklow, she is the mother of four young children. She is a published writer of short stories and is currently working on a novel.

JOSEPH WOODS: A poet and Director of Poetry Ireland. A winner of the Patrick Kavanagh Award, his two poetry collections *Sailing to Hokkaido* (2001) and *Bearings* (2005) are published by The Worple Press (UK).

PADDY WOODWORTH: Born in Bray, Co. Wicklow in 1951. A former *Irish Times* arts editor and foreign desk journalist. His books include *Dirty War, Clean Hands* and *The Basque Country: A Cultural History*. He is currently working on *Restoring the Future: the Race to Repair a Damaged Planet*, on ecological restoration projects around the world.

ENDA WYLEY: Born and still living in Dublin, she has published three collections of poetry, *Eating Baby Jesus, Socrates in the Garden* and *Poems for Breakfast*.

GRACE WYNNE-JONES: Author of four critically-acclaimed novels.